1

THE ENGLISH REFORM BILL OF 1867

STUDIES IN HISTORY, ECONOMICS AND PUBLIC LAW

EDITED BY THE FACULTY OF POLITICAL SCIENCE
OF COLUMBIA UNIVERSITY

Volume XCIII]   [Number 1

Whole Number 210

THE ENGLISH REFORM
BILL OF 1867

BY

JOSEPH H. PARK

AMS PRESS
NEW YORK

COLUMBIA UNIVERSITY
STUDIES IN THE
SOCIAL SCIENCES

210

The Series was formerly known as
Studies in History, Economics and Public Law.

Reprinted with the permission of Columbia University Press
From the edition of 1920, New York
First AMS EDITION published 1969
Manufactured in the United States of America

Library of Congress Catalogue Card Number: 76-78002

AMS PRESS, INC.
NEW YORK, N. Y. 10003

To
MY UNCLE
J. C. WILLEVER

PREFACE

THERE is no more important event connected with the story of the development of democracy in England than the passage of the Representation of the People Act of 1867. It is not unfitting, therefore, that attention should be paid to the circumstances under which the measure was carried.

The present study is an attempt not only to tell the history of great party leaders and political cliques of the period but also to calculate the extent to which England reacted to the *esprit du siècle* after the triumph of the democratic cause in the American Civil War and more especially to trace the influence of the political agitation of those social classes not within " the pale of the Constitution " during a season of stress. A recital of facts proving that the urban working class was advancing in knowledge does not of itself explain why the working class was admitted to a share of England's government, else the arguments brought forward by the friends of Reform in 1866 would have accomplished the passage of the bill of that year. Nor yet was it mob violence in 1866-1867 which was effective, for the lower classes displayed more violence in 1832 and during the Chartist movement than in the 'sixties and did not attain success. But as in 1828 O'Connell, by displaying through his remarkable control of the Catholic Associations that he had power over those capable of immoderate action, caused a worried Parliament to legislate, so in 1866-1867 middle-class leaders of workingmen, cooperating with organizations such as the Reform League and the trade unions, obtained results by stating that their well-planned parades and quietly-conducted Reform meetings were but "dress rehearsals" for more dramatic scenes in case demands were not granted. Political leaders, recognizing that action must be taken by one party or the other, bid for popular support. England started on the road to democracy although that road was not to broaden out to Mr. Lowe's dreaded "wide plain" until other measures, notably among them the acts of 1884-1885 and 1918, had been passed.

Acknowledgment is made by the author of a very free use of certain secondary works although material for the survey is based in the main upon newspapers, magazines, and pamphlets. Frequent notation will show the service to which Lord Morley's *Life of Gladstone,* Mr. G. M. Trevelyan's *Life of John Bright,* and the excellent biography of Disraeli by Monypenny and Buckle have been put. Statistics concerning the electoral system in Mr. Charles Seymour's *Electoral Reform in England and Wales* have been regarded as authoritative. The work of writers in the *Journal of the Royal Statistical Society* has proved very helpful indeed. And much inspiration has come from Mr. J. Holland Rose's *The Rise of Democracy,* Mr. Gilbert Slater's *The Making of Modern England,* and Mr. Preston Slosson's *The Decline of the Chartist Movement.*

The writer wishes to acknowledge the kind interest of Professor James T. Shotwell under whose general supervision this monograph was started. He is indebted to Professor Carlton J. H. Hayes for whose encouragement, advice, and criticism he is deeply grateful. And he is under obligation to Professor Robert L. Schuyler for criticizing the manuscript and to Professor Edwin R. A. Seligman for the use of pamphlets in his private library. Mr. Clinton Mindil of New York University and Miss Isabel McKenzie have given helpful suggestions. It seems fair to state that this thesis was practically finished when the writer was called into military service on March 5, 1918, and was therefore obliged to defer its publication.

CONTENTS

CHAPTER III

THE POPULAR ATTITUDE TOWARD REFORM

CHAPTER IV

THE OFFICIAL ATTITUDE TOWARD REFORM

CHAPTER V

DISRAELI'S SUCCESS WITH REFORM IN 1867

CHAPTER VI

Conclusion

CHAPTER I

INTRODUCTION

THE Reform bill of 1832 [1]—the Great Reform bill—has merited much attention and praise, especially from those students who have desired to trace the rise of democracy in England. But, as is well known, the measure is not the one which made England democratic, and was not without its defects: both in the provisions concerning redistribution and in those pertaining to the enlargement of the franchise it was open to the attacks of the Radicals and of the working class.

Although some of the grossest anomalies of the period preceding 1832 were removed by its redistribution clauses, there had been no pretence of adopting the principle of equal electoral districts. Many of the smaller boroughs still were given the same political influence as the larger ones. And, because of the great influence of property, not a few of them fell under the power of the property-owning class to such an extent that they approached the character of those boroughs in which direct nomination had formerly prevailed.[2] Indeed, a list of over forty was made out with the name of the patron of each.[3] Moreover, the transfer of part of the representation of those boroughs which had

[1] 2 and 3 William IV, c. 45, 65, 88 (including the measures for Scotland and Ireland).

[2] *Vide* the speech of Lord John Russell, *Annual Register*, vol. xciv, p. 18.

[3] G. Lowes Dickinson, *The Development of Parliament during the Nineteenth Century* (London, 1895), chap ii, gives a long description of anomalies of distribution after 1832.

been disfranchised, to the counties where the influence of
the landlord was predominant, gave power to property and
was displeasing to the Radicals.[1]

And the anomalies which were bad enough in the 'thirties
became greater and greater as the years went by and the
Industrial Revolution wrought its changes. Those cities
which grew very rapidly during the thirty years following
1832 retained the old number of representatives in Parliament—as did also those towns and districts which showed
little increase in population and wealth. Statistics depict
an England becoming half again as populous during this
period; they tell of the increasing crowds of the cities—of
the number of persons engaged in manufactures mounting
during the twenty years between 1841 and 1861 from
1,789,000 to 3,117,000, in commerce from 499,000 to
1,110,000, in mines from 210,000 to 425,000, in building
from 353,000 to 539,000; they tell, on the other hand, of a
relative decline in agriculture wherein the recorded increase
of persons engaged is only from 1,297,000 to 1,700,000.[2]
The industrial map of England was showing great changes;
many a Silas Marner found that factories had taken the
place of the familiar Lantern Yard. If the new situation
were not met by a new redistribution bill, the anomalies of
the later nineteenth century would be as great as they had
been at the beginning of that century. It is not surprising,
therefore, to find the pamphleteers and the magazine writers discussing the subject. The *Westminster Review* declared in 1865 that it was impossible upon any rational
principle to contend that Honiton with a population of
3300 ought to have—as it then had—as many members as
Liverpool or Glasgow with half a million of people and in-

---

[1] J. H. Rose, *The Rise of Democracy* (London, 1897), p. 49.

[2] M. G. Mulhall, *The Dictionary of Statistics* (London, 1899), pp.
420 and 421.

calculable wealth of commerce.[1]   In *Macmillan's* it was
said that a majority of the House of Commons consisting
of 328 members, all of whom (except 11) represented borough constituencies of the smaller class in England (including Wales) and Scotland, was returned by 250,291
electors, or about one-fifth of the whole electoral body;
while about the same number of electors (244,459) in the
larger boroughs returned only thirty-six members or about
one-eighteenth of the whole House;[2] in the *Fortnightly
Review* it was asserted that such an unequal and anomalous
system of representation as was then existing in England,
if proposed to a new community by any statesman, would
be considered absurd.[3]   To the writer in the latter magazine the fact was startling that Rutland with 1,772 electors on the roll should return as many members as the
West Riding of Yorkshire, with 40,476, and that the little
town of Knaresborough with 271, and Thetford with 223
electors, should be as largely represented as the great cities
of Birmingham, Liverpool and Manchester, with constituencies of from 15,000 to 22,000.   The result of the whole
system was that one-third of the constituents sent two-
thirds of the Parliamentary representatives for all Great
Britain and Ireland, and what great practical good—it was
asked—could spring from a system so theoretically unjust!
Indeed, a person of a mathematical turn of mind may show
anomalies at will from the nicely constructed tables of the
pamphleteers;[4] and he may find some foundation for their
statements that when the enormous increase of population
and the still greater increase in the value of property were

[1] *Westminster Review*, April, 1865, p. 512.

[2] *Macmillan's*, January, 1866, p. 260, article by Lord Hobart.

[3] *Fortnightly Review*, vol. iv, p. 430, article by Edward Wilson.

[4] *Vide*, for instance, *The Reform Problem* by " Political Euclid,"
(London, 1866).

taken into consideration, the anomalies of the existing system of representation were almost as great as those that
existed prior to 1832.[1]   That Parliament was well aware
of the main facts of the case may be seen from an extract
from Mr. Laing's speech before the House of Commons
given shortly after the introduction of the 1866 Reform
bill:

He found a number of boroughs—forty—in which the population was under 7,000; the number of electors averaging 400 in
each; those forty boroughs, therefore, with a united population
of 200,000, and an aggregate number of voters of 16,000, returned sixty-four Members to that House.   Contrast that with
the single county of Lanarkshire, with a population of 530,000
by the last census—more than that of the whole forty boroughs
united—and returning only one Member to Parliament . . .
Dundee, the capital of a staple branch of industry with a
population approaching 100,000, had a single Member—exactly
one-sixty-fourth of the representation enjoyed by the forty
small boroughs, whose united population only doubled that of
Dundee.   Glasgow, again, with a population of about half a
million, and more than 20,000 electors, only returned two representatives as against the sixty-four returned by these small
boroughs.   But the case for redistribution became even
stronger if the table of boroughs was examined with an eye to
the increase or diminution which had taken place in the population of the large towns and small boroughs since 1832.   In
eighteen boroughs, returning twenty-three Members, the population had actually diminished since that date, whilst in the
eleven largest manufacturing towns in the North, the number
of £10 householders in the same period had increased by 178
per cent.   The contrast was not merely remarkable as regarded
the population relatively to the Members; but while, on the one
side, they had a set of small boroughs stationary or declining

[1] *Ibid.*, p. 5.

in population, on the other they had a number of large towns
rising rapidly into importance, with electors in each of those
towns increasing more rapidly than the electors in all the small
boroughs put together; and yet they commanded no adequate
proportion of the representation.[1]

But justly complained of as were those defects, already
mentioned, of the great Reform bill, a much greater cause
for complaint was found in its enfranchising clauses. Before 1832 the landed and commercial classes had been the
rulers of England. Both the manufacturing class and the
working class expressed, during the years immediately preceding the passage of the bill, their opposition to the existing situation. Francis Place, a Radical, who had secured
partial liberty for trade unions in 1824, became influential
in the formation of a National Political Union (October,
1831), designed to give cohesion to the provincial bodies
which were interested in Reform, and to unite the middle
and laboring classes in common political action.[2] His activity and the agitation of the working class were important
factors in causing the bill to be passed.[3] But the measure
gave the franchise to only those occupiers of premises of
the clear yearly value of not less than £10 in the boroughs
and those copyholders and leaseholders of land worth £10 a
year, and tenants-at-will of lands worth £50 a year in the
counties.[4] Such provisions meant that the industrial middle
class was to be added to the rulers of the country and that
the working class had been given nothing. To the latter it
soon became patent that Lord John Russell, important leader

[1] *Hansard*, third series, vol. clxxxii (March 12, 1866), pp. 78 and 79.

[2] Rose, *op. cit.*, pp. 46 and 47.

[3] *Cf.* Gilbert Slater, *The Making of Modern England*, new revised
edition (Boston, 1915), pp. 94-97.

[4] In boroughs resident freemen created before 1831 kept their vote
and in the counties the forty-shilling freehold qualification was retained.

of the Whigs, did not intend to have any further extension of the franchise after the passage of the Reform bill and that both those Parliamentary leaders who had supported and those who had opposed the measure were alike determined to go no further, but to use their best endeavors "to preserve the renovated constitution, entire and unimpaired." [1] There had been ushered in the Victorian compromise, described by Chesterton as "the decision of the middle classes to employ their new wealth in backing up a sort of aristocratical compromise, and not . . . insisting on a clean sweep and a clear democratic programme." [2]   Doomed to disappointment, therefore, was any hope of betterment of social conditions through the exercise of the franchise that the working class and the Radical Reformers and Radical Clubs had in mind when they demanded universal suffrage, vote by ballot, short Parliaments, and the abolition of the property qualification for members of Parliament.   The House of Commons was still to remain the "comfortable rich man's club," [3] caring too much for the interests it represented.

Hence it happened that any alliance between the Whigs, the Radicals and the working classes could not be formed permanently when the latter two groups saw the Whigs play the part of Tories. [4]   Whig ministries found it expedient to do nothing to protect trade-union organizations or cooperative societies.   "Taxes on knowledge" were allowed to continue, an obstacle to efforts on the part of the workingman to gain opportunities for social, mental and

[1] Speech of Lord John Russell, *Hansard*, third series, vol. xiii, p. 462.

[2] G. K. Chesterton, *The Victorian Age in Literature* (London, 1913), p. 30.

[3] So called by *Westminster Review*, January, 1867, p. 185.

[4] Rose, *op. cit.*, pp. 61 and 62.

moral improvement. The " Moral-force " Chartists might
well protest.

It can be pointed out, of course, that something was done
for the working class. The famous Factory Act of 1833 [1]
—in the opinion of a section of England's representatives,
the factory owners as typified by John Bright, " one of the
worst measures ever passed in the shape of an Act of the
legislature "—was put through by the aid of Tories deeply
moved by the existing conditions in the factories and not
unmindful of an opportunity to injure the interests of the
manufacturing capitalists.[2] The Tory Lord Ashley succeeded in carrying the Mines and Collieries Act [3] of 1842
by which some of the evils connected with the employment
of women and children in mines were remedied. The same
reformer was able to carry an act in 1844 [4] which bettered
the condition of young persons and women in factories, and
in 1847 the Ten Hours Act [5] (not, however, through any
aid rendered by John Bright and the Radicals). Moreover,
the factory acts were extended during the years 1845 to
1861 to industries allied to textiles, and during the 'sixties
to non-textile factories and workshops.[6] But, in contrast
to the little done, there was much more left undone. The
Fortnightly Review declaimed against this lack of legislation on important topics:

[1] 3 and 4 William IV, c. 103.

[2] George C. Brodrick and J. K. Fotheringham in *The Political History
of England* (edited by William Hunt and R. L. Poole), vol. xi, p. 327,
and Arnold Toynbee, *Lectures on the Industrial Revolution*, third im--
pression (London, 1913), pp. 231 and 232.

[3] 5 and 6 Vict., c. 99.

[4] 7 and 8 Vict., c. 15.

[5] 10 and 11 Vict., c. 29.

[6] B. L. Hutchins and A. Harrison, *A History of Factory Legislation*,
second edition revised (London, 1911), chap. vii and viii.

The doctrine of *laisser faire* in such matters may be philosophical, but it may also be the result of cowardice, selfishness, and stupidity; and there is an amusing inconsistency in the manner in which men will tell you almost in the same breath that Parliament can do little or nothing for the welfare of the masses of the people, and then quote some recent Act as indicative of the profound consideration of the same Parliament for their welfare.[1]

Much, too, which was done was regarded as having been done for self-interest. The new Poor Law of 1834,[2] opposed by Cobbett and Disraeli, who believed it bore " fearful tidings for the poor," [3] cut down the rates for the property owner; it did little for the destitute who had not been trained to care for themselves, and when the measure was vigorously enforced by the commissioners with little disposition to allow any temporary relaxation of the system, and during a time of poor harvests, the suffering was great, and the cry arose: " Let us end the power of the Whigs. Vote for the Tories in preference to the Whigs, the authors of the accursed Poor law." [4] The exclusion of all councillors who did not possess a certain amount of real or personal property, from the elective town councils had caused the Municipal Corporations Act of 1835 [5] to appear as another middle-class measure.[6] And again, later—in 1846—a section of the Whigs was anxious to have the corn laws repealed, influenced greatly, doubtless, by the existing distress and by the chance, perhaps, to injure land-owners (many of

---

[1] *Fortnightly Review*, vol. iv, p. 425.

[2] 4 and 5 William IV, c. 76.

[3] William F. Monypenny, *The Life of Benjamin Disraeli*, 4 vols. (New York, 1910-16), vol. i, p. 374.

[4] Rose, *op. cit.*, p. 61, citing an election speech of 1841 at Leicester.

[5] 5 and 6 William IV, c. 76.

[6] Rose, *op. cit.*, p. 61.

whom were Tories), and also touched by the thought of cheap bread and low wages. Thomas Cooper, in *The Life, Written by Himself,* gives a speech of a Chartist leader in which the hearers are earnestly exhorted not to be led away from their adherence to the People's Charter by the corn-law repealers; not that the corn-law repeal was wrong but

when we get the charter, we will repeal the Corn Laws and all other bad laws. But if you give up your agitation for the Charter to help the Free Traders, they will not help you to get the Charter. Do not be deceived by the middle classes again. You helped them to get their votes—you swelled their cry of " The bill, the whole bill, and nothing but the bill! " But where are the fine promises they made you? Gone to the winds! They said when they had gotten their votes, they would help you to get yours. But they and the rotten Whigs have never remembered you. Municipal Reform has been for their benefit—not yours. All other reforms the Whigs boast to have effected have been for the benefit of the middle classes—not yours. And now they want to get the Corn Law repealed—not for your benefit—but for their own. " Cheap Bread," they cry. But they mean " Low Wages." Do not listen to their cant and humbug. Stick to your charter. You are veritable slaves without your votes.[1]

There *were* members of Parliament who wished the work of reform to go on. In this connection the proposals of the year 1837 are often mentioned.[2] Hume,[3] for instance, stood for household suffrage, Tennyson,[4] for the repeal of the Septennial Act, Molesworth,[5] for reform of the upper

[1] *Life of Thomas Cooper* (London, 1872), pp. 136 and 137.

[2] *Vide*, for instance, Brodrick and Fotheringham, *op. cit.*, vol. xi, p. 374.

[3] Joseph Hume (1777-1855) voted early as a Tory but later became a Radical and carried the repeal of the combination laws.

[4] Charles Tennyson (1784-1861), Liberal.

[5] Sir William Molesworth (1810-1855), " Radical" and friend of J. S. Mill.

House, but such proposals made up no part of the Whig program. Lord John Russell, indeed, opposed the amendment to the address in answer to the Queen's speech in 1837 which demanded an extension of the suffrage, on the ground that the reopening of the question would destroy the stability of institutions! [1]

And, in the meantime, the protest against the existing order of things became stronger as the distress grew. The poor harvests of the late 'thirties, the enforcement of the new Poor Law when corn was rising to an average of more than sixty shillings per quarter, the suffering due to the supersession of manual labor by machinery and the displacement of agriculture and rural industry by manufactures, did not make the protests less vociferous. The politically active working class agitated for the six demands of the People's Charter: manhood suffrage, equal electoral districts, annual Parliaments, abolition of the property qualification for members of the House of Commons, vote by ballot, and salaries for members of Parliament. By the Charter they intended to obtain what they had not secured from the Reform bill of 1832: namely, control of the government to procure for themselves betterment of their social and economic position. Their agitation played an important part in the history of England for over ten years, especially during the lean years, but in the end did not attain its immediate objects. For various reasons the Chartist movement began to die out after 1848: [2] the failure of a great petition may have caused an unfavorable re-

---

[1] *Hansard*, vol. xxxix, p. 70.

[2] W. Nassau Molesworth, "History of the Reform Question from 1832 to 1866," *Fortnightly Review*, vol. vii, pp. 733 and 734, mentions: (1) failure of the monster petition; (2) failure of O'Connor's land scheme; (3) repeal of corn laws and success with free trade; (4) Poor Law beneficial by this time; (5) spread and success of the co-operative movement.

action; the leadership was defective; the middle class never came to be connected intimately with the movement; and—perhaps most important of all—the betterment of economic conditions brought on a period often designated as a period of torpor.[1]

For, in the 'fifties, the prosperity in trade tended to contract the area of misery and unemployment.[2] In the fifteen years from 1850 to 1865 imports nearly trebled and exports more than doubled. During this period, although prices were rising, nominal wages were rising faster, with the result that there was a considerable increase in real wages.[3] Stimulus was given to industry by the discovery of gold in California in 1848 and in Australia in 1850 and 1851—as the writers of the economic history of the period point out — and although financial crises brought ruin to many, favorable forces overbalanced the destructive influences.[4] Railways were opening up districts hitherto inaccessible—hence came a fresh stimulus to manufacturers—more capital was forthcoming and more railways were built.[5] Emigration to Australia and New Zealand multiplied the number of customers abroad. Great quantities of manufactures went to pay for the influx of gold with a consequent impulse to the shipbuilding trade. Agriculture, too, was thriving.[6] The result of the general prosperity

[1] Preston W. Slosson, in *The Decline of the Chartist Movement* (New York, 1916), chap. iv, gives a good discussion of the causes of the decline of the Chartist movement and stresses the influence of economic factors.

[2] H. D. Traill, *Social England*, 6 vols. (London, 1897), vol. vi, p. 423.

[3] G. R. Porter, *The Progress of the Nation*, revised by F. W. Hirst (London, 1912), p. 56.

[4] Traill, *op. cit.*, p. 433.

[5] A. L. Bowley, *A Short Account of England's Foreign Trade in the Nineteenth Century*, revised edition (London, 1905), pp. 58 *et seq.*

[6] The London *Times*, Dec. 31, 1859, speaks of this as a period of an unprecedented duration of agricultural prosperity.

was such an increased demand for labor that the *Times*
could declare in 1859:

It may be doubted whether greater accumulations of wealth
have ever taken place in a period of ten years in any age or
country, and for the first time within recent experience the reward of labor has increased even more largely than the profits
of capital. . . . In every department of skilled industry able
workmen find it in their power to command almost any price
for their services.[1]

And with the coming of prosperity, " the six points had
almost passed out of the range of practical politics and
only provoked a good-humored smile." [2]

The whole period under discussion, so far as the attitude
of the working class toward the franchise question is concerned, is to be found in summary in the *Edinburgh Review:*

As regards the classes which are not within the limits of the
franchise, a very great change has been operated in the course
of the five-and-thirty years of which we have been speaking.
The first part of that period was occupied in the abortive Chartist agitation. It was a period of great commercial depression
and manufacturing distress; labor was cheap, employment precarious, wages low. It seemed to be a problem how the increasing masses in our manufacturing towns were to be fed or
housed, and whether the means of subsistence could be made
to keep pace with the ratio at which the population was increasing. Since then, time has solved all these problems—the
discovery of the gold fields of California and Australia, the absorption caused by the Crimean war, and latterly, the enormous
increase of our commerce and manufactures, resulting from
our successful commercial policy, have changed the whole com-

[1] *Ibid.*

[2] Sir Spencer Walpole, *The History of Twenty-five Years*, 4 vols.
(London, 1904-08), vol. i, p. 65.

plexion of our laboring classes. Penury has given way to
plenty; idleness to employment; disaffection to content. . . .
The good which they (the workingmen) expected to result
from the six points of the Charter has descended upon them
from an unexpected quarter. Although the feeling among
them in regard to their admission to the franchise is genuine
and strong, it is altogether different, not in degree only but in
kind, from that which animated the Chartist agitators in 1848.[1]

During this period of torpor, however, the official class
had seen fit to take up again the question of Parliamentary
Reform. It was suggested here and there[2] that the Reform question was reopened by Lord John Russell because
his Government was declining in popularity and power and
needed such support as would probably come from those
newly enfranchised under Liberal auspices. According to
this interpretation, the agitation on the subject resulted
from the activities of political leaders. It must not be supposed, however, that outside interest in Reform was entirely lacking: large and important meetings held early in
1852 at Manchester, Sheffield, Westminster and elsewhere,
indicate that this was a question which still belonged among
the great political questions of the day.[3] The Queen's
speech of 1852, in which appeared the following words,
showed that at least some consideration was actuating the
Government:

It appears to me that this is a fitting time for calmly considering
whether it may not be advisable to make such amendments in
the Act of the late reign relating to the representation of the
Commons in Parliament as may be deemed calculated to carry

[1] *Edinburgh Review*, vol. cxxiii, p. 283.
[2] *Vide* the *Times*, December 31, 1859, editorial, "A Review of the
Decade."
[3] Molesworth, *op. cit.*, pp. 734 *et seq.*

into more complete effect the principles on which the law is
founded.[1]

And on the seventh of February Lord John Russell moved
for leave to bring in a bill to extend the right of voting for
members of Parliament. He proposed to lower the qualifications for the franchise in both county and borough, to
raise the constituency of the small boroughs by adding
neighboring places, to abolish the property qualifications of
members, *etc*. But the bill was shortly afterwards withdrawn when the Government was defeated on a Militia bill.

Lord Aberdeen, the head of a coalition ministry of Whigs
and Peelites, assisted by Lord John Russell as leader in the
House of Commons, came into power within a year's time.
It was announced that the Reform question would receive
serious consideration. Meetings were held in Manchester
and elsewhere to stir up interest in the subject. The bill
which Russell brought forward in February, 1854, proposed the disfranchisement of several boroughs which together had twenty-nine members, the reduction to one
representative of thirty-three of the smaller boroughs and
the apportionment of the sixty-two seats to more populous
places. Franchise qualifications were to be reduced and a
whole series of new and fantastic methods for the enfranchisement of particular sections of the people was devised.[2]
But this measure, too, had to be withdrawn when the minds
of the members of the House and of the public in general
were taken up with the Crimean War. At the close of the
war the popularity of Palmerston, who had become head of
the Government and was opposed to Reform in England,
the consequent rejection of some of the more Radical
Whigs in the election of 1857, and the Indian Mutiny all

[1] *Annual Register*, vol. xciv (1852), p. 4.
[2] *Annual Register*, vol. xcvi (1854), pp. 110-120.

tended to injure the prospects of having the question successfully taken up at the moment.

In 1858, however, Palmerston's popularity began rapidly
to wane when the Government, influenced by a plot [1] against
Louis Napoleon, brought in a bill to prevent foreign refu-
gees from abusing the hospitality of the country. A suggestion that the Government was yielding to foreign dictation was enough to cause the rejection of the bill, and
Lord Derby of the Conservative party was called upon to
form a new ministry.[2] The Conservatives, perhaps thinking
that the Liberals for their own interests had been identified
with the Reform question for too long a period, decided to
break the monopoly.[3] Acting upon the supposition that a
bill would be brought forward, agitators led by Bright became very active, hoping to gain large concessions.

On February 28, 1859, Mr. Disraeli, Chancellor of the
Exchequer under Derby, brought in his bill. By this it
was proposed not to alter the limits of the borough franchise but " to introduce a new kind of franchise, founded
upon personal property, and to give a vote to persons having property to the amount of £10 a year in the Funds, Bank
Stock, and East India Stock "; to enfranchise any persons
having £60 in a savings bank, recipients of pensions of £20
in the naval, military or civil services, graduates, ministers
of religion, members of the legal and medical professions,
etc. The bill was to do away with the distinction between

---

[1] A plot against the French Emperor's life had been planned by for-
eigners in London. The attempt to assassinate him failed but the
French demanded in dictatorial terms that the English Government
prevent such plots in future. *Cf.* Walpole, *op. cit.,* vol. i, pp. 113 *et seq.*

[2] It was in this year that Mr. Locke King's bill for the abolition of
the property qualifications required of English and Irish members (the
21 and 22 Vict., c. 26), was carried.

[3] But *cf.* J. H. Murchison, *The Conservatives and " Liberals," Their
Principles and Policy* (London, 1866), p. 45.

the county and borough franchise. Some little attention was given to redistribution.[1] Lord John Russell and Mr. Bright agreed in opposing the measure for the serious omission of any important proposal for the working class. Mr. Bright, speaking for the Radicals, thought that a Government representing a party which had always opposed the extension of political power to the people ought not to have undertaken to settle the question. In addition to the opposition from the Radicals, there was the opposition of those Conservatives[2] who did not like a measure which made the county and borough qualifications the same and the opposition of a large section of the Whigs who stood against Reform on general principles. Hence 291 voted for and 330 against the second reading, and the Government appealed to the country.

The result of the election was not favorable to the ministry, and Lord Palmerston assisted by Lord John Russell took office. This Government in turn decided to " supply the omissions and remedy the defects of the Act of 1832." Molesworth remarks that there was little distress, and public feeling in favor of their measure was slight: " The nation looked on, not certainly with indifference, but with comparative calmness, and regarded the contest as though the ascendency of a party, rather than the welfare and prosperity of the nation, was involved in the issue." [3] The bill itself provided for a £10 county and a £6 borough occupation franchise, and some little redistribution.[4] But little enthusiasm in the Government accorded with little enthusiasm in the nation and after the second reading delay fol-

[1] *Annual Register*, vol. ci (1859), chap. iii.

[2] Henley, the President of the Board of Trade, and Walpole, the Home Secretary, retired from the Government, dreading " that identity of suffrage which is the principle of the Government Bill."

[3] Molesworth, *op. cit.*, p. 741.

[4] *Annual Register*, vol. cii (1860), chap iv.

lowed delay. Finally on the eleventh of June Lord John Russell withdrew the bill. Henceforth no Reform bill was brought forward by the Government until 1866.

Before the Liberals and Conservatives were again to manœuver over the Reform question events happening beyond England's shores helped the cause of democracy and affected opinion in England itself. It is true that the results of the turmoil of 1848 on the Continent had not been very fruitful for democrats: instead of the republic of a Louis Blanc or the government of the middle-class republicans there came the empire of Louis Napoleon in France; instead of the reform projected by the Frankfort Assembly of 1848 there came a reactionary triumph with the restoration of the 1815 Confederation in Germany; instead of unity and democracy there came Austrian restoration in Venetia and to the various Italian thrones conservative princes and a Pope converted to conservatism. Nevertheless democracy still remained an ideal for the workingmen [1] and to both Sardinia and Prussia had been granted a constitution.

France had its Napoleon — but Napoleon ruled in the name of democracy. He was careful, however, to retain for himself control of the ministry, the power of initiating legislation, command of the army and navy, together with decisions upon questions of peace and war and the power of concluding treaties. The *Corps législatif* of two hundred and fifty-one members elected by direct manhood suffrage was carefully restricted in its powers. As Lecky points out, in spite of the fact that Legislative Assemblies were elected by universal suffrage, the government was an almost absolute despotism during the greater part of the

[1] Carlton J. H. Hayes, *A Political and Social History of Modern Europe*, 2 vols. (New York, 1917), vol. ii, p. 144.

reign.[1]   Enemies rather than friends to an extended suffrage could therefore get inspiration from events across
the Channel.   When John Bright, the great English champion of Parliamentary Reform, reminded an audience in
1866 that universal suffrage existed in France, the *Saturday Review* reminded him that " in France universal suffrage produces an assembly of Crown nominees, which has
no voice on peace or war, on the policy of the country, or
on the appointment of a single clerk in a public office." [2]
Blackwood's, a Conservative magazine, declared universal
suffrage ineffective in France where " the result obtained
by the ballot-box no more represented the real opinions and
wishes of the inhabitants than if they had been marched up
to the poll under an escort of military and compelled to
vote, at the point of the bayonet, according to the dictates
of the French Emperor, whose subjects they have now become." [3]   The pamphleteers of illiberal leanings likewise
pointed to the failure of universal suffrage as a means
of giving freedom to the French people.   One declared that
manhood suffrage in France had been consistent with a
fettered press and trammels on speech and motion.[4]   Another asked : " France—is this a freer country than Eng-

[1] William Edward Hartpole Lecky, *Democracy and Liberty,* 2 vols.
(New York, 1896), vol. i, p. 38.

[2] *Saturday Review,* September 1, 1866. *Vide* the attitude of this
weekly on April 21, 1860, April 28, 1860, May 20, 1865, June 24, 1865,
January 12, 1867, *etc.*   In the number dated February 17, 1866, it
acknowledges, however, that " no one can doubt that there is something both elevating and inspiriting to the masses, both of the American
and the French people, in the conviction which they feel that their
Government belongs to them, represents them, embodies their views,
and expresses their wishes."

[3] *Blackwood's,* vol. lxxxviii, p. 107. The quotation is descriptive of
conditions in Savoy and Nice but succeeding pages of the article show
that the statement is regarded as true of France as a whole.

[4] Frederic Hill, *Parliamentary Reform, How the Representation may
be Amended* (London, 1865), p. 5.

land? . . . What does the present show us? Her most
eloquent orators, writers and statesmen silenced, her press
gagged—neither liberty of knowledge nor utterance, nor
opinion, nor combination—her parliament packed; her elections a mockery." [1]

Moreover, little happened in German affairs between the
middle of the century and 1865 to rouse the enthusiasm of
the more liberal of the English. Austria had been given
over completely to reaction, and in Prussia, Bismarck, firm
believer in divine-right monarchy, was master. In the
spring of 1866—when the Reform question was becoming
important once more in British politics—Bismarck surprised
the world, however, by advocating a reform of the confederation in such a way that there should be representation of
the people by universal manhood suffrage. J. H. Rose points
out that hostility to bureaucratic Austria moved him to make
Prussia the champion in German affairs of the principle of
a very slightly restricted suffrage.[2] Hypocrisy was the
term applied to Bismarck's action in many quarters. But
after the victory over Austria in the Seven Weeks' War
there was formed the North German Confederation,[3] the
legislative power of which was vested in a *Bundesrath,* an
assembly of deputies from the states, and a *Reichstag,*
whose members were elected by equal, secret, direct and
manhood suffrage.[4]

[1] "L," *Queries on the Franchise, an Examination of " the Seven
Reasons "* (Norwich, 1866), p. 29.

[2] Rose, *Rise of Democracy,* p. 180, but *vide* the statement of Heinrich
von Sybel, *Die Begründung des Deutschen Reiches durch Wilhelm I,*
7 vols. (München, 1890-94), vol. iv, pp. 317 and 318, that Bismarck,
believing in the interest of the masses in the maintenance of public
order, considered universal suffrage a guaranty of conservatism.

[3] The invitation to form such a Confederation had been given June
16, 1866; the scheme was adopted February 2, 1867.

[4] A contrast to the situation within Prussia where because of the three-
class system the suffrage was indirect and unequal.

German affairs interested the English public, as articles in the London *Times* testify. But Reform speakers referred to movements in Germany comparatively seldom. John Bright told an audience:

In Germany a vote is to be given to every man of twenty-five years of age and upwards, so that, if we were to propose a measure that would give a vote to every man of twenty-five years of age and upwards in this country, we should not be in advance of that great country of Northern Germany which is now being established. What is it that we are now come to in this country, that what is being rapidly conceded in all parts of the world is being persistently and obstinately refused here in England, the home of freedom, the mother of Parliaments? [1]

To this statement the *Saturday Review* retorted that Mr. Bright had dwelt with too much complacency on the " promiscuous suffrage " which Count Bismarck had announced as the proper basis of election for a German parliament and suggested that the eminent German champion of parliamentary privilege had probably little thought that he would be quoted by Mr. Bright as a pattern Reformer. It further warned that when the attributes of the new German parliament should be known, and when its relation to the Prussian House of Deputies should be defined, it would then be " time enough for the Mother of Parliaments to take a lesson from her youngest and least promising descendant." [2]

Occasionally speeches made in Reform meetings contained a few sentences concerning Germany [3] or France,* a

[1] Quoted from the *Saturday Review*, September 1, 1866.

[2] *Ibid.*

* *Vide* speech of Colonel Dickson quoted *infra*, p. 112.

[3] Replying to congratulations of the workingmen of London to the people of North Germany on recent events, Bismarck wrote on May 17, 1867: " I have the honor to acknowledge the receipt of a resolution

pamphlet now and again referred to events on the Continent,[1] a Reform writer and speaker like Professor Beesly [2] might declare to a newspaper that he approved of the French type of democracy as contrasted with American democracy.[3] Yet Rose's statement — that since 1830 the influence of Continental democratic movements on British politics has steadily declined [4]—is applicable to the influence of Germany and France upon England in 1867.

Italy is the one Continental country whose influence upon British politics was of such importance that the foregoing statement would hardly hold true. Italian unity was destined to come from the leadership of Sardinia, the only Italian state where absolutism after 1849 had not conquered constitutionalism. Skilfully led by Cavour, Sardinia in 1859 won the assistance of Louis Napoleon in a war to drive Austria from the peninsula. Although that assistance did not free Venetia, the struggle did stir central Italy to demand unity under the Sardinian king. In southern Italy the activity of Garibaldi and his Thousand led to the overthrow of the Bourbons and the expressions of a desire on the part of the Sicilians and Neapolitans for union with the North. Plebiscites showed the strength of this desire. By 1861, Italy was well on the way to unity under a constitutional government.

passed at a meeting of metropolitan delegates from trades, friendly and temperance and other societies, and from a hundred London branches of the Reform League, congratulating the people of North Germany on the achievement of full representation and vote by ballot, and commenting very kindly on my conduct in advising and defending that Reform . . . " The *Times*, May 23, 1867.

[1] *Cf.* " L," *Queries on the Franchise.*

[2] E. S. Beesly had a professorship at University College, London. He wrote much in favor of trade unionism.

[3] The *Spectator*, April 21, 1866.

[4] Rose, *Rise of Democracy*, p. 146.

England was greatly influenced by this Italian movement for national unity. Louis Blanc made mention of the " impassioned interest " which England, considered as a whole, took in Italian affairs.[1]   Her moral support, amid the strongly expressed disapprobation of the great Continental powers, gave, says Lecky, " both force and respectability to the Italian cause, and broke the isolation to which it would have otherwise been condemned." [2]   It is true that the Conservatives, led by Lord Derby and Disraeli, with a feeling akin to that of the great Continental leaders, cherished antipathy to Italian independence and declared for the cause of legitimacy,[3] but they were taking the unpopular attitude.[4]   Lord John Russell, on the other hand, urged that the Italian people should be allowed to form their own government freely without the intervention of either France or Austria, although — true Whig that he was—he refused to put stress on the verdict of universal suffrage as expressed by the plebiscites, but regarded the voice of the duly authorized representative bodies as the only legitimate expression of the people's wishes.[5]   Men of more liberal bent had greater enthusiasm for the Italian cause.   Fawcett,[6] for instance, feeling that the emancipa-

---

[1] Louis Blanc, *Letters on England*, translated from the French by James Hutton and revised by the author, 2 vols. (London, 1866), letter i.

[2] W. E. H. Lecky, *Democracy and Liberty*, vol. i, p. 495. *Vide* Herbert Paul, *A History of Modern England*, 5 vols. (New York, 1904), vol. ii, p. 224, for a still stronger statement of England's influence.

[3] The *Saturday Review*, April 26, 1862.

[4] *Saturday Review*, July 1, 1865. *Vide*, also, *Frazer's* vol. lxiv, July, 1861.

[5] Lecky, *Democracy and Liberty*, vol. i, pp. 493-495.

[6] Henry Fawcett was a vigorous but as yet subordinate member of the Radical party. Accidentally blinded in 1858 he remained actively concerned with public affairs and was elected to Parliament July, 1865, as member for Brighton.

tion of Italy was only one of the many struggles going on
in society to give the lesser man a fair chance, correlated
this movement with that of the British laboring class, which
he championed. He was thus "a lusty swimmer on this
tide of freedom." [1] Gladstone, important in the counsels
of the Liberals, [2] was referred to by a weekly as a patron
and associate of Italian exiles and liberals. [3] In April, 1862,
he made a great speech in the House of Commons in which
he approved of Italian yearnings. His attitude helped to
secure for him a hold "upon all of the rising generation
of liberals who cared for the influence and the good name
of Great Britain in Europe, and who were capable of sym-
pathizing with popular feeling and the claims of national
justice." [4] The majority of educated men and the middle
class in general felt sympathy for Italy; [5] the working
class showed its interest on one occasion by presenting to
Garibaldi as a testimonial a gold watch and chain pur-
chased by penny subscription. [6] So intense was their feeling

[1] Winifred Holt, *A Beacon for the Blind Being a Life of Henry
Fawcett the Blind Postmaster General* (Boston, 1914), p. 157. *Vide,*
also, *Saturday Review*, September 17, 1864, "The New Reformers."

[2] Details of his life and importance are given in chap. iv.

[3] *Saturday Review*, July 1, 1865.

[4] John Morley, *The Life of William Ewart Gladstone*, 3 vols. (London,
1903), vol. ii, p. 108.

[5] *Saturday Review*, January 31, 1863.

[6] This was done by the townspeople of Brighton. *Vide* the *Times,*
April 18, 1861. The acknowledgment of Garibaldi came to Mr. Coning-
ham, M. P.,—"Be pleased to express my feelings of great gratitude to
the English working men, to which good and laborious class I am
proud to belong, for the valuable gift which they have transmitted to
me through you. I knew that the hour of Italian nationality was marked
on the dialplate of time; but, observing that in my own country many
denied this, because the counsels of the foreigner and dastardly fears
would have it so, it is a great comfort to me to find that hour indicated
by the watch which the people of Brighton have given to me."

that it seemed probable to one writer [1] that England would
not have hesitated to join France in recovering Italy for
the Italians in 1859 had the working class been fully represented in Parliament at that time.

The full effect of Italian events upon British politics
was probably first felt as a result of Garibaldi's visit to
England in the spring of 1864. Seldom has a foreign hero
met with the reception accorded Garibaldi by the London
populace. To the working class he appeared as one striving for liberation of enslaved peoples all over the face of
the globe,[2] a soldier who bore the sword for human freedom.[3] It was such a belief that gave him great popularity.
" In those days," says Morley, " there were idealists;
democracy was conscious of common interests and common
brotherhood." [4] Thus was there being created an atmos-
phere in which democracy could triumph.[5]

The enthusiasm aroused by Garibaldi's visit among the
millions of unenfranchised workingmen alarmed both Whig
and Tory leaders. Disraeli, regarding the hero as the foe
of constituted authority in both church and state, refused
to meet him, although other Tories paid their respects.[6]

[1] R. H. Hutton, *The Political Character of the Working Class.*
(London, 1867), pp. 31 and 32.

[2] *Saturday Review*, December 16, 1865, speaking of the attitude of
the Reform League toward him. When later Garibaldi accepted the
Honorary Presidency of the Reform League, the League thanked him
for accepting the honor and addressed him as the proved champion of
true liberty in all countries. *Vide* the *Times*, May 20, 1867.

[3] Morley, *Life of Gladstone*, vol. ii, p. 109.

[4] *Ibid.* Qualifications for the franchise were not such, of course, as
to give anything like democracy to the Italians, but by the activity of
men like Garibaldi and by the expression of opinions in plebiscites, the
desires of the great masses for unity had been obtained.

[5] George Macaulay Trevelyan, *The Life of John Bright* (London,
1913), p. 331.

[6] Monypenny and Buckle, *Life of Disraeli*, vol. iv, pp. 327-328.

Whigs received him in their homes but kept him from contact with the people, " to whom he might act as a flame of tinder." [1]   After the reception in London what might not happen in the manufacturing centers?   "Fears of this sort were added to other reasons why Palmerston's Government wished to prevent his longer stay in England." [2]

Although Garibaldi did not make a projected tour of the " provinces ", his stay in England was long enough to react upon the feelings of the great Liberal leader Gladstone. In May of 1864 the latter uttered in the House of Commons words which could mean only that he was willing to break the Victorian compromise.   Speaking of Parliamentary Reform, he said: " I venture to say that every man who is not presumably incapacitated by some consideration of personal unfitness or of political danger is morally entitled to come within the pale of the constitution." [3]   Of the effects of such a statement upon Gladstone's position among the official class, explanation will be made later; that such sentiment came directly from the Italian influences is vouched for by Gladstone's great opponent, Disraeli himself.   Referring to the foregoing quotation in a letter to Lord Derby, Disraeli wrote: " Though Gladstone's move was matured, and, indeed, for a considerable time contemplated, I have no doubt the visit and reception of Garibaldi have acted on his impressionable nature, and have betrayed him into a far more extreme position than was at first intended." [4]   Gladstone's own biographer has summed up the effect of Italian liberation as follows:

It is easy to see some at any rate of the influences that were

[1] Trevelyan, *Life of Bright*, p. 331.
[2] *Ibid.*
[3] *Hansard*, vol. clxxv, p. 324.
[4] Monypenny and Buckle, vol. iv, p. 404.

bringing Mr. Gladstone decisively into harmony with the movement of liberal opinions, now gradually spreading over Great
Britain.   The resurrection of Italy could only be vindicated on
principles of liberty and the right of a nation to choose its own
rulers.   The peers and the ten-pound householders who held
power in England were no Bourbon tyrants; but just as in
1830 the overthrow of the Bourbon line in France was followed
by the Reform bill here, so the Italian revolution of 1860 gave
new vitality to the popular side in England.[1]

Important as was the influence of Italy upon democracy's
cause in England, still more important for the growth of
democratic tendencies was the outcome of the Civil War in
America.   In this struggle democracy was on trial.   England had already learned of the benefits of American democracy.   John Bright for many years had carried its fiery
cross, as the *Saturday Review* complained,[2] through the
length and breadth of the manufacturing districts preach-
ing Reform in all weathers, as Peter the Hermit preached
crusades.

With the outbreak of the Civil War in April, 1861, the
Saturday Review itself was to have the opportunity of
going on a crusade—a crusade against democracy and John
Bright.   The failure of the " Model Republic " to keep an
undivided household was suggestive enough of the unhappy
ending of a great experiment in government, but the expedients to which America had recourse in attempting to
preserve itself intact were in the opinion of the magazine
absolutely damaging to the democratic cause.[3]   The reckless expenditure of funds,[4] the absolutism of the adminis-

----

[1] Morley, *Life of Gladstone*, vol. ii, pp. 123 and 124.

[2] *Saturday Review*, February 2, 1867. *Vide* issues for November 26,
1859, January 21, 1860, December 8, 1866.

[3] *Saturday Review*, October 12, 1861, and February 1, 1862.

[4] *Saturday Review*, September 14, 1861.

tration with its repression of free discussion, the disappearance of every guaranty of liberty, the ubiquitous police, the muzzled press, gave to those opposed to democratic movements an estimation of the opinion in which future true lovers of liberty would hold democracy. If the Radicals still rallied around Bright when all his prophecies had failed, when the delusive confusion between freedom and democracy was being finally banished from the minds of Englishmen,[1] scarcely could it be said that the ages of faith had passed away.[2] Since the United States which practised universal suffrage had become involved in hopeless difficulties, it would be madness to lower the qualification for the suffrage in England and " overthrow the only free representation of sound public opinion which exercised sovereign power in any part of the world." [3]

Against democracy and John Bright the *Saturday Review* was not a solitary crusader. The press, almost as a whole, joined on its side of the struggle. To *Blackwood's* the evils of democracy were not accidental, as might be concluded from the example of the French Revolution, but inherent, as was shown in the result of the experiment conducted under the most favorable circumstances in America.

That example should teach both rulers and peoples moderation . . . And we have written in vain if we have not also deduced a moral for those who would seek to improve our own condition by assimilating our institutions to those of America. Our own agitators, in their clamour for reform, are descending towards universal suffrage. Universal suffrage means, the government of a numerical majority, which means oppression—which means civil war. What civil war, even in its mildest form, means, we know from the *Times'* correspondent; and most heartily do we,

[1] *Saturday Review*, September 14, 1861.
[2] *Saturday Review*, October 12, 1861.
[3] *Saturday Review*, November 23, 1861, and February 23, 1861.

in concluding this article, echo his wish—" *God defend us from mob law.*" [1]

Frazer's [2] and the *Quarterly Review* joined the forces of those mentioned. The latter could now rejoice that Bright no longer had America to fall back upon because " the great Republican bubble has burst." [3] The London *Times*, the opinions of which counted for more in both England and the United States than those of any other English publication, had a warm sympathy with the aristocracy across the sea. [4]

Yet the press, in its hostility to the North, merely represented the opinions of the classes which were powerful in society and in Parliament. Palmerston, leader of the Government, was distrusted by Charles Francis Adams, the American minister to England. [5] Gladstone, friendly to Italian unity, was guilty in 1862 of uttering words whose connotation he later found it difficult to explain: " There is no doubt that Jefferson Davis and other leaders of the South have made an army; they are making, it appears, a navy; they have made what is more than either — they have made a nation. . . . We may anticipate with certainty the success of the Southern States so far as regards their separation from the North." [6] Disraeli thought that the United States was breaking down. He and most of

---

[1] *Blackwood's*, October, 1861, "Democracy Teaching by Example," p. 405.

[2] *Vide* issues of November, 1859, and July, 1862.

[3] *Quarterly Review*, vol. cx, pp. 254-256.

[4] *Vide* Charles Francis Adams, *Charles Francis Adams* (Boston, 1900), p. 349, and James Ford Rhodes, *History of the United States*, 8 vols. (New York, 1900-19), vol. iv, pp. 82-84. The *Spectator* often opposed the opinions of the *Times*.

[5] Adams, *Charles Francis Adams*, p. 241.

[6] The *Times*, October 9, 1862.

his followers took it that the disruption of Bright's ideal democratic community showed the instability of an extended suffrage as the foundation of a state, and believed that the collapse of republican institutions would tell greatly in favor of aristocracy.[1]   But Disraeli had the wisdom to keep his opinions to himself.

The aristocracy and the upper middle classes were hostile to the United States because pure democracy was hateful to them, wrote Cobden.[2]   Mr. Trevelyan, in the *Life of John Bright* declares that " the Conservative classes, Tory and Whig, were nervously aware that Bright's democratic movement was threatening their own monopoly of political power.   If democracy triumphed in America, nothing could long delay its advent over here.   But if democracy in America failed, the reaction would be strongly felt in Europe and most of all in Great Britain."   He goes on to say that Motley [3] found the situation unbearable and wrote after Bull Run, " The real secret of the exultation which manifests itself in the *Times* and other organs over our troubles and disasters is their hatred, not to America so much as to democracy in England." [4]   The *Quarterly Review* wrote that the American proceedings would have been discussed less eagerly in England and criticized with less freedom if they had not been made the turning point of a political controversy at home.   Battles on American soil were deciding the status of Mr. Bright's theories.[5]   Mr. W. E. Forster at

[1] Monypenny and Buckle, vol. iv, pp. 328 and 402.

[2] T. Wemyss Reid, *Life of the Right Honorable William Edward Forster*, 2 vols. (London, 1888, 2nd edition), vol. i, p. 341.

[3] The historian, Motley, was in England from 1859 to the middle of 1861.   In August, 1861, he left the United States to which he had returned two months before, as minister to Austria.

[4] Trevelyan, *Life of John Bright*, pp. 304-305.

[5] *Quarterly Review*, vol. cxii, " The Confederate Struggle and Recognition."

a Reform meeting of May 16, 1865, at Manchester clearly stated that dislike of democracy was the cause of the hostile attitude toward the North:

What was it made such a large portion of our aristocracy espouse the cause of the South? He did not believe it was love of slavery, or even hatred to a republic, though that might have had something to do with it (Applause). He believed it was an instinctive feeling that there was a chance for aristocratic government such as had not been seen before; that in that manœuvring oligarchy of the South, although they might not be proud of them as a very good imitation of themselves (a laugh)—yet, after all, there was the hope that there, in a young Anglo-Saxon country, an aristocracy was taking root, which, if the South obtained power, would be a strong force in the world. It was an instinctive feeling of that kind which made the aristocracy rally to the South, and made one of their most talented representatives (Lord Robert Cecil) say in the House of Commons that the South were our natural allies. (Loud laughter and groans.) They certainly were natural allies of Lord Cecil's order, but not the natural allies of England. (Applause).[1]

There were also other reasons for a hostile attitude. According to Louis Blanc, not only the democratic institutions but the prodigious development of power under those institutions grieved aristocratic England.[2] The feeling of jealousy toward the power of the great republic of the West and the wish that it might be weakened by the success of the rebellion did exist.[3] The high tariff of the North contrasted poorly in the Englishman's eye with the free trade of the South. Commercial and manufacturing interests

[1] *The Times*, May 19, 1865.

[2] Louis Blanc, *Letters on England*, letter xlviii.

[3] *Vide* William Harris, *History of the Radical Party in Parliament* (London, 1885), pp. 447-448.

desired an early end to a war that was preventing the importation of raw cotton in England and the exportation of manufactured goods to America.[1] Moreover, many of the English believed that the South was within its constitutional rights in withdrawing from a distasteful union, and others argued that the South had the doctrine of the rights of nationalities on its side.[2] A " sporting spirit," on one hand, led to a partisan interest in the welfare of the comparatively small power skilfully carrying on a desperate struggle with an unwieldy and gigantic adversary;[3] a conservative judgment, on the other, might decide that final subjugation of five and a half millions of people was impossible and that continuation of warfare was a useless waste of life.[4]

Fortunately for the United States, these causes of English hostility did not appeal to certain leaders of the lower classes or to those classes themselves. Bright, Cobden and W. E. Forster were the three important men of the middle-class element who remained friendly to the United States,[5] " the friends of free labor and advocates of a democratic republic."[6] Confederate statesmen knew their influence and feared much their opposition to the recognition of a slaveholders' Confederacy.[7] Mention of Bright and Cobden has been made before. They understood the real meaning of the struggle going on across the water. Bright told

---

[1] Rhodes, *History of the United States*, vol. iv, pp. 77 and 78.

[2] *Vide* Lecky, *Democracy and Liberty*, vol. i, pp. 487 and 488.

[3] *Ibid.*, p. 487, and Morley, vol. ii, pp. 85 and 86.

[4] Rhodes, vol. iv, p. 78, and Lecky, vol. i, p. 488. *Vide*, also, Leslie Stephen, *The " Times" on the American War*, reprinted in the *Magazine of History*, vol. x.

[5] Reid, *Life of Forster*, vol. i, p. 338.

[6] Adams, *Charles Francis Adams*, p. 156.

[7] *Ibid.*, pp. 262, 299, 302.

a meeting of skilled laborers, held in London on March 26, 1863, that the struggle was between two sections of a country, in one of which labor was honored more than elsewhere in the world and men might " rise to competence and independence," and in the other of which labor was degraded and the laborer made a chattel.[1] W. E. Forster was rather young in parliamentary life, having first been elected as a member of the House of Commons from Bradford in 1861. He proved to be, in the opinion of Charles Francis Adams, " the most earnest, the most courageous, and the most effective friend the United States had among men prominent in English life." [2] All three were influential in guiding the opinions of the working class.

To the workingmen, especially to the Lancashire operatives, honor has continued to be given for holding to the cause of the North when dire distress caused by the cotton famine [3] naturally would have led them to demand an end to the Northern blockade of Southern ports. Their *interest* in the matter, far deeper than that of the professional classes, an interest opposed to the line of policy they adopted, did not blind them to the great idea involved in the struggle; [4] freedom contending with slavery called not in vain for their support. Even when the outcome of the war seemed destined to be unfavorable to the Union—toward the close of 1862 and in the early months of 1863—their public meetings gave strong manifestation of sympathy for the North. Writing of their attitude, Louis Blanc said:

[1] John Bright, *Speeches on Questions of Public Policy*, edited by James E. Thorold Rogers (London, 1868), vol. i, pp. 248 and 249.

[2] Adams, *Charles Francis Adams*, pp. 263 and 188.

[3] For details, *vide* chap. ii.

[4] R. H. Hutton, *The Political Character of the Working Class*, pp. 30 and 31.

While the members of the aristocracy, the landed proprietors, the great manufacturers, and the politicians of the drawing room or the club, breathe nothing but vengeance, war, and victory, it is to what an imbecile pride is accustomed to call the lower stratum of society, that we must descend to look for calmness, moderation and a thoughtful love of peace.[1]

Until July, 1863, the foes rather than the friends of democracy had cause for happiness. Neither abroad nor at home was the American government reaping advantages. In the latter part of 1861, the American Captain Wilkes of the *San Jacinto* nearly caused war with Great Britain by stopping the British mail steamer *Trent* and taking forcibly from it two accredited Confederate emissaries; in 1862 Louis Napoleon and English public men were pressing the British government towards recognition of the South.[2] Feeling among the upper classes was so intense that the Emancipation Proclamation was interpreted as a sham to deceive Europe. Moreover, Union forces in the field were not successful. The *Saturday Review* declared that American events were causing the influence of radicalism to wane.[3] *Blackwood's* shows very well the satisfaction of the conservative press:

It would perhaps be too much to say that the tendencies of our constitution towards democracy have been checked solely by a view of the tattered and insolvent guise in which republicanism appears in America. The right instinct and good sense of the country had already preserved it from following the Reform leaders in their downward strides to the declivity that overhangs chaos. . . . As the pause, however, proceeded from indifference rather than conviction, that season might have arrived, and

[1] Louis Blanc, *Letters on England*, letter xlviii, p. 252.

[2] Adams, *Charles Francis Adams*, p. 278.

[3] *Saturday Review*, August 2, 1862.

the effort might have been renewed. But the events which have since passed in America have made a deep impression on the public mind. Theorists might have uttered warnings through an entire generation without producing a tithe of the effect which has followed from the spectacle of floundering democracy. . . . The only result at present of a proposal to "Americanise our institutions" on an audience who are witnessing the Transatlantic exhibition, would be to induce a belief that the proposer was insane. Possibly the time is not very distant when what have lately been propounded as great political truths may, for a season at least, be classed among the most astonishing delusions; when faith in political equality and universal suffrage will appear as absurd and unintelligible as in right divine and the infallibility of the Pope.[1]

But the aristocracy was shocked by the victories of Gettysburg and Vicksburg in July, 1863.[2] A possibility of war between England and America was contingent upon the escape of iron-clad rams which were being built in England for the breaking of the blockade. Their escape would probably have been much more damaging to the cause of the North than had been the escape of the *Alabama*.[3] Earl Russell's activity warded off that danger in the fall of 1863. Thereafter there was little chance of intervention. By March, 1865, the *Spectator* declared that the House had at last become convinced that the North must win.[4] Cobden in a letter dated February 5, 1865, wrote to the American minister at Copenhagen:[5]

[1] *Blackwood's*, April, 1862, p. 514.

[2] R. Barry O'Brien, *John Bright, A Monograph* (London, 1910), pp. 157 and 158.

[3] The *Alabama* escaped from Liverpool in July, 1862, and during her career burned fifty-seven vessels of a value of over six and a half million dollars. *Vide* Rhodes, vol. iv, pp. 365 and 366.

[4] The *Spectator*, March 18, 1865.

[5] Bradford R. Wood was the minister to Denmark in the early part of 1865.

Democracy has discovered how few friends it has in Europe among the ruling class. It has at the same time discovered its own strength, and, what is more, this has been discovered by the aristocr cies and absolutisms of the Old World. So that I think you are more safe than ever against the risks of intervention from this side of the Atlantic. Besides, you must not forget that the working class of England, who will not be always without direct political power, have, in spite of their sufferings and the attempt made to mislead them, adhered nobly to the cause of civilization and freedom.[1]

Democracy came out of the struggle triumphant and the workingmen were vindicated. By their clearness of insight into the merits of a great national question and by their resolute determination to support the right, they had proved that they might be called upon to take part in their own government with safety and advantage.[2] Mr. Forster told them that " if any community had done anything towards helping the right cause, and taking care that England was not disgraced in all future history by going on the wrong side in this contest, it had been the working men of Lancashire." And he added : " If they had a care about Reform they would be repaid for what they had done, by the lesson which the triumph of freedom, the triumph of popular government in America taught those who refused the workingmen their rights."[3] For their part the workingmen continued to look with enthusiasm toward the American Republic. The *Saturday Review* complained that " even the audacious anticipation of one speaker, that in the course of years England would be absorbed by the Western Republic, was received [by them] certainly without any too patriotic

[1] The *Times*, April 3, 1865.

[2] William Harris, *The Radical Party in Parliament*, p. 448. *Vide,* also, Winifred Holt, *A Beacon for the Blind*, p. 157.

[3] At a Reform meeting at Manchester. *Vide* the *Times*, May 19, 1865.

discomposure, and even with a measure of approval, as if it were probably about the best thing that could happen to us." [1]

The various magazines, indeed, bear witness to the fact that the victory of the Union reacted for the cause of democracy, just as the expected failure had reacted for the power of aristocracy. The *Spectator* declared that democracy in America had come victorious out of a war which would have crushed any European monarchy except the British, and had overcome a rebellion before which even Great Britain might possibly have succumbed.[2] In 1866 the *Fortnightly Review* pointed out that a few years ago republican government had been on its trial in America and its success seemed to be uncertain. " There was then a lull in the Reform movement in England, and a very moderate measure would have satisfied its supporters. . . . The United States have exhibited a wealth, a strength, an organization, a temperance and moderation after their great successes, which show that universal suffrage and the freest institutions are compatible with a well-ordered state." [3]

The outcome of the American struggle had a great effect, too, upon the opinions of certain of the political leaders like Gladstone. He had learned that " universal suffrage had proved itself compatible with the display of certain great qualities." [4] Gladstone's biographer mentions that American events had " reversed the fashionable habit of making American institutions English bugbears, and gave a sweeping impulse to that steady but resistless tide of liberal and popular sentiment that ended in the parliamentary

[1] *Saturday Review*, December 16, 1865.

[2] The *Spectator*, July 1, 1865; *vide*, also, the number for February 17, 1866.

[3] *Fortnightly Review*, September 15, 1866.

[4] *Saturday Review*, April 14, 1866.

reform of 1867." [1]   As the Americans themselves foresaw, the liberal, democratic, progressive party headed by John Bright and his friends had a prodigious increase of power.[2]

The evidence showing the influence of America upon England has been striking enough to call forth the statement that " it is hardly too much to say that the Reform Bill of 1867 was a direct product of the Northern triumph in the American war." [3]   In April, 1866, Professor Beesly, when addressing a Reform meeting, attributed the revival of the Reform agitation to the result of the American war and observed that republicanism was looking up in the world.[4]

Nevertheless, succeeding chapters will show that the power of the urban artisan class, especially as exerted through their trade unions, made their admission to political power inevitable [5] when once their feeling had been aroused by economic pressure, the eloquence of their middle-class leaders and the openly-expressed hostility of the majority of the members of Parliament. For, it will be seen,[6] the majority of members, even in the lower House, were still hostile to anything approaching democracy in 1866, although they could not point to its failure. But events in Italy and America were of influence at least to this extent: they gave inspiration and confidence to men like Bright and Forster and had not a little to do with the changing attitude of a less radical person like Gladstone, and they

[1] Morley, *Life of Gladstone*, vol. ii, p. 124.

[2] *Vide* the *Times*, April 16, 1866, quoting the *New York Times*.

[3] William Archibald Dunning, *The British Empire and the United States* (New York, 1914), p. 230.

[4] The *Times*, April 12, 1866.

[5] *Cf.* Bernard Holland, *The Life of Spencer Compton, Eighth Duke of Devonshire*, 2 vols. (London, 1911), vol. i, pp. 64 and 65.

[6] In chap. iv.

kept England from becoming reactionary, from being
handed over for years, as it was after 1815, to an administration resolved to resist all changes as "dangerous to
our institutions." [1]

[1] *Cf.* the *Spectator*, July 15, 1865.

CHAPTER II

CONDITION OF THE WORKING CLASS IN THE 'SIXTIES

IN the foregoing pages note was made of the fact that the working class, during the prosperous years of the 'fifties, ceased that violent agitation which was carried on in the unfortunate decade of the 'forties. During the years 1866 and 1867, it will be seen,[1] an agitation for political Reform once again was taken up. Naturally the question arises: did the economic situation in the 'sixties help to stir up discontent?—Such is the question with which the present chapter will deal.

The early 'sixties, indeed, need very little attention, inasmuch as conditions in general show much the same prosperity as was evident during most of the preceding ten years. Agricultural prosperity may be said to have lasted from 1854 to the end of 1865. 1860 ought to be mentioned as an exception although even during the winter of that year free trade happily obviated to a great extent the effects of domestic scarcity. For owing to the very large importations of grain from Europe and America, the cost of "the prime necessary of life"—as the *Annual Register*[2] points out — was kept within moderate bounds and occasioned but little pressure upon the poorer classes. With commercial, financial and industrial conditions, there was little room for complaint. The revenue was proving the satisfactory state of industry; the returns issued by the

---

[1] *Cf. infra*, pp. 101 *et seq.*
[2] *Annual Register.* vol. ciii (1861). p 2

Board of Trade were testifying to the continued expansion and development of commerce.

1865, as representing the middle section of the decade, likewise gave an encouraging report.   The circulars sent to the *Economist*, with scarcely an exception, were filled with congratulations on the prosperous results of the trade of that year.   The woolen, cotton, iron, linen, shipping, hardware, chemical, timber, and building trades were all active.[1] The cessation of the Civil War in America and the consequent demand of the American market doubtless contributed largely to this result during the latter part of the year.[2] There was no great number of commercial failures.   Uncertainty in the cotton market caused some difficulty, however, and a demand on the Bank of England due to the remittance of gold in an attempt to hasten the arrival of raw cotton meant a considerable drain of bullion and frequent and severe variations of the rate of discount.[3]   Wages were advancing.   The harvest, though not highly productive, was generally of a fair average character.[4]   In short, the main elements of the national strength—agriculture, commerce, manufactures—were well sustained and gave promise of increased development; public finances were eminently buoyant and transactions of foreign commerce were on the largest scale.[5]   And, had there been a great "abatement in the painful contrast" which still existed even in a prosperous year between enormous wealth and luxury on one hand and painful destitution and pauperism on the other, England's annalist might have been still more cheerful.

[1] The *Economist*, March 10, 1866—supplement, "Commercial History and Review of 1865."

[2] *Ibid.*, p. 1.

[3] *Ibid.*, p. 2.

[4] *Annual Register*, 1865, new series, p. 160.

[5] *Ibid.*, p. 185.

Noteworthy exceptions there were, to be sure, to this generally favorable description, the most important of which was the cotton famine due to the American Civil War. Although possibly many cotton spinners would have been ruined by a surplus of raw material at hand at the opening of the war and an overcrowded market of manufactured goods which must have been sold at a sacrifice, the surplus was quickly used up when the regular supply was cut off, and soon factories had to cease work and the millhands found themselves out of employment. Just how important the cotton industry was, may be seen from the fact that the trade profits of Lancashire in 1860 constituted nearly one-fifth of the entire amount classed under that head for all England.[1] Consequently the distress occasioned by the partial or total stoppage of the cotton mills was great. The situation was the most pressing a short time prior to Christmas, 1862:[2] the weekly loss of wages in the cotton manufacturing districts at that time was estimated at approximately £168,000.[3] The number of paupers relieved in the distressed unions of Lancashire and Cheshire the first week of December, 1862, was 284,418; during the first week of January, 1863, 266,450, and during the first week of February, 1863, 236,780.[4] By the first week of September, 1863, the number had dropped to 155,163. Thereafter, except for a reaction[5] from October, 1863, to February, 1864, there was improvement in employment until September and October of 1864 when rumors of peace caused fluctuations in the prices of cotton. By 1864, however, the difficulties

[1] *Journal of the Statistical Society of London*, 1862, p. 536.

[2] *Accounts and Papers*, 1863 (100-I) lii, 157 *et seq.*

[3] *Annual Register*, 1863, new series, p. 140.

[4] *Accounts and Papers, op. cit.*

[5] *Vide* Thomas Mackey, *History of the English Poor Law* (London, 1899), p. 415, and *Accounts and Papers*, 1863 (515) lii, 220.

of the operatives had been lessened by imports of the raw
material from various quarters of the world and by the
absorption of the redundant labor in other channels, and
the cotton famine may be considered to have terminated.[1]

The distress had been alleviated somewhat, and the losses
of wages made up, to a partial extent, by the rates levied
under the poor law and the voluntary contributions of the
public—the latter yielding by far the larger amount.   Before the end of January, 1863, these voluntary contributions,
from the various parts of the United Kingdom and from
the Colonies, had exceeded three quarters of a million sterling.[2]   The fund was controlled and allocated in weekly sums
by committees.   The amount thus obtained by the operatives plus that granted by the poor rates gave just bare subsistence.   The poor rates were obtained by the Union Relief Aid Act [3] from such an extensive territory that the
burden of the distressed parishes was relieved by contributions from adjoining districts.   By the same Act loans on
mortgage of the rates could be raised for the purpose of
affording relief.   This Act, limited in its operation to the
first of March, 1863, was extended to June and then passed
again.   In the early part of the summer of 1864 a new
plan to help—the Public Works Act [4]—was passed.   By its
provisions loans were to be issued by the Government, at a
low rate of interest, to the local authorities in the cotton
manufacturing districts, for the purpose of enabling them
to employ the operatives who were thrown out of work in
executing improvements required in the various towns, such
as drainage, construction of roads, water works, and similar
undertakings.

[1] The *Times*, June 19, 1865.

[2] *Annual Register*, 1863, p. 2.

[3] 25 and 26 Vict., c. 110; *cf. Annual Register*, 1863, pp. 151-4.

[4] 27 and 28 Vict., c. 104.

Yet the calamity produced by the cotton famine was, to
the *Annual Register,* not without its alleviating circumstances.[1] It was endured by the working class with a
patience which did not escape notice, it excited universal
sympathy, and it was not attended with that degree of
demoralization which might have been anticipated from so
great a dislocation of ordinary habits and industrious pur-
suits. The sufferers felt that the distress to which they
were reduced was owing to no neglect or errors of the
Government, no injustice of the laws under which they
lived. In fact, with but a single exception there was no
disturbance, no outrage, scarcely any agitation or audible
complaint throughout the heavily afflicted districts. That exception—an outbreak of two or three days in March, 1863,
at Ashton-under-Lyne and adjacent territory — occurred
over payments in tickets instead of money by the relief committee. Several shops and houses were plundered by the
mob. Troops assisted in stopping the rioting. Forty-two
persons were finally convicted and sentenced to terms of
imprisonment varying from one to six months, but it was
believed that the majority of the disturbers were people who
had never worked in the mills.

Closely connected with the cotton famine was a commercial crisis of the year 1864.[2] Since the commencement of
the war, cotton had been a favorite article for speculation,
as was also, to a lesser extent perhaps, sugar, tallow, jute,
rice and fruit. Quotations had reached a very high point
when rumors of peace were freely circulated. The price
of cotton and of the other articles that were unduly advanced, began to recede, and soon came the announcement
of several failures. Joint stock companies felt the strain.

[1] *Annual Register,* 1863, p. 2.

[2] *Vide Economist,* March 11, 1865, supplement, "Commercial History
and Review of 1864."

The extraordinarily low prices of all classes of production, however, soon began to attract buyers; a favorable reaction set in and before the end of October the commercial prospect began to brighten.

The year 1865 also had its exception to the generally favorable conditions in the appearance of the cattle plague or rinderpest — an event which, because of its continued duration and influence, belongs to the year 1866 as well as to 1865. Whole herds of cattle around London died off;[1] one inspector who had charge of a great part of the north and northeast of London stated that in his own district more than four-fifths had either died or been slaughtered. By the early winter of 1865 the disease had spread in many counties of England, in Scotland and Wales, and continued to work destruction during the whole of the following year.   The effect of the plague upon the price of commodities was a cause of public anxiety: mutton and beef were charged by the butchers in the autumn of 1865 at twenty or twenty-five per cent above the rates of preceding years, and the price of milk rose twenty per cent.[2]

On the whole, however, the period of the early 'sixties may be said to have been prosperous. The one great exception is, of course, the distress in the cotton manufacturing districts, but the cause of that distress, it seems, was patent to the workingmen and no blame could be placed either upon the Government or upon the ruling classes. Because of the cotton famine the percentage of unemployed during 1861, 1862, and 1863 was very large, indeed. On the other hand, the average money wages rose, if 1850 is taken as the base year,[3] from 114 in 1860, 116 in 1862,

---

[1] *Annual Register*, 1865, p. 161.

[2] *Ibid.*, p. 170.

[3] When a year or a fixed period is taken as the standard, or base, its

117 in 1863, to 124 and 126 in 1864 and 1865 respectively, while average retail prices went from 111 in 1860 and 114 in 1861 to 106 in 1864 and 107 in 1865. Real wages for a workman of unchanged grade rose from 99 and 97 in 1860 and 1861 respectively to 100 in 1862, 104 in 1863, and 110 in 1864 and 1865, a point which was not again reached in the 'sixties. And trade was increasing by leaps and bounds.

A study of the years 1866 and 1867, however, gives by no means so favorable a picture of economic conditions. The harvest during both years was poor. In the critical months of August and September, 1866, the weather was unusually wet and stormy and the wheat crops suffered much.[1] With a yield decidedly below the average, prices were much enhanced. This circumstance, combined with a contraction of the demand for labor, arising from commercial failures, and the exceptionally severe weather, made the winter of 1866-1867, as will be seen,[2] a period of considerable suffering to the poorer classes. A generally poor harvest of 1866, moreover, extended over all Western Europe, presaging a restriction of the purchasing means of the bulk of the population.[3] In 1867, too, the yield of the cereal crops was so decidedly below the average that large importations were necessary.[4] The average price of wheat per imperial quarter for the calendar year 1863 had been

staples are represented by an index arbitrarily fixed at 100. The ratios obtained by comparing staples at a given time with the base, give index numbers.

The index numbers of George H. Wood in the *Journal of the Royal Statistical Society*, 1909, "Real Wages and the Standard of Comfort since 1850" are here used.

[1] *Annual Register*, 1866, p. 186.

[2] *Cf. infra*, pp. 75 *et seq.*

[3] The *Economist*, March 9, 1867, supplement, "Commercial History and Review of 1866," p. 1.

[4] *Annual Register*, 1867, p. 204.

44s. 9d.; for 1864, 40s. 2d.; for 1865, 41s. 10d.; but so
unfavorable was the harvest of 1866 that the average price
was 49s. 11d.   From 45s. 9d. at the first of May it had
risen to 60s. by the last week of December.   It stayed
around this figure through March and then gradually advanced until at the end of May, 1867, it stood at 65s. 3d.
Since July, 1866, the country had had a price of wheat
from sixty to eighty per cent above the prices which prevailed in the last three years, 1863-1865; the same remark
would hold good of a large part of Europe and America.
" In the wide diffusion of a calamity of this magnitude,"
said a writer in the *Economist*, " there is afforded at once
an explanation of a large part of the difficulties of 1866
and 1867, and the present time." [1]   It was estimated that
the harvest of these two years entailed an extra cost of at
least forty millions sterling on the country [2]—at the very
time, too, when a severe collapse of enterprise and credit
was having its bad effects.

With regard to financial and commercial matters the
year 1866 started off in a fair condition.   It is true that
even during the first part of the year a high rate of interest
and a mania for speculation was causing some foreboding
but it was commonly asserted that trade was healthy,[3] and
the failure of one or two country banks was attributed to
local causes.   The *Quarterly Review* thought the material
condition of the country was furnishing no cause for
anxiety.   " Our wealth is overflowing," it said, " our
commercial prospects are unclouded, save by the excess of
our own activity; and nothing seems likely to disturb either

[1] The *Economist*, March 14, 1868, supplement, " Commercial History
and Review of 1867," p. 2.

[2] *Journal of the Statistical Society of London*, 1869, p. 82.

[3] *Annual Register*, 1866, p. 184.

the peace of Europe or the profound contentment which this island is enjoying." [1] The *Times*, in discussing what the ensuing twelve months were likely to bring to pass, felt " cheerful and thankful." [2]

February, however, saw severe liquidation on the stock exchange, and there were some important failures in April. On the ninth of May the Bank rate rose to nine per cent; on the tenth the failure of a firm of world-wide reputation— Overend, Gurney & Company, whose business as bill-discounters had been transferred in the preceding year to a joint-stock company with limited liability — produced terrible consternation. On the following day, Friday, great restless crowds collected in the streets, especially in the banking quarters of the city.[3] The *Times* depicts the tumult becoming a riot by midday:

The doors of the most respectable Banking Houses were besieged, more perhaps by a mob actuated by the strange sympathy which makes and keeps a mob together than by creditors of the Banks, and throngs heaving and tumbling about Lombard street made that narrow thoroughfare impassible. The excitement on all sides was such as has not been witnessed since the great crisis of 1825, if, indeed, the memory of the few survivors who shared that Panic can be trusted when they compare it with the madness of yesterday. Nothing had happened since the day before to justify such a fear as was everywhere shown.[4]

" Black Friday " was not soon forgotten in London; other great commercial cities of the kingdom which had been affected by the news likewise had cause for remembering

[1] *Quarterly Review*, January, 1866, p. 250.
[2] The *Times*, January 5, 1866, editorial.
[3] *Vide Annual Register*, 1866, chronicle, pp. 44 and 45.
[4] The *Times*, May 12, 1866, editorial.

the day. The Government found it necessary to suspend the Bank Act, but the Bank of England did not extend its note issue beyond the amount permitted by the Act of 1844.[1]

Unfortunately the effects of the crisis were not destined to pass away so suddenly and rapidly as the crisis itself had come. The *Times* vouches for the fact that nothing had happened the week before to excite universal alarm.[2] The Bank rate of discount was not so high as it had been again and again in the last three years, and though the glories of finance companies had begun to pale, and it was known that the Imperial Mercantile Association was tottering, there was no reason to apprehend any panic in consequence of a collapse which was distinctly foreseen.[3] It had been the suspension of Overend, Gurney & Company on the tenth of May which awoke the terror of the creditors. The name of the firm was historical, and the magnitude of its liabilities would tend to show that the mass of depositors had confidence in the public company with limited liability. But the influence of the panic was to be seen through many of the succeeding months. Two or three banks failed within the week.[4] The rate of ten per cent discount which was imposed on the Bank of England as a condition of the additional power of issue lasted from the eleventh of May to the seventeenth of August; and when the rate did decline from eight to six, to five, to four per cent, the price of the Funds and of shares in railway and joint-stock companies scarcely rose at all. Moreover, an intense foreign

---

[1] By the Bank Charter Act of 1844 (the 7 and 8 Vict., c. 32) issues of the Bank were to be covered by bullion, three-fourths in gold, except for £14,000,000 covered by Government securities.

[2] The *Times*, May 15, 1866, editorial.

[3] *Ibid.*

[4] *Annual Register*, 1866, p. 184.

distrust [1] of every English signature was engendered by
the suspension of the Bank Act. Lord Clarendon's circular [2] to British Embassies and Legations throughout
Europe, explaining the distinction between scarcity of
money and insolvency, and giving as the causes of the
panic overspeculation due to prosperity, the derangement in
commercial transactions produced by events on the Continent, which hindered a return to a sound state in monetary
matters, and as immediate cause the stoppage of the great
discount house of Overend, Gurney & Company did little
to check the prevailing suspicion. [3]

So bad was the situation that the royal speech at the
prorogation of Parliament on August 10 expressed great
concern over the monetary pressure which had weighed
upon the interests of the country so long; and although on
the first of October the *Times* was still optimistic, claiming
that in spite of all commercial troubles people had been
well employed and the rate of wages had permitted the
masses to live well, [4] by the latter part of November complaint was heard in this newspaper:

Trade is slack. Wherever we turn this is the report which
meets us. Whether it be the hardware of Birmingham or the
soft goods of Yorkshire, the flax-spinning of Scotland or the
mining industry of the West, which is the subject of inquiry,
the answer is the same monotonous croak. There is little or
nothing doing. Bankers won't look at new and promising investments. Merchants are inaccessible to the most glowing
descriptions of untried foreign and colonial markets. Stocks
hang on hand and accumulate in spite of all the care of pro-

[1] The *Economist*, March 9, 1867, supplement, p. 5.

[2] To be found in the *Times*, May 22, 1866. Lord Clarendon was Secretary of State for Foreign Affairs.

[3] *Annual Register*, 1866, p. 184.

[4] The *Times*, October 1, 1866, editorial.

ducers and warehousemen to keep them low. Towards the end of the month slight demand for money arises, but it is only for the payment of debts when bills mature on the coming fourth. It is in no case occasioned by the growth of trade or the revival of speculation. Paris echoes the complaint of London.[1]

Such was the heritage of 1867. The *Annual Register* points out that during this year " commerce and credit did not display their wonted elasticity " in recovering from the disasters of 1866, that a gloom was cast over the surface of society and embarrassment and distress were spread among thousands of families.[2]   The sufferers belonged not only to the section of society classified by the *Times* as those who could ill afford pecuniary sacrifices or those who could find but little consolation in the discussed indirect advantages following from the bursting of commercial bubbles [3] but to that section whose incomes were dependent on those investments which had greatly depreciated in value. Railway securities, for instance, became less valuable when troubles with railway property and railway management in general came as a result of the exposure in 1866 of the financial condition of the *London, Chatham and Dover Company,* the *Great Eastern Company,* and the *North British Company.*[4]

As an example of the unhappy influence of the panic upon private individuals, the *Globe* quotes that in the inland revenue department at Somerset House, where was kept a register of all those persons paying duty on carriages

[1] The *Times,* November 28, 1866, editorial.

[2] *Annual Register,* 1867, p. 202.

[3] The *Times,* December 31, 1866, editorial.

[4] The *Economist,* October 19, 1867, under the article " Railways," discusses the depreciation in value of railway property.

and horses, 1600 persons in less than two months gave notice of the intention to discontinue keeping their carriages.[1] Even traveling was checked somewhat, we read,[2] and places of public amusement were less resorted to.

A more intimate knowledge of the latter part of 1866 and of 1867, however, can be gained from reports on trade. The official tables of exports and imports seem to testify to a continued expansion of foreign trade for 1866.[3] And it is true that the amount of commerce carried on was still immense and growing, but it was not increasing with that percentage of augmentation which marked the preceding year. The real truth may be disguised too easily by looking at the trade figures for the year and refusing to note the effect of trade during the early months upon the total: a comparison of the returns for 1866 month by month with those of the preceding year shows no great increase during the latter part of 1866. In fact, there was a diminution in percentage of augmentation.[4] 1867, moreover, saw no improvement over 1866.

The reports on the condition of the leading trades as given in the *Economist* were discouraging. In the cotton industry—outside of the first seven months of 1866 when the supply of raw cotton was in excess of the demand, while the demand for the manufactured article fully equalled the supply—the high price of the raw material, together with the slackened demand for goods, kept England's largest branch of the manufacturing industry in a fluctuating,

---

[1] The *Globe*, February 2, 1868—cited in the *Economist*, March 14, 1868, supplement, p. 2.

[2] *Annual Register*, 1866, p. 185.

[3] For a discussion on revenue returns, *vide* R. D. Baxter, *National Income* (London, 1868), p. 28; for graphs, *vide* Bowley, *England's Foreign Trade.*

[4] *Cf. Accounts and Papers*, 1867 (46-xii) lxv, 607, 629.

feverish and unprofitable state. 1867 opened with a general adoption of short time as the only mode of enabling the manufacturers to keep in check the price of the raw material, and to clear their warehouses of unsold goods. Trade throughout the year remained unsatisfactory both to the importers of raw material and to the exporters of the manufactured articles.

The iron industry—next to the cotton trade the most important industry of the country—likewise felt the depressing influences which were generally prevailing. There was a decline in prices of articles in 1866 and a demand insufficient to keep the works going full time; the great disorganization of the home demand, consequent on the commercial crisis, and the disrepute falling on railways and other companies, explained in part the condition. In 1867 the iron trade was dull and unsatisfactory, and the general course of prices, at least to the middle of the year, tended downward.

In the linen trade the year 1866 was the worst which had been experienced for some years past, and the dullness and inactivity which prevailed at the close of 1866 and which led to a partial stoppage of flax-spinning machinery, continued throughout 1867; and, if the descriptions of the condition of other industries such as the chemical trade, the leather trade, the woolen trade, were somewhat more favorable in 1866, the reports of 1867 presented expressions of hope for the coming year rather than of rejoicing over the past.

Other events there were which add little to the good reputation of these two years. The cattle plague, which during the earlier months had not been checked, was proving so ruinous to farmers and graziers, especially to those of the northwestern counties, that many an ancient pasture had to be given up. The money loss for 1866 due to the

disease was computed at not less than £3,500,000.[1] The
Government found it necessary to act. It prohibited markets and fairs for the sale of lean and store cattle, and,
among other regulations, gave the local authorities power
to kill animals which had been exposed to contagion. Some
compensation was to be given to the owners. Again, the
Austro-Prussian War disorganized and checked Continental
trade. Prospects of war had a bad influence on the market
some time before the actual declaration. Some of the reports to the *Economist* placed a considerable amount of
blame upon the Continental situation for the English trade
conditions.

Two other events, not strictly economic, helped to de-
press the public: the activity of the Fenians,[2] who were
causing so much disquietude that Parliament in February,
1866, passed a bill for the suspension of the *habeas corpus*
act in Ireland, and the presence of cholera, which, though
not causing many deaths, was alarming, especially in the
eastern parts of London, during the latter part of July and
the first of August.

Gloomy enough, then, is a general description of economic conditions during the period of the Reform agitation,[3] yet it is only by going to the statistician that there
can be found the definite statement concerning the condition of that class to which the Reform bill was to give the
franchise. His figures on prices, wages, and unemployment
must tell much concerning the workingman. In his attempt
to get the desired material, to piece together from here and
from there the economic history of the nineteenth century

[1] *Annual Register*, 1866, p. 182.

[2] The word is derived from an old Irish word meaning "champion
of Ireland." The aim of the Fenians was to throw off British rule.

[3] This is described in chap. iii.

he has had to expend much energy;[1] and the information obtained, he may warn,[2] gives only general trends and is not to be used carelessly for fine distinctions. Nevertheless, the results of his work, supplemented by more or less typical accounts taken directly from contemporary writers, give the best account now available for the years 1866 and 1867.

PRICES

Difficulty is met at once when data on retail prices are sought. Investigations on this topic have, as yet, made little headway[3] although material upon wholesale prices is at hand for this portion of the nineteenth century. The following cases, however, chosen more or less at random, will make clear the trend of retail prices. The London *Times* for July 10, 1866, gives the following data regarding the cost of living for workingmen in Lancashire:

The clamor among operatives of Lancashire for increased wages is no doubt attributable principally to the great rise that has taken place during the past three years in the price of provisions. This rise is illustrated by the following facts: seven men of the county constabulary have for some years lodged at a certain house in Preston, the whole joining in a common stock of provisions, and each at the end of the week paying his proportion of the cost. As an accurate record has been kept of all provisions consumed, and the price paid for each article, they are enabled to make an exact comparison of the weekly

---

[1] *Vide* Mr. A. L. Bowley's discussion of Mr. Wood's paper in the *Royal Statistical Society Journal*, vol. lxxiii (1910), pp. 626-629, for a statement of the difficulties which the statistician has had to overcome in compiling his information.

[2] *Vide* A. L. Bowley, in the *Royal Statistical Society Journal*, vol. lxix (1906), "The Statistics of Wages in the Nineteenth Century."

[3] *Vide* Mr. G. H. Wood in the *Royal Statistical Society Journal*, vol. lxv (1902) under the article "The Investigation of Retail Prices," p. 685.

cost per head during the whole of the time they have lived together. In the first week of July, 1863, the cost was 7s. 8d;
of July, 1864, 7s. 11d.; of July, 1865, 8s. 5d.; of July, 1866,
9s. 5d. . . . Food in July last was hence about twelve per cent
cheaper than at present and in 1863 about twenty-two and one-
half per cent cheaper. As cloggers, cobblers, shoemakers,
tailors, dressmakers, etc. all raised their prices immediately the
factory operatives obtained their recent advanced wages (from
five to ten per cent), it is more than probable that with the present price of food, and the increased charges for nearly all other
necessities, they are not so well off as they were in 1863 or
even last year at this time.[1]

In the Parliamentary Reports of 1889[2] is to be found
specially supplied to the Board of Trade the annual balance sheet of a working cabinet-maker. Housekeeping cost
£1 4s. 3d. a week in 1865, £1 7s. in 1866, and £1 11s. in
1867. Notable advances took place in the prices of bread,
some kinds of meat, and beer. A summary shows that in
this particular household the item including rent, taxes,
water, was very high in 1866 but that much less was spent
for clothing during the year than in either 1865 or 1867.[3]
Retail prices of bread as taken from the Greenwich Hos-
pital bread prices show the effect of the poor harvests mentioned above.[4] A four-pound loaf sold for 5½d. in 1865,
for 6d. in 1866 and for 8d. in 1867. A detailed statement
of retail prices of provisions can be obtained from extracts
from the books of a Mr. George Dix, grocer and general
dealer, as given by Brassey: [5]

[1] The *Times,* July 10, 1866.

[2] *Accounts and Papers,* 1889, (c-5861) lxxxiv.

[3] The wages earned were less in 1866 than in 1865 and 1867.

[4] *Journal of the Royal Statistical Society,* vol. lxv (1902), p. 690.

[5] Thomas B. Brassey, *On Work and Wages,* 3rd edition (London,
1872), pp. 164 and 165.

TABLE A

	1864			1865			1866			1867		
	£.	s.	d.	£.	s.	d.	£.	s.	d.	£.	s.	d.
Flour per sack.	1	8	0	1	10	0	1	14	6	2	0	6
Cheese per lb..........	0	0	8	0	0	8½	0	0	10	0	0	9
Butter " "	0	1	4	0	1	5	0	1	6	0	1	3½
Bacon " "	0	0	8	0	0	9	0	0	9	0	0	8
Tea " "	0	3	8	0	3	8	0	3	8	0	3	6
Coffee " "	0	1	4	0	1	4	0	1	4	0	1	4
Sugar " "	0	0	5	0	0	5	0	0	5	0	0	4½
Candles " "	0	0	6¼	0	0	6	0	0	6¼	0	0	6¼
Soap " "	0	0	4½	0	0	4½	0	0	4½	0	0	4½
Beef " "	0	0	7½	0	0	8¼	0	0	8	0	0	7½
Mutton " "	0	0	8	0	0	8	0	0	8½	0	0	7½
Bread " "	0	0	1⅛	0	0	1¼	0	0	1⅜	0	0	2

A glance at wholesale prices for the period confirms the impression of the increasing cost of living obtained from retail prices. The index numbers used to represent 1866 as given in the *Economist* and elsewhere must be understood to take into consideration the prices of raw materials of manufacture. The great drop in cotton, flax, *etc.*, from the end of May on, therefore, will greatly affect the index number representing prices for the year although the condition of the workingmen may not be much bettered by the change in these articles.[1] In such a case a table as the following, containing some data on those articles of food asserted by Professor Leone Levi to be necessities for the British workingman may take the place of a weighted average:

[1] Leone Levi, *Wages and Earnings of the Working Classes* (London, 1867), p. xxxviii, says about two-thirds of the income of workingmen was spent on food.

TABLE B [1]

	Jan., 1865	Jan., 1866	June, 1866	Sept., 1866	Jan., 1867	June, 1867
Wheat per quarter [2] (Gazette prices)	37s. 10d.	46s. 3d.	47s. 5d.	49s. 7d.	60s. 2d.	65s. 5d.
Beef per 8 lbs.[2] (Inferior middlings)..	42d.[3]	36d.	44d.	48d.	44d.	44d.
Mutton per 8 lbs.[2] (Middling)	50d.[3]	52d.	56d.	60d.	48d.	50d.
Pork per 8 lbs.[2]	52d.[3]	58d.	56d.	56d.	40d.	46d.
Sugar per cwt. (Bengal good).......	24s.[3]	27s.	24s.	23s. 6d.	24s. 6d.	24s. 6d.
Tea per lb.	9½d.[3]	12d.	12d.	10½d.	9½d.	6d.
Butter per cwt.	119s.	123s.	123s.	115s.	115s.	115s.
Bacon per cwt. (Hamburg)	54s.	61s.	62s.	71s.	71s.	....
Barley per quarter.[2].....	28s. 5d.[4]	32s. 9d.	35s. 1d.	37s. 2d.	44s. 3d.	36s. 2d.

The preceding pages seem to show that Wood [5] has not gone astray in representing average retail prices in 1866 and 1867 by higher index numbers than those used for the preceding years.[6]

But it is obvious that prices taken by themselves cannot mean anything. The real condition of the workingman can be ascertained only by additional data on wages and unemployment. If wages rise faster than prices the workingman will find himself in a more prosperous condition even though prices are soaring. What data, then, can be obtained on wages?

[1] Material for such a table can be found conveniently in the *Economist*.

[2] Professor Levi says that bread and meat absorbed the largest portion of the laborer's income devoted to food: *Wages and Earnings*, p. xxxix.

[3] Lowest figures given are used.

[4] Average Gazette prices (monthly) to be found in *Accounts and Papers* 1867-1868 (4028) lxx, 100 and 101.

[5] *Cf. Journal of the Royal Statistical Society*, 1909, p. 102.

[6] Wood shows a fall after 1867. Articles in the *Economist* on 1867 and 1868 seem to confirm his work.

WAGES

Unfortunately material upon this topic is not even so
good as it is upon prices. The Parliamentary *Accounts
and Papers* do give many figures concerning wages, but
how difficult it is to deduce a table from them, for year-
periods, can be judged only by an actual attempt to accomplish the task. As Mr. Bowley says,[1] one's impression on
first taking up the question of the statistics of wages as in
the cotton trade is one of simple chaos; the various lists
give no guide as to hours, the rates vary from place to
place, and the minute grades of occupation also vary from
place to place. The statistician again warns that his work
must not be accepted for fine distinctions. Nevertheless his
labor may give some material on the general trend of
wages. A review of the work of Bowley and Wood in the
Journal of the Royal Statistical Society shows [2] the year
1866 somewhat favorably as contrasted with 1865 or
1867. Evidently during a part of 1866 wages were rising,
although a fall is seen for the year 1867. When the laborer's wages in 1886 are taken as 100, his wages in 1865,
1866, and 1867 are represented by the index numbers 87,
88, and 87 respectively. Wages of pattern-makers are represented for those years by the index numbers 152, 158,
155; ironmoulders by 166, 166, 166; machinists 118, 122,
121; shipwrights 173, 178, 162, and so on. Index numbers
of average rates in engineering and shipbuilding in nineteen districts [3] give about the same results. Likewise when
actual figures are used in place of index numbers, the above
data is upheld. Weekly wages of all workpeople in the
cotton industry during the three years averaged 144, 157,

[1] *Journal of the Royal Statistical Society*, vol. lxxiii (1910), pp. 626-627.

[2] *Vide* tables, vol. lxix (1906), pp. 174-175.

[3] *Ibid.*, pp. 162 *et seq. Vide* also average figures from seventeen
sets of workingmen, vol. lxii (1899), pp. 664-665.

and 158*d*.[1] The *Accounts and Papers,* in showing the
wages of carpenters and joiners for the years 1862 to
1890, give the following for 1865, 1866 and 1867: 24*s.*,
26*s.*, 26*s.*[2] According to Bowley in *Wages in the United
Kingdom,* Scotch brewers received 4*s.* 1*d.*, 4*s.* 6*d.*, 4*s.*
1¼*d.* daily.[3] Webb's *Industrial Democracy* gives the average standard rate of wages per week of a stonemason at
Glasgow, as 28*s.* 6*d.* (1865), 27*s.* 7*d.* (1866), 28*s.* 8*d.*
(1867) ; and the standard rate of wages of compositors in
London per week as 33*s.*, 36*s.*, 36*s.*[4] The quarters of wheat
purchasable with the wages in each case is given as 0.68,
0.55, and 0.45; 0.79, 0.72, 0.55.   Provided a workingman
lived entirely on bread his condition was much worse in
1866 and 1867 even though his wages had increased somewhat.

The facts so far given do not, of course, tell what part
of the year 1866 caused the increased index number for
wages.   For any changes which took place during any
months of the year, we must go to the newspapers, weekly
and daily.   And they cannot be expected to give the exact
statistical information desired.

The year opened under favorable auspices, according to
the *Fortnightly Review;* [5] in the issue of May first, com-
ment is made upon the prosperity and the content of the
mass of the people, the general rise of wages and the better
understanding between capital and labor, and finally, the
lack of response on the part of the workingman, because
there was not distress in the country, to the attempts to

---

[1] *Journal of the Royal Statistical Society,* vol. lxxiii (1910), p. 599.

[2] *Accounts and Papers,* 1890-91 (c-6475) xcii, 504.

[3] A. L. Bowley, *Wages in the United Kingdom in the Nineteenth
Century* (Cambridge, 1900), p. 105.

[4] Webb, Sidney and Beatrice, *Industrial Democracy* (London, 1902),
appendix iii.

[5] *Fortnightly Review,* vol. iv, p. 756.

arouse him for Reform. The *Times* here and there sub-
stantiates the opinion that wages were rising. We read of
the London carpenters and joiners receiving an extra half-
penny per hour on the existing rate of wages, or 8*d*. per
hour.[1] We read [2] that in North and East Lancashire an
extensive agitation was going on regarding wages and
hours of labor—a movement confining itself to no particular class but permeating all sections, " from scavengers
up to sub-editors, and from high-class artisans down to
' half-penny shavers ' and washer-women." And while
some of the claimants received no concessions and realized
no improvements, either in reference to the rate of remuneration or the hours of labor, many obtained almost all
they sought for. At Preston, for instance, all the operative
weavers received an advance of ten per cent upon the standard list of prices; the spinners and minders likewise obtained an increased rate of remuneration; the printers were
given an advance of wages, ranging from 2*s*. to 4*s*. or 5*s*.
per week. The shoemakers had to remain out for three
days and then obtained the extra money they had demanded;
the stonemasons were on strike for a month before they
were able to get the reduction of hours which they asked
for, and the joiners and the flaggers and slaters were, at
the writing, still on strike, the former for more money, the
latter for certain alterations in their rules. Some wanted
increases in wages, which they did not get—the scavengers
for instance, and the warehousemen in the employ of the
North Union Railway Company. Many barbers who had
charged ½*d*. for a single shave demanded and received 1*d*.
The washerwomen, too, in some of the East Lancashire

---

[1] *Vide* the *Times*, April 19; a discussion on the subject is to be found
in the issues for April 26 and April 30. By May 17 most of the firms
had paid the advance.

[2] A résumé is to be found in the *Times*, June 22.

towns tried to secure an advance of wages. At Bacup the painters were striking for an advance of ½d. per hour; at Accrington the shoemakers received an increase; at Blackburn the plumbers and glaziers and some factory operatives were on strike, and the stonemasons were demanding fewer hours; at Chorley the weavers had their wages raised and yet were not content.

In contrast to the upward trend of wages during the first half of the year, however, a trend in the opposite direction will be found during the later months. The *Economist* mentions [1] that wages fell in 1866 in several large trades from ten to twenty per cent, and declares the most decided fall occurred in the iron trade [2] and iron shipbuilding trades, in the midland and northern districts. The reductions were submitted to only after protracted strikes. The strike among the ironworkers on the Tyne, Wear, and Tees lasted for nineteen weeks, from July to November, and ended in the unconditional surrender of the men. The explanation given for the change in wages was that for four or five years capital had been bidding for labor, and there was, consequently, a continuous rise of wages. Suddenly capital was paralyzed [3] and now labor had to bid for capital. In the building trades, too, there came a severe check and employment was scarce.

By January, 1867, [4] the factory operatives of North and East Lancashire were protesting against a proposed reduction of five per cent in wages; they preferred short time. Most of them apparently thought the market was over-

[1] The *Economist*, March 9, 1867, supplement, p. 2.

[2] The *Times* of September 12 tells of iron workers locked out for refusing to accept a reduction of ten per cent; it mentions, too, a raise given to hand mule weavers employed by one man at Preston and a reduction of hours to bricklayers.

[3] That is, after the panic.

[4] *Vide* the *Times*, January 7, 1867.

stocked, although here and there the suggestion was made that a reduction in the profits of the manufacturers and merchants might help matters. A memorial presented to the employers set forth that the five per cent conceded them in February last had been more than swallowed by increased rents, and that since that time the prices of meat, coal, and the necessities of life had been advanced to the extent of twenty-six and a half per cent. They, therefore, respectfully prayed that their wages might not be reduced, but that short time might be substituted and the market by that means surely but gradually relieved. But within a month's time a large number of men agreed to accept the reduction.[1]

UNEMPLOYMENT

That the condition of the workingman was not so good after the middle of 1866 as it had been before, is probably a safe conclusion from the facts given above. That a better detailed knowledge of his condition could be obtained if we knew something definite about unemployment will not be disputed. Anything like exact and final figures on unemployment cannot, of course, be obtained. Mr. Wood in articles[2] in the *Journal of the Royal Statistical Society,* however, has been able to tell something concerning the progress made by the workingman since 1860 by tracing the percentage of unemployed as shown by the records of the more important trade unions.[3] His results[4] show that

[1] *Vide* the *Times,* January 9, January 15, January 17.

[2] *Journal of the Royal Statistical Society,* vol. lxii (1899) and vol. lxiii (1900).

[3] *Vide* also an article by E. L. Hartley in the *Journal of the Royal Statistical Society,* vol. lxvii (1904), where marriage and pauperism are suggested as tests for unemployment and also diagram on this by Wood, vol. lxii, in the *Journal of the Royal Statistical Society,* p. 660.

[4] Mr. Wood, in the *Journal of the Royal Statistical Society,* vol. lxii, p. 643, has something to say concerning the understatement of the evil in the fifth report on trade unions.

1866 was not so favorable a year as was 1865, and that
1867 was much worse in unemployment than was 1866.
Whether the average percentage of members in want of
employment be used or the average expenditure per head
on unemployed and traveling benefit, the conclusion is much
the same. The Registrar-General's Report gives a decrease
in pauperism for the March and June quarters of 1866 as
compared with the same period of 1865 but an increase in
1866 over 1865 for the December quarter. And the opening months of 1867 show a great increase over the corresponding months [1] of 1866. Written pictures of pauperism
as given to the *Times* suggest, moreover, a much worse
condition than the actual statistics show. Statistics cannot
tell the whole truth because many workingmen were unwilling to receive parish relief not only because such a course
of action would tend to break down their self-respect but
because it would disqualify them from taking advantage of
benefits connected with their trade and friendly societies.
On the other hand, the descriptions of the newspapers may
be too gloomy. Yet there can be found in the *Times,* almost
at random, during the period of greatest stress, letters de-
picting the condition in London:

At certain doors of those districts (waterside districts of East
London) are to be seen daily, crowds of men jostling, striving,
almost fighting, for admission—to what? . . . to gain the privilege of breaking hard stones for two or three hours in a cold
muddy yard attached to the parish workhouse, for the reward
of threepence and a loaf of bread.

These men, too, are not clad in the usual stoneyard apparel,
they wear good coats—rags are scarcely to be seen. They are
men who, not very long ago, were earning from 18*s.* to £2
weekly, to whom the very mention of the workhouse would have

---

[1] 1867 as a whole had a worse record than 1866.

been contamination; and here they struggle and wrestle for its most meagre advantages.

There are many other parishes, I believe, similarly situated.[1]

The Lord Mayor, calling the attention of a meeting of bankers, merchants, magistrates and others to the prevailing distress among the laboring population in the eastern part of London, said:

Mr. Jeffries, the relieving officer for the South District, . . . reported the total number of persons relieved out of the house that week was 8,319, being an increase on that of the corresponding week of last year of 5,453. . . . A gentleman residing in the West Indies road, writing on Sunday last, states that he had visited many of the working people at their houses in that neighborhood, and that the distress among the mechanics and laborers is appalling. Many of them, he says, are quite disheartened, sitting within bare walls, with neither bed nor clothing and with their children almost naked and famishing. Strong young men had burst into tears on seeing him enter, and pointed to their starving wives and children in silent despair. Some among them had been very improvident; but others quite the reverse. He had that day relieved a young man with four children, who was an ironworker, and had been out of employment for many months. He was a teetotaller, and husbanded his saved earnings to the last, and now, with his family, had nothing to lie upon but the bare floors, and nothing to cover them but a single sheet. The writer adds that he could fill a volume with cases of like destitution and that he fears the late conduct of the Shipwrights' Union at the Thames Ironworks will do much harm and subject many innocent persons to suffering.

The Rector of Bethnal Green writes that there is a great deal of distress there; that the commercial panic, the cholera, and the frost have severely affected the working classes; that

[1] The *Times*, January 12, 1867.

the rates are now in the proportion of 8*s.* in the pound a year;
that the workhouse is full, every spare space being occupied
by a bed; and that on Tuesday last eight hours were spent in
inquiring into the outdoor cases. . . . The Secretary of the
Docks and Wharfs Laborer's Association, High Street, Shad-
well, writing on Saturday last, thinks he may safely say 20,000
of those classes are now quite out of employment and had
not earned a shilling for the last two months; that probably
15,000 of them are dragging out a miserable existence by
pledging little things and selling articles of furniture. . . . Another correspondent writes: " Sickening and heartrending have
been the scenes of distress I have witnessed during my four
months' voluntary employment of doing what I could, in my
humble degree, to assist in alleviating the misery of some of
my fellow creatures. Upwards of 500 families during that
time have been brought under my notice, and I can unhesitat-
ingly affirm such a season of distress and misery was never
before experienced in the locality." He adds that during all
the summer months, owing to the scarcity of work and the
visitation of cholera, many families had to part with articles
of clothing, bedding and everything upon which money could
be obtained, so that when winter set in they had nothing left
to dispose of, and the pawnbrokers, whose shops are already
crammed with goods, care but to give the merest trifle. . . Now
the distress was fearfully and palpably developed by the
continuance of cold weather. To particularize cases of distress, he says, is almost beyond his power. It is widespread
and almost universal.[1]

The January return of the Poor Law Board showed the
large amount of distress in England elsewhere than in London.[2] In the northmidland division, the district least affected, the number of persons in receipt of relief was only
2.7 per cent more than in the corresponding period of 1866,

[1] The *Times*, January 22, 1867.
[2] *Vide* statement of the Rev. Rowsell in the *Times*, February 7, 1867.

but in the southwest division the increase was 4.4 per cent, in Wales 4.6 per cent, in Yorkshire 5.3 per cent, in the south-midland division 6.1 per cent, in the northern 8.8 per cent, in the westmidland 11.4 per cent, in the southeastern 12.6 per cent, in the northwestern 27.4 per cent, and in the metropolis 72.6 per cent.[1]

Thus the data on prices, wages and unemployment—neces_sarily rather vague—suggest that the period when Reform was being made an important public question was a time of serious economic difficulty for the people who were to be affected by a change in the franchise law. Additional material, not statistical, showing that it was a period of gloom is not lacking.   For instance, the *Economist* says:

In our review of 1866, we said that the year had " left behind it sinister influences which will penetrate far into '67, or perhaps into '68 " and the events of the last twelve months have confirmed this expectation.   Nearly the whole of 1867 has been occupied in converting the mistakes which preceded, and retrieving, as far as possible, the losses which were inflicted by the crisis of 1866.   The year has been, therefore, throughout its whole course, a period of arrangements, liquidations, compromises, retrenched expenditure, circumscribed trade, and general indisposition to trust the future.   It has been a year of strict supervision of all elements of cost—a year of declining wages and of stern comparisons between English and Foreign capabilities of commanding neutral customers.[2]

Elsewhere it speaks of 1866 and 1867 as two dark years—the period of rough discipline.   The tone of these circulars already referred to, which were sent to the *Economist* to give information concerning various trades for the year 1866 is almost without exception unfavorable.   The writers,

---

[1] *Cf.* the *Times*, April 16, 1867.

[2] The *Economist*, March 14, 1868, supplement, " Commercial History and Review of 1867," p. 1.

each speaking of facts of his particular business, complained of expectations unfulfilled, losses incurred and former relations of trade broken up. The report on the cotton trade begins with this statement:[1] " From nearly every point of view regarding the material interests of the country, the past year has been one of the most disastrous on record ;" the report on the linen trade with this :

In reviewing the progress of our staple trade during 1866, we regret that we cannot continue the same favorable account of it as we had to give in our last annual circular, the year that has just expired having *been the worst*[2] that has been experienced for some years back, especially to those engaged in the *spinning trade* ;

the one on the woolen trade with this :[3]

The year which has just closed will be long remembered, not only in this district, but in the country at large, as one of the most disastrous in the present century. The severe and, perhaps, unprecedented monetary panic, the Austro-Prussian war, cholera, deficient harvest, and the strikes in the iron trade, have all combined to restrict the natural operations of business, and entailed loss and inconvenience on nearly every class of the community ;

and the one on the iron trade with this : " The Iron trade has been in an unsatisfactory condition throughout the year, prices of all descriptions having steadily declined, whilst the demand has been insufficient to keep the works going full time." Sir Robert Giffen, at one time president of the Royal

[1] These quotations are to be found in the *Economist*, March 9, 1867, supplement.

[2] The original is in italics.

[3] The report from Bradford; the report from Leeds has a more cheerful tone, although reports from Huddersfield and Halifax show the effects of the panic.

Statistical Society and also chief of the statistical department of the Board of Trade, although believing that the
trade depression of this period came entirely from a very
moderate change as compared with a period of prosperity,
speaks of this as a time when " men's hearts were failing
them for fear of what the consequences of the great panic
of 1866 might be." Writing sometime afterwards he expressed himself in his *Essays in Finance* [1] as recollecting no
period when trade was spoken of in more desponding terms
than it was in 1867. " The city was dull," he states, " as
every one said, beyond all previous experience, with money
at two per cent for an unprecedented time; a remarkable
article appeared in the *Edinburgh Review,* discussing the
strike of capital; no symptom was wanting to what is called
a marked period of depression."

And now arises the important question: did the period of
depression help stir up discontent against the existing conditions; could the Reformers make use of distress to cause
those who cared little for Reform in prosperity to demand
it in adversity? Did the writer judge correctly when he
said: " The country clamors for Reform—Parliamentary
Reform—Reform somehow. Something is felt by Great
British starvation to be vitally wrong?" [2]

There can be little doubt, indeed, that the commercial
panic and the subsequent period of depression did much to
awaken the nation. As the *Westminster Review* pointed
out:

When a commercial panic brings disturbance to trade and industry, then the evils of pauperism and crime in their more

[1] Sir Robert Giffen, *Essays in Finance,* 2nd series (New York, 1886),
pp. 2 and 3.

[2] W. F. Stanley, *Proposition for a New Reform Bill* (London, 1867),
p. 6.

aggravated form excite attention, and the community are
hurried into hasty and spasmodic action.   The financial disasters of 1866 have been felt through the whole community, but
more severely by the humbler orders who have to depend upon
precarious employments.   The ranks of the pauper classes
have been swollen, and the burthens upon the rates and upon
every kind of public and private charity are heavier than they
have been for many preceding years.[1]

That the " humbler orders " and the working class as a
whole, might be stirred by economic pressure even to demand political privileges, was a possibility remarked upon
by the *Spectator:*

It is quite possible,—we desire carefully to guard ourselves
against any positive anticipation—but it is quite possible, that
Parliament has postponed this Reform question one year too
long, and will have to settle it during a season of very considerable popular distress, and therefore of earnest popular agitation.
The reports which come in from all sides are not very reassur-
ing.   The Iron Trade is in deep trouble, so deep that the best
organized Union in England, that of the Southern Ironworkers,
has accepted a blank reduction of ten per cent, which at another
time would have encountered sharp resistance, and that men
who were thought to be millionaires find finance their most
serious occupation.   Bread, though not positively " dear," according to the ante-Free-Trade standard of prices, is very
much dearer than it has been, and the average rate of wages
has not yet adjusted itself fully to the slow but visible rise of
prices.   Agricultural laborers still swarm to the towns.   The
emigration towards the great cities has been of late so rapid
that the number of men outside the regular grooves of labor is
large, and it is on these men that pressure falls with its first
severity.   Finally, the effects of the " panic " have at last
reached down to the lowest class, the sediment, as it were, of

[1] *Westminster Review*, April, 1869. p. 438.

our reservoirs of labor. . . . A contractor refuses all but the least riskful enterprise. This does not ruin his best workmen, who have savings and are indeed seldom discharged, but it presses terribly on vast classes beneath them, on the unskilled laborers in particular. Add to these causes temporary circumstances, like the suspension of river traffic, great fleets unable to enter the Thames, the quarrel in the ship building trade, on the merit of which the public is, we suspect, still misinformed,—and the cessation of dockyard labor, and we can readily understand that there have been " bread riots " in Liverpool, and terrible distress in the riverine parishes of London. In Greenwich, Deptford, and Poplar this distress has taken a dangerous form, almost threatening large masses of human lives. There are said to be 30,000 " shipwrights," but rather shipwright's laborers and dockyard people, out of work, exclusive of the number always thrown out by a frost, of new immigrants, and of the wives and families of all these persons. The poorhouses are full beyond the possibility of receiving more, and " liberal out-door relief," the usual panacea, involves this terrible difficulty. It means additional taxation upon parishes already so heavily taxed that every additional shilling in the pound throws hundreds of self-supporting persons upon alms. Thousands of bakers, pork-butchers, green-grocers, and petty linendrapers are dependent on these ship laborers, and of course can get nothing from them at present, are compelled in fact, at once by policy and feeling, to be as lenient as they dare. They struggle on, often amid real deprivation, eating one meal a day, and so on, and imploring forbearance from the larger dealers who supply them, but any peremptory demand for cash overweights them at once. They have not got it, and they cannot get it, and they sink.[1]

Others there were, like the chairman at the meeting of dock laborers, a meeting called to consider the hard times, who stated distinctly that nothing could be done until the

[1] The *Spectator*, January 26.

working classes had a money interest with the capitalists
and until, as a class, the workingmen were represented in
Parliament.[1] The " commercial morality " of the business
class was to blame for 1866's great disaster, said one of
England's magazines;[2] and the *Beehive*,[3] the official organ
of the trade unions, was quick to declare that workingmen's
representatives in the House of Commons would soon make
it known that the present terrible situation was due to the
capitalists and the middle class, that portion of the country
political powerful. With a few such representatives in the
House public opinion on the subject of trade unions would
be revolutionized, and (it continued)

the fallacy of the cry of " Tradesunions driving trade to foreign countries "[1] would speedily be shown, and the real object
of that cry—the reduction of wages, that employers may still
keep up their enormous profits to maintain the luxury and ex-
travagance indulged in, if not by themselves personally, by
their families—mercilessly exposed. With a few such men in
the House, the ridiculous and miserably false statement, that
the present stagnation of trade, and distress of the unemployed
workmen, had been brought about by Trades-Unions and
strikes, would be exposed and scattered to the winds, and the
real cause would be made patent to the world—viz., the late
monetary panic, brought about by the reckless over-trading,

[1] The *Times*, January 29, 1867.

[2] The *North British Review.*

[3] The *Beehive*, a weekly organ of the trade-union world, was published
from 1861 to 1877 under the editorship of George Potter. Because of
the contributions of such writers as Frederic Harrison, E. S. Beesly,
and other friends of trade unionism, it became, Mr. Sidney Webb says,
the best labor newspaper which has yet appeared, and is of the greatest
possible value to the student of trade-union history. Unfortunately
there is to be found no complete file. So far as can be discovered,
Mr. John Burns is the only person possessing a set for the years 1865,
1866, and 1867.

[4] Articles or letters on this topic appeared frequently at this time.

fraudulent speculations, Stock Exchange gambling, bank and company swindling, and general cupidity, avarice, and roguery of a large portion of the capitalists and middle classes, all eager to get rich by any other than honorable and legitimate means.[1]

The pampleteers, too, agreed with the *Beehive*. One declared that the present unsatisfactory condition of every branch of trade and industry throughout the country was due to bad currency and money laws which the House of Commons did not tend to;—but, " were the Directors and other Proprietors of the (so-called) ' Bank of England ' losers by monetary panics, in the ratio that they have been gainers by them, the Public may be quite certain that monetary panics would not occur." [2]   Another placed the blame for the increase of pauperism upon the panic of 1866 and the depression of trade which in turn was due to the lack of honesty and prudence in the management of the great public undertakings in which a large portion of the savings of the country was formerly invested.[3]   Another gave his explanation of the situation:

The working-classes, through their organ, the *Beehive*, are perfectly aware of the injury " Monetary Panics " periodically inflict upon them, often depriving them partially or wholly of that employment by which alone they can obtain bread for themselves and families; and they also well know that the cause of such panics are our Currency laws, commonly called Bank laws, which were made by the wealthy to suit their own purposes. If the working-classes are told upon authority that these laws cannot be altered because it is necessary that the Bank of England should have in its coffers a huge mass of gold coin and bullion, in order to enable the importer of foreign

[1] The quotation can be found in *Blackwood's*, February, 1867.
[2] Richard Dover, *Progress versus Collapse* (Westminster, 1869).
[3] John Noble, *Free Trade, Reciprocity and the Revivers* (London, 1867), p. 38.

goods to pay his creditor in gold when the Exchanges are against us, they will naturally ask, *Why such necessity? Why not trust to the laws of supply and demand?* Then the truth will come out. It is not that the law of supply and demand would not always enable the importer of foreign goods to obtain whatever gold he required, but he might occasionally have to pay for it, in which case he would have to charge a higher price to his wealthy customers, whether lords or ladies, who would therefore have to pay more for their expensive wines, laces, silks, velvets, and other luxuries; and, rather than such an event, it is far better that the country should be periodically inflicted with " Monetary Panics," and the working-classes deprived wholly or in part of that employment by which alone they can obtain bread for themselves and families! How long can such injustice prevail? [1]

So important was the economic aspect of the question that the opponents of Reform effectively argued that the working classes would use their political power, when obtained, for their own selfish economic and social interests. Thus the *Times* summed up the feeling of the pessimists, although it professed not to take this gloomy view itself:

Almost universally without the first elements of political knowledge it is readily concluded that they will use the franchise for the objects which animal life or their social condition will enable them to appreciate. They are hard-worked and ill-fed, so their cry at the hustings will be for eight hours instead of nine, and sixpence more a day. They are envious, and they will want to have divided among them the land and the incomes of their more fortunate neighbors. They want employment so that they will ask for infinite paper money, to keep up enterprise.[2]

[1] Rigby Wason, *The Currency Question* (London, 1869), pp. 24 and 25.
[2] The *Times*, May 23, 1867.

Indeed, to those students of History who believe that many of the agitations for reforms, which stirred England at various times during the nineteenth century, were brought about by a discontent arising from economic conditions, the foregoing pages will tend to suggest that here again a period of stress had decisive influence upon the popular attitude toward Parliamentary Reform.

CHAPTER III

The Popular Attitude Toward Reform

THE demand for Reform "from without" had been of little importance during the early 'sixties. The bill of 1860 had to be abandoned and no new bill was brought in by the Government because of the apathy of the nation. So said Lord John Russell. In a speech in Parliament in March, 1861, and again in a speech at Blairgowrie in September, 1863, he admitted that a strong feeling existed in the country against changes in the system of representation.[1] Lord Palmerston, in explaining his opposition to Mr. Locke King's County Franchise bill of 1864, said,[2] "I hardly think it was expedient for my honorable friend to bring forward his bill at the present juncture, for it is plain that there does not now exist the same anxiety for organic change that was observable some time ago."

Those who were indifferent to Parliamentary Reform could point out that in 1860 there were no petitions in its favor; in 1861 there were fourteen, signed by 2225 persons; in 1862 there were two, signed by 1097; and in 1863 there were no petitions.[3] The middle classes were in power; their political and economic wants were satisfied and they troubled themselves very little about the working classes.

[1] *Vide Hansard*, vol. clxi, pp. 1920-1926, and J. H. Murchison, *The Conservatives and "Liberals,"* p. xi.

[2] Joseph Irving, *The Annals of Our Time* (London, 1875).

[3] *Cf.* Mr. Whiteside's speech, April 13, 1864, in *Hansard*, vol. clxxv, p. 331.

And even these " humbler neighbors," [1] as they were called, were fairly prosperous—for them. Agitation was checked, however, not only because of the influence of good harvests, increasing trade, and rising wages, but also because of the influence of Lord Palmerston,[2] that typical mid-Victorian gentleman who was at the head of the Liberal ministry. He and Lord Derby, leader of the Opposition, were in agreement upon this question of Reform; both were willing to " rest and be thankful." Lord John Russell summed up the situation as follows:

With regard to domestic policy I think we [*i. e.*, Liberals under Palmerston and Conservatives under Derby] are all pretty much agreed, because the feeling of the country and of those who have conducted great reforms is very much like that of a man, who, having made a road in your own [Scottish] high-lands, put a stone on the top mountain with an inscription, " Rest and be thankful." That seems to be very much like our feeling, not that there are not other roads to make and other mountains to climb; but it seems to be the feeling of the coun-try, in which I cannot help joining, that our own policy is rather to " rest and be thankful " than to make new roads.[3]

The nation at large was conversant with this attitude of Lord Palmerston and knew that there was little chance for an agitation to be successful, but here and there respectable newspapers and magazines [4] and even men [5] of good stand-ing at times averred that some of the more intelligent work-ingmen were anxious for the franchise; anything like

[1] Term of *Westminster Review*, April, 1865, p. 529.

[2] *Cf.* views of *Quarterly Review*, July, 1865.

[3] Murchison, *op. cit.*, p. xi. *Vide*, also, Sir Spencer Walpole, *The Life of Lord John Russell*, 2 vols. (London, 1889, 2nd edition), vol. ii, p. 402.

[4] Letter to the *Times*, May 11, 1865; *Frazer's*, August, 1865.

[5] Reference to Messrs. Baines, Locke King, Bright, Forster, *etc.*

household suffrage was not taken seriously by either of the great parties.

In the spring of 1865 there were a number of Reform meetings held in various cities of the Kingdom, probably with the purpose of trying to commit one party or the other on this question in the coming elections. Some of the speakers criticized [1] the House of Commons and the leaders of both parties as having failed to fulfill the pledges solemnly given to the country six years before; others made known no lesser expectations than universal manhood suffrage and the redistribution of seats. In an effort to make the whole question as important as possible the Reformers organized the Reform League under the leadership of which most of the agitation for the next two or three years was to be carried on. The following notice giving definite information as to the purpose and organization of the League appeared in the London *Times* for February 21, 1865:

A new Reform Association—For some weeks past negotiations have been on foot between a body of influential gentlemen, members of Parliament and others, and several of the leaders among the working classes in the metropolis, for the purpose of ascertaining whether the working men are really desirous of obtaining the franchise, and, if so, whether the existing organizations of the working classes could be made available for furthering a measure of Reform which would accomplish that object. Among other gentlemen who have taken a deep interest in the movement may be enumerated the following members of Parliament: Messrs. Cobden, Bright, Forster, *etc.*, and also several well-known public men, such as Mr. Samuel Morley, Mr. E. Beales, Mr. T. B. Potter, Mr. Mason Jones, *etc.* These gentlemen state that they are prepared, if they see the working classes themselves moving earnestly in the

---

[1] *Vide* especially the Reform meeting at Leeds, an account of which is to be found in the *Times*, February 2, 1865.

matter, to put down a sum of £5,000 to carry on the agitation. The result of these negotiations has been the sending out by a committee of working men of a circular to upwards of 250 representative men among the working classes, comprising the secretaries and officers of the principal trades, friendly, and other working-class organizations, requesting them to attend a meeting at St. Martin's-hall, on Tuesday evening next. Should that meeting respond to the appeal thus made, a deputation will be appointed from it to meet the gentlemen above named on an early day to make the necessary arrangements for establishing the association, which it is intended shall be inaugurated by a great public meeting at one of the large metropolitan halls, over which a leading Liberal member will preside, supported by a large number of the advanced Liberal members of Parliament. An important part of the programme will be the appointment of sub-committees in each metropolitan borough, whose especial duty it will be to watch the election and the candidates who may offer themselves, with a view to obtain the return of members who will honestly carry out the principles of the association, *viz.*, the extension of the franchise to the working classes. The exact basis on which the association is to be formed will be settled at the delegate meeting to take place as above, but whether it be that of a residential manhood suffrage, or household and lodger franchise, or a less extended suffrage, one of the principles of the association is to be that it will accept any installment of Reform that may be offered, from whatever party it may proceed. Should the proposed association be successfully established, it cannot fail in exercising considerable influence over the future of Reform, and in all probability become a power that no Goverment, to what party so ever it may belong, will be able to despise with impunity.[1]

After being formed, the association did not exercise much influence during the year 1865, and the Reformers were

[1] Quoted from *Observer*.

unable to get either party to pledge itself at the election, although a meeting of delegates, held at Manchester in May, passed resolutions expressing " dissatisfaction with the present state of the people as a gross injustice to the working classes, regret that the Government has abandoned the Reform question, and an opinion that Reformers throughout the country should support at the next general election only such candidates as are favorable to the introduction of a comprehensive measure of Reform in the next session of Parliament." [1]

Palmerston apparently was influenced no more by the Reform League than he had been by the friends of the Baines' bill of 1865. This bill, proposing the reduction of the borough franchise, if of any effect, hurt the cause of Reform. The author of it himself admitted the apathy out of doors; he urged, however, that the question be discussed and settled in time of calm " lest some day it should take the shape of a demand for universal suffrage." [2] Other speakers corroborated his statements with respect to the attitude of the nation, and the majority of the House agreed with Mr. Horsman when this gentleman, although avowing a sincere desire that the working classes should have some voice, urged that the votes of mere numbers never ought to and never should govern the country.

The first election for the new Parliament took place on the eleventh of July and on the twenty-fifth the *Times* was able to announce that the " restful and thankful " nation had given Palmerston 367 Liberal as against 290 Conservative members. The *Annual Register* thought this election noteworthy for its lack of excitement; the *Times* [3] thought it memorable for the evidences of national pros-

[1] The *Times*, May 16, 1865.

[2] *Hansard*, vol. clxxviii, pp. 1371 *et seq.*

[3] The *Times*, July 4, 1865, editorial.

perity and the contentment which its history would afford.
In fact there had been no definite issue.   As for Reform—
" willingly or unwillingly " said the *Quarterly Review*,[1]
" they (the Palmerston Administration) have brought the
. . . . movement to a deadlock, and have made it almost
impossible for anyone who comes after them for a considerable number of years to call it into activity again."
Mr. John Bright declared that Reform should be postponed
till the close of the official life of Lord Palmerston, " the
only man in the Liberal party able and willing to betray
it :" [2] a part of this statement Mr. Bright within a year
found to be untrue.   It must be added that many members
in election speeches had given individual pledges to take
up the question.

Lord Palmerston died on October 18, 1865, and with
the formation of the Russell-Gladstone ministry there
seemed to be hope for the Reformers.   It was thought in
some quarters [3] that Russell would have to do something lest
he forfeit a long-standing pledge, and Gladstone was felt to
be in favor of Reform.   In 1864 the latter had uttered the
fated words of which mention has been made in a preceding
chapter: " I venture to say that every man who is not presumably incapacitated by some consideration of personal
unfitness or of political danger, is morally entitled to come
within the pale of the constitution."   Vague as were these
words, and qualified as they had been by a protest against
sudden or violent or excessive or intoxicating change, nevertheless they caused distrust among the Conservatives and the
Whigs.[4]   Now that the retarding influence of Palmerston

[1] *Quarterly Review*, July, 1865.

[2] *Cf.* the *Times*, September 20, 1865, editorial.

[3] *Cf. Frazer's*, June, 1866, pp. 683 and 684.

[4] *Vide* John Morley, *The Life of William Ewart Gladstone*, vol. ii,
pp. 126-131.

was gone, what might Gladstone not do? And his defeat
in 1865 at Oxford and his election from Lancashire would
tend all the more to unmuzzle him. Hence the Reformers
claimed him as their own and quoted his words again and
again. They were encouraged, too, by the addition to the
Government of Mr. Forster and Mr. Goschen, two men of
the Radical wing.[1]

Reform meetings held in the latter part of November and
during December, compared with those held one year later,
appear to have been very unimportant, although enough
interest was shown to warrant the statement of the *Times*
on the eighteenth of December, that the question of Reform
seemed to have revived,[2]—a statement later contradicted. A
meeting held in London on the twelfth of December, is important as showing what reforms the working men expected
to result from a wide extension of the franchise.[3] Here
as at many of the meetings of the following two months
manhood suffrage was demanded, but few really had hopes
that such a request would be listened to. As Mr. Tom
Hughes said at a Reform meeting at Lambeth: " They might
just as well ask for the whole loaf, and they would be more
likely to get half of it than if they went for only two-
thirds." [4] Some of the speakers, however, did not want the
full loaf or even the two-thirds. Members of the House of
Commons of the Liberal or Radical denomination who
were trying to guide or to make public opinion, gave various
solutions to the Reform problem in their " out of door "
speeches. The meetings went on, without impressing the

[1] The *Times*, November 25, 1865, editorial. *Vide* the *London Review*,
October 12, 1867, for a life of Goschen.

[2] The *Times*, December 18, 1865, editorial.

[3] *Cf. infra*, pp. 130-133, for a complete discussion of this topic.

[4] The *Times*, January 13, 1866.

Government very much, however, for in the Queen's speech
Reform was the last of more than twenty subjects and the
two sentences about it were very vague: the question had
been " ushered in with the modesty proper to an experience
of many failures," [1] and if we are to believe the *Times*, a
franchise bill,[2] which was brought in on March 12, 1866,
conservative as it could well be, produced no applause: "We
have listened in vain for the faintest note of approval, or
the contrary or bare recognition from the provinces. . . .
Not even the workingmen make the least sign, or seem to be
aware that they are to be presented with a very considerable
slice of the British Constitution." [3] The *Saturday Review* [4]
expressed a like opinion; " The organs of the Government may put as good a face on the matter as they like,
but the fact is that the Reform Bill has fallen dead.
The country does not care for it an atom. There is no
loud outcry against it, but there is scarcely a whisper of
approval of it." The Radicals claimed there *was* a popular
desire for the bill. Their arguments may be seen from Mr.
Bright's Manchester speech of March 27, 1866:

These gentlemen who oppose this Bill tell us in the House of
Commons and some of their newspapers tell us outside, that
really nobody wants this Bill, and that a few men who have
objects of their own to serve are constantly talking about it,
but that the great body of the people have really no interest in
it whatever. They said exactly the same of the Bill of 1831.
I stated in the House of Commons the other night that in the
years from 1821 to 1831 there were scarcely any petitions presented to Parliament in favor of Parliamentary Reform, and
yet in the year 1831 the whole thing was an explosion. The
House of Commons was terror-stricken, and men of great

[1] The *Times*, February 8, 1866, editorial.
[2] For detailed information on the bill, *cf. infra*, pp. 142-3.
[3] *Ibid.*, March 20, 1866, editorial.
[4] The *Saturday Review*, March 24, 1866.

families were almost hiding themselves from popular indignation. What do these gentlemen want now? Are they content to be taught by great and peaceful meetings, and by the presentation of great petitions, or do they want something more?[1]

Bright then urged the holding of monster meetings and elsewhere[2] declared that " if Parliament Street from Charing Cross to the venerable Abbey were filled with men seeking a Reform Bill, ... these slanderers of their countrymen would learn to be civil if they did not learn to love freedom."

As a matter of fact, the Council of the Reform League determined to support the Government measure, and the various Reform meetings held during the Easter recess, many of them under the auspices of the Liberals, it is true, also passed resolutions favoring the measure but expressing a desire for greater reductions in qualifications. It seemed for a long time during the first weeks of April that the agitation was to become general. Meetings were held[3] in Edinburgh (April 2), in Sheffield (April 2), in West Riding of Yorkshire (April 3), in Burnley (April 3), in Rochdale (April 4), in Lambeth (April 4), in Hanley (April 4), Exeter (April 4), Manchester (April 5), Liverpool (April 5), and so on. Mr. Forster, Mr. Bright, and Mr. Gladstone made important speeches. The last named in the famous speeches at Liverpool (April fifth and sixth) declared that the Government was staking its political character on the adoption of the bill in its main provisions, that the trumpet had been blown with no uncertain sound, that the Rubicon had been passed, the bridges broken and the boats burned behind them.

[1] The *Times*, March 28, 1866.

[2] In a letter to a Reform meeting at Birmingham; *vide Annals of Our Time*, March 26, 1866.

[3] Following announcements in issues of the *Times*.

The result, gentlemen [said he] is in other hands than ours. . . .
I can't doubt from the extraordinary working and movement
of society that there is on the part of the masses of the community a forward and onward movement, which forward and
onward movement will be perfectly safe and harmless, and not
only safe and harmless, but infinitely profitable if we only deal
with it wisely and in time.   But read the signs of the times.
The voice that once spoke as never man spoke rebuked those
in authority who could not read the signs of the times.   Does
any man really suppose that the political limit signified by the
number ten is to be forever and ever, from generation to generation, the limit within which all are to enjoy, but beyond which
every man is to be deprived the enjoyment of the franchise?
Certainly not.   The defeat of the Bill, what would it procure?
—an interval, but not an interval of repose; an interval of fever,
an interval of expectation, an interval for the working of those
influences which might possibly arise even to the formidable
dimensions of political danger.   Let the great English nation
be wise, and be wise in time.[1]

The audience cheered him to the echo not only upon the expression of this sentiment but also upon his attack [2] on a
conservative section of the Liberals called the Adullamites [3]
who refused to follow him in the question of Reform and
especially upon an invective against the Adullamite leader,
Robert Lowe.

But the enthusiasm which the Chancellor of the Exchequer
attempted to kindle by his visit to Liverpool seemed, like
a fire of tow, hastily lit and soon extinguished.   Such was
the opinion of the *Times.*   From the middle of April until
the middle of June there were scarcely any Reform meetings.
A graph roughly representing the agitation for Reform as

[1] The *Times*, April 7, 1866.

[2] On the previous day.

[3] More detailed information on the Adullamites and their leader is
given in the next chapter.

shown by the number and enthusiasm of the meetings held from the summer of 1865 to the summer of 1866, would give a curve rising gradually during the late autumn of 1865, keeping to a level during January and February, 1866, falling slightly the first of March, rising again toward the middle of the month and really gaining respectable height during the first weeks of April, after which it would fall rapidly and remain low in the scale until the first of July.

In fact the demand from without had not been great enough to produce the desired effect upon the House of Commons,[1] although it looked for a time as if the meetings of the Easter recess might be the beginning of a real agitation. The failure to impress the Conservatives and Adullamites was due to several things: the agitation had not been carried on for any considerable time; enthusiasm at the meetings took the form of praises for greater reductions of qualifications rather than for anything which the bill contained; the Conservative press[2] felt that Liberal leaders were getting up the agitation and that noted speakers such as Bright and Gladstone took people to the meetings rather than any desire on the part of the working class to force Reform; the all but universal opposition of the London press[3] and the censorious tone of London society counterbalanced favorable comments upon the bill. Moreover, a large number of the recently elected members of the House were quite unwilling to pass a measure which would have the effect of causing them to appear before their constituents and of exposing them to the risk and cost of

[1] *Cf. Fortnightly Review*, vol. vii, p. 745 (Molesworth's article); *Blackwood's*, February, 1866, pp. 147-148; *Fortnightly Review*, vol. v, June 15 and July 15, 1866.

[2] *Cf. Blackwood's*, February, 1866, and letter to the *Times*, February 3, 1866.

[3] *Cf. Edinburgh Review*, April, 1866.

a contested election. Another cause, economic at least in part, would tend to make many members oppose change: the working class, it was felt,[1] wanted the franchise for a reason other than that of merely casting a vote, and their interests might not always coincide with the interests of capitalists and landowners. The workingman could see the need of great improvement in governing the country; for in spite of the prosperity of the early 'sixties already described, scenes of misery were not few or hard to be found. As the *Fortnightly Review* pointed out,[2] one had only to wander from the lace makers of Devonshire to the strawplaiters of Hertfordshire, the glovers of Worcestershire, and the hosiers of Nottinghamshire to find the usual close rooms, long hours, inadequate payment, bad food, disregard of physical wants, undue pressure, and everything calculated to make life miserable. In the town, in the country, on the surface and beneath it, one would see a dreadful catalogue of human sufferings; poor wretched creatures laboring among the mineral deposits in danger of death alike from poisonous vapors and from lack of proper safeguards; children working in glass foundries day and night without intermission, or mixing in gangs in the fields under the eye of a ruffian taskmaster. The member of Parliament might console himself over the situation with the philosophy of an Emerson or the theories of a Ricardo or Malthus; the workingman as a lawmaker would mend matters. For instance, Mr. Odger, shoemaker, speaking at the National Reform League meeting at St. Martin's Hall a fortnight before Christmas, 1865. declared that if the working classes were given the vote they would do away with the present class legislation and would see " that the

---

[1] *Vide, infra*, the arguments presented by the Conservatives and Adullamites against the bill.

[2] *Fortnightly Review*, vol. iv, article by Edward Wilson.

poor man's daughter, who was worked 12, 14, and 16 hours a day, should have time to go abroad and view the face of nature.   They would prevent the poor man's child from going in early life into mines and workshops before it was educated.   They would prevent the poor agricultural laborer from working for 8s. per week." [1]   Professor Beesly [2] at a Reform meeting held in St. Martin's Hall, April 11, 1866, instanced as grievances the unequal pressure of indirect taxation on the workingmen, who paid 4s. a week out of 20s. wages, the operation of the game laws, the punishment of servants for breach of contract, the excessive expenditure on the army and navy as compared with the education grant, the treatment of the poor in workhouses, and the monopoly of land by large proprietors.   These were grievances which a reformed Parliament might be expected to redress, but which were not likely to be redressed under the present system.

The middle class and the skilled workingmen, however, were prosperous and the lot of the unskilled workingmen was improving,[3] notwithstanding these complaints which could have been made during any period from 1815, so that the need for social reform was not pressing enough to keep an agitation going.   " If there were distress in the country " said the *Fortnightly Review,*[4] " we cannot say what might be the effect of representations made to the working classes that the extension of the franchise would improve their condition, but as wages are rising, and no political grievances are felt, the working classes have certainly not hitherto responded to any efforts to rouse them."

[1] From the *Quarterly Review*. January, 1866, pp. 264 *et seq.*; also to be found in the *Times.*

[2] The *Times*, April 12, 1866.

[3] *Blackwood's*, February, 1866, p. 144.

[4] *Fortnightly Review*, vol. iv, " Public Affairs," p. 756.

The *North British Review* of March, 1866, pointed out that people thought Reform was bound to come but that if anything should occur to disturb that confidence, those who maintained the indifference of the people would find themselves unpleasantly startled from their fond belief.[1] And it so happened that the arguments of the conservative Liberals who go by the name of Adullamites against any extension of the suffrage and the defeat of the bill with the consequent resignation of the Liberal leaders did help to shatter the indifference at about the same time that the economic condition of the country was rapidly growing worse.

With the fall of the ministry the agitation was renewed. The Adullamites, ably led by Lowe, had caused the defeat of the bill; their arguments against the present bill were equally applicable to any change in franchise qualifications whatsoever, and Lowe's speeches so successful in their immediate purpose were used by the Reformers with great advantage in arousing the working classes to demand their rights. Mr. Frederic Harrison,[2] writing for the *Fortnightly Review*,[3] expressed the opinion that full justice had not been done to the speeches of Mr. Lowe. "In our memory," he wrote, "it has not been known that the arguments of one independent speaker have accomplished so much; checked the current of constitutional development, roused the upper classes to resistance, terrified the middle classes into hesitation, and stung the working classes into action."

Frazer's declared the spirit of the unenfranchised classes had been kindled by Mr. Lowe's "contumelious speeches, so delightful to the Tory part of his audience."[4] The

[1] The *North British Review*, March, 1866, p. 232.

[2] Frederic Harrison wrote much in favor of trade unions.

[3] *Fortnightly Review*, vol. vii, p. 261.

[4] *Frazer's*, November, 1866, "Why we want a Reform Bill," p. 559.

speakers at the meetings of June and July and later were bitter against the Adullamites. At a conference of the National Reform Union,[1] an association largely of the middle classes but originating at the suggestion of the workingmen of Leeds for a platform upon which the two classes could co-operate, a Mr. Partridge gave a typical speech [2] in which he declared that the obstacles to their representation were not the Tories, who were their " natural enemies," nor the Liberals, who were their friends, but " this mongrel party, which was neither for nor against them, but which was for itself always and only." [3]   It was remarked that the bill of 1832 had been passed under circumstances by no means peaceful, that the French Revolution ought to serve as a warning to the reactionaries.   Lowe, in fact, and others of his group received disapproving letters [4] from their constituents, since, without a dissolution, no other means of expression was possible.

The renewed agitation was manifest by the important meetings of early July—one of July 2, 1866, in Trafalgar Square, and one of July 5, 1866, at Birmingham.   Seven or eight thousand persons were present at Birmingham where resolutions were passed against the Tories and Adullamites and in favor of a dissolution.   There was an expression of want of confidence in any ministry Derby might form.   At the demonstration at Trafalgar Square there was present a large number of well-behaved people; Mr. Beales, head of the Reform League, spoke of the " thunder of the crowd's gratitude to such real patriots as Mr. Gladstone and Mr. Bright."   Mr. Lucraft, a Hoxton journeyman and

[1] Held June 22, 1866, at Manchester.

[2] To be found in the *Times*, June 25, 1866.

[3] It was sometimes stated that Lowe was anxious for the downfall of the Liberals because he had been given no position in the cabinet.

[4] These can be found in the *Times*.

reformer, gave the rallying cry of " Reform, and Gladstone
and Liberty." Later in the evening " Lucraft and his mob,"
—8,000 of them—marched with due enthusiasm to Gladstone's house, but found only the ladies at home. Such
meetings, however, seem unimportant when compared with
the Hyde Park incident.

The Hyde Park affair, described with considerable detail
in almost every English history of the nineteenth century,
was a somewhat spectacular incident about which a great
number of particulars have been given, some true, a number
not to be verified, most of them unimportant compared with
the effect of the " riot."[1] When the Reform League announced that a great demonstration in favor of the extension of the suffrage was to be held in Hyde Park, Mr.
Walpole, the Home Secretary of the Conservative Government, which had recently come into power, had the Commissioner[2] of Police of the Metropolis insert in the newspapers a notice to the effect that no such meeting would be
allowed. It was stated that the meeting was illegal, would
lead to disorderly conduct and would endanger public peace.
Mr. Beales in reply said that the meeting would be held unless
he were shown the law by which the Commissioner had
authority to prohibit it. The Reformers regretted exceed-
ingly, they said, that the Home Secretary was determined
to put himself " in a position of wanton antagonism " to
the people, but were willing to put the blame of any possible collision between themselves and the police—a collision
which they promised would take place if the meeting were
forcibly interfered with—upon the Home Secretary.

Accordingly on the twenty-second of July, the Reformers marched[3] in goodly numbers to Hyde Park, found the

[1] Walpole's *History of Twenty-five Years* gives a very good account.
[2] Sir Richard Mayne.
[3] *Vide Annual Register*, chronicle, July, 1866.

gates closed and sixteen or eighteen hundred police waiting
for them. Mr. Beales formally demanded admittance. This
was refused, of course, and having raised the legal question
desired, he with the other leaders proceeded to Trafalgar
Square, there to hold the program as prearranged. The
greater part of the crowd, however, did not follow the
leaders but finding the railings around the park none too
strong began to push them over,[1] and rushed upon the forbidden ground. Thereupon began a scuffle with the police,
resulting in a few injuries on both sides. Some " roughs "
were a little troublesome; all in all about eighty or ninety
persons were taken into custody. Those who were bold
enough to make speeches after their entrance into the park
were not interrupted by the police. As a matter of fact
little damage was done except to the shrubbery and the
flower beds.

But the influence of the Hyde Park affair was very great.
The *Times* protested that such a gathering was a display of
numbers to overawe the Legislature and the ruling classes,
that it was useless for political discussion but might easily

[1] Justin McCarthy in his *History of Our Own Times*, 2 vols. (New
York, 1880), vol. ii, p. 344, gives the following account: " Emerson has
said that every revolution, however great, is first of all a thought in the
mind of a single man. One disappointed Reformer lingering in Park
Lane, with his breast against the rails, as the poetic heroine had hers,
metaphorically, against the thorn, became impressed with the idea that
the barrier was somewhat frail and shaky. How would it be, he vaguely
thought for a moment, if he were to give an impulse and drive the
railing in? What, he wondered to himself, would come of that? The
temptation was great. He shook the rails; the rails begun to give way.
Not that alone, but the sudden movement was felt along the line, and
into a hundred minds came at once the grand revolutionary idea which
an instant before had been the· thought in the mind of one hitherto unimportant man. A simultaneous impulsive rush, and some yards of
railing were down, and men in scores were tumbling, and floundering,
and rushing over them." Unfortunately, McCarthy has not seen fit to
give to the world the name of his hero of original thought.

produce serious danger to the public peace, that finally, excepting some decent people, it was a mass of the coarsest mob.[1] The Reformers, on the other hand, claimed that the ministry, by employing the police to prevent forcibly the working classes from a peaceable meeting in Hyde Park at which they wished to complain of their exclusion from the suffrage, had shown that it possessed all the old spirit of Toryism and distrust of the people and hence had forfeited all claims to the confidence and support of the country.[2] In fact the president of the Reform League seems to have outgeneraled his opponents completely. After the Home Secretary had forbidden the use of the park without any specific right to do so, the attempt of Beales to hold the meeting in spite of opposition was bound to advertise the Reform cause. Had the Reformers been kept out of the park, a cry against class government would immediately have been taken up by every association in the country; had the crowd been allowed in after various notices had forbidden the meeting, the Government's surrender would have been demonstrative of the force of the people's will and hence would have been suggestive of further fulfillments of their demands. As it was, the best possible happened for Mr. Beales. The people after being refused admittance, had managed to get their demands in a semi-forcible manner but with responsibility unfixed. The Reformers could point to victory; the upper classes had the power only to decry the act as violence. What, in fact, could be done by the Government in such a situation? The police had been unable to control the people; the Chief Commissioner of Police, on the evening which succeeded the disturbance, had

[1] The *Times*, July 24, 1866, editorial.

[2] The *Times*, July 31, Reform League demonstration in Agricultural Hall (July 30, 1866); the *Times*, July 25, London Working Men's Association; the *Times*, July 28, editorial from *Pall Mall Gazette*, etc.

even asked that troops be held in readiness for him.[1]   The
Reform League attempted to help matters by agreeing to
get the mob from the Park upon the understanding that the
legal right of meeting therein should be tested.   But the
issuance of its placard, without authority, that there should
be no further attempt to hold " a meeting in Hyde Park except only by arrangement with the Government. on Monday
afternoon, July 30," connoted that the Home Secretary had
consented, as the price of the League's assistance, to concede
the whole principle by allowing a meeting.   Mr. Walpole
because of this unfortunate incident was almost driven from
office![2]   Reform had been brought before the country in a
startling manner.   Mr. Beales is authority[3] for the statement that there was a general feeling prevalent throughout
the country that the events of the last month had done more
to hasten the progress of Reform than all the exertions of
the last thirty years.

There can be no doubt as to the influence of the League
after the Hyde Park affair.   In the first place it was able
to keep going a series of monster meetings, and in the second
place it entered into an alliance with the trade unions.[4]

[1] Walpole, *History of Twenty-five Years*, vol. ii, p. 175.

[2] *Ibid.*, pp. 175 and 176.   Mr. Walpole was the private secretary to his
father, the Home Secretary, in 1866, and was in closest communication
with him.   Further data on the mistake of the leaders of the Reform
League in issuing the placard may be found in George Jacob Holyoake,
Sixty Years of an Agitator's Life, 2 vols. (London, 1900, 4th edition),
vol. ii, chap. xcii.

[3] *Cf.* the *Times*, August 16, 1866.

[4] Sidney and Beatrice Webb in the *History of Trade Unionism*
(London, 1911, new edition), pp. 223, 224, and 231, emphasize the influence of the "Junta," an informal cabinet of five trade-union leaders
who lived in London and were in constant communication with one another, toward having the trade unions agitate for political Reform, even
in spite of "a strong traditional repugnance to political action."   Under the influence of the "Junta," the London Trades council "enthusiastically threw itself into the demonstration" in favor of Reform in

The great demonstrations of the autumn of 1866 were tried out first " in the provinces." On the twenty-seventh of August there was a demonstration at Birmingham where, according to the reports, " thousands and thousands " were present.[1] In honor of the occasion all the nearby towns turned out and business in the city was stopped. Members of trade and co-operative societies collected at nine o'clock in the morning and proceeded in six divisions to the meeting grounds. Here resolutions were passed in favor of manhood suffrage and the ballot, and expressing gratitude to Gladstone, Bright, Mill, and Beales. The great event at the evening meeting was a speech by John Bright; " let us do as your forefathers did thirty-four years ago, — let us have associations everywhere; let every workshop and every factory be a Reform Association," was his plea.

During September there took place a great number of fairly well attended meetings. The *Times* contains data, for instance, as follows: September 1, Reform meeting at Bristol, —10,000 present; [2] September 1, Reform demonstration at Bolton,—3,000 present;[3] September 5, Reform meeting at Leeds:[4] September 10, Reform meeting at Bermondsey,— 7,000 present;[5] Reform demonstration at Hanley on September 12 with 15,000 to 20,000 present; [6] and finally on September 24, a big Reform demonstration at Manchester.[7] The

---

1866. The London trade unions with the exception of two small clubs, did not, however, join the Reform League in a corporate capacity, although many of the local Birmingham trade unions became directly affiliated with that organization.

[1] *Vide* the *Times*, August 28, 1866.

[2] *Cf.* the *Times*, September 3, 1866.

[3] *Ibid.*, September 4, 1866.

[4] *Ibid.*, September 7, 1866.

[5] *Ibid.*, September 11, 1866.

[6] *Ibid.*, September 12, 1866.

[7] *Ibid.*, September 25, 1866.

following short summary concerning this latter meeting is given in the *Annual Register*:

This afternoon [September 24] a meeting, supposed to be larger than any hitherto assembled in England, was held at Manchester. During the morning many local divisions marched into the town from the various populous districts around, carrying flags inscribed with the words "National Reform Union," and proceeded to the square called Camp-field, a center surrounded by ten acres, in which six platforms were erected. Notwithstanding the torrents of rain which continued throughout the day, the numbers assembled were estimated by the reporters, both of the local and of the London press, at between 100,000 and 200,000 persons. At each of the above sections these resolutions were carried, namely, 1. "That this meeting protests against the perpetuation of class government to the exclusion of the great majority of the people from the franchise; refuses to allow itself to be made an instrument to further the means of contending parties or the selfish interests of any class; and pledges itself to adopt all means of organizing and agitating for the only just basis of representation — registered residential manhood suffrage and the ballot." 2. "That this meeting rejoices in the formation of the northern department of the Reform League, and pledges its support to the executive council in the organization of branches throughout the north of England, and hereby declares its confidence in Mr. Edmund Beales and the executive of the Reform League in London." 3. "That this meeting tenders its warmest and most grateful thanks to the Right Honorable William Ewart Gladstone, John Bright, Esq., John Stuart Mill, Esq., and all friends of Reform who, throughout the late discussions in Parliament, vindicated the character and protected the rights of the people; and further expresses confidence in the honesty and ability of Mr. John Bright to champion the people's cause in Parliament during the coming parliamentary struggle." [1]

[1] *Annual Register*, 1866, chronicle, pp. 137 *et seq.*

At the evening meeting John Bright was the principal speaker; so great was the crowd that only one-fourth of those who applied, could enter Free Trade Hall.

On the eighth of October occurred another great Reform meeting of the working classes—this time at Leeds. The weather was favorable and there were present nearly 200,000 persons. As early as four o'clock in the morning—says the *Annual Register* [1]—came some arrivals into Leeds from distant localities, and during the greater part of the forenoon every highway and byway leading into this city was overrun by large or small parties of operatives, the majority well clad and in holiday trim—all of them hastening with exuberant cheerfulness to some rendezvous which had been fixed upon as their rallying point. Along the Bradford road, as well as the roads of Dewsbury and Halifax, and by the country lanes leading from the many clothing villages of the districts, came trooping along on foot at short intervals large bodies of men with music and banners; for at many of the mills and workshops of Bradford and the adjacent towns as well as of Leeds, there was a complete holiday. The procession contained some 70,000 persons—an orderly line of men walking five abreast four miles long, with its marshals and musicians, with its flag-bearers carrying banners, mottoes and ensigns. Arriving at Woodhouse Moor the crowd was addressed by the speakers who offered the following resolutions: protest against and denial of the charges of venality, ignorance, drunkenness, and indifference to Reform brought against the working classes during the last session of Parliament; pledges of co-operation in the cause of registered residential manhood suffrage and the ballot; acknowledgment of the services of Gladstone, Bright and Mill. At the evening meet-

[1] *Annual Register,* 1866, chronicle, pp. 141 *et seq.*; *vide* the *Times,* October 9, 1866.

ing Mr. Forster and Mr. Bright spoke, the latter declaring to the assembly: " The workingmen must combine, and they must subscribe a penny a week or a penny a month from the thousands and from the millions to raise funds that will enable you to carry on the most gigantic and success-ful agitation that this country has ever seen.   It is mainly your own voice that will decide your own fate." [1]

On the sixteenth of October there was a Reform demon-stration at Glasgow—such a demonstration as has not been seen since the year 1832, said the *Fortnightly Review*.[2]   So large was the parade that it took two hours to get past any given spot.[3]   At the meeting there were the usual resolu-tions.   In the evening Mr. Bright again was the chief speaker.   Before he delivered his speech an address was made to him which is highly significant as showing the economic and social conditions which a reformed Parlia-ment might well improve.   The speaker declared:

We dread that gulf, pauperism, the scandal of the world, amid unparalleled wealth, which is swallowing up our aged and infirm, and in which so many of our youth are abandoned to misery and crime.   We protest against the domination of sec-tional parties, who, professing to govern for the people, have failed to provide education for the nation, which popular Governments in other lands have secured, leaving us far be-hind.   We point to the wasteful expenditure which has pro-duced and fostered our dangerous national debt, sapping the energies of the country, and burdening it in the race of na-tions.   In the city from which Smith taught we point to the unsatisfactory laws of banking, and the attendant paralyzing of our trade.   We denounce the system of misgovernment in certain colonies. . . . We protest against the present sectional

[1] The *Times*, October 9, 1866.
[2] *Fortnightly Review*, vol. vi (November 15, 1866), p. 748.
[3] The *Times*, October 17, 1866.

representation, its restricted basis, its gross inequalities, the interference with tenant voters, the shameful bribery and corruption. . . . We seek . . . to assist in solution of these great problems on which the future of our country depends . . . but warn our rulers against the continued breach of the Great Charter wrung from reluctant hands at Runnymede, which provides that the rulers "shall not deny nor delay justice to anyone." [1]

Mr. Bright, in replying, denounced the landed interests; he acknowledged that the class which had hitherto ruled in the country had failed miserably, that it reveled in power and wealth, while at its foot, a terrible peril for its future, lay a multitude which it had neglected. " If a class has failed," he shouted, " let us try the nation. That is our faith, that is our cry. Let us try the nation."

With the exception of a demonstration at Edinburgh [2] on the seventeenth of November there was no great activity among the Reformers until the third of December, when the London workingmen were given a chance to show their interest in the question of the day. For weeks this trades' Reform demonstration had been the talk of all London.[3] Rumor had it that 200,000 would take a part in the procession, and many and various were the suggestions sent to the newspapers by interested parties as to the marching and handling of such a crowd. As a matter of fact there were some 23,000 in the parade, according to the Inspector of Police. The members represented about fifty societies, and each trade or society had one or more banners.[4] Some of these contained mottoes of rather general application,[5] as

[1] *Ibid.*

[2] *Cf.* the *Times*, November 19, 1866.

[3] The *Times*, November 30, 1866.

[4] *Annual Register*, 1866, chronicle, p. 189.

[5] *Cf.* the *Times*, December 4, 1866.

"Taxation without representation is tyranny"; others were rather piquant. The tallow chandlers had a motto " Bright and Light"; the cabinetmakers, the inscriptions: " No more oligarchical rule—the people are determined to be the cabinetmakers ", " Bright cabinetmakers wanted—no Adullamites need apply "; the shoemakers, an elegant boot on a pole, with words, "It's the wearer that feels where the shoe pinches." The Workingmen's Association was represented by a banner with the inscription, " to procure the political enfranchisement and promote the social and general interests of the industrial classes." The Reformers, of course, had their song, the sentiment of which may be seen from the concluding verse:

> " Then shout with all your might
> God save Gladstone, Beales, and Bright;
> Wave your banners, let your ranks closer form,
> And let your watchword be—
> Old England, Liberty,
> Manhood Suffrage, Vote by Ballot and Reform."

The demeanor of those in procession was irreproachable; even the *Times* declared that the day's proceedings showed what the sturdiest Conservative would have to admit, that the more intelligent mechanics were at least the equals, in all that constitutes good citizens, of the small shopkeepers who did possess the franchise.[1]

The crowd of spectators, many thousand strong in spite of mud, slush, and a cold, drizzly, uncomfortable rain, behaved in seemly fashion, and listened good-naturedly to readings by some of their members. The following speech especially produced much merriment:

And now, dearly beloved, the Gospel of the day is the Hyde Park railings and the cause of their destruction. Now it was shortly after the premature death of the Russell Administra-

[1] The *Times*, December 4, 1866.

tion that the Tories took office, and that a couple of chiefs of
the tribes of the Derbyites and Disraelites laid their heads
together to consider in what way they might . . . bamboozle
the working man. And behold there sprang on the face of the
earth a new race of people called Adullamites, who were like
unto their namesakes of old, a dissatisfied and a two-faced
people, and like the chameleon, could change their color at
will. And their chief was a Low(e) man, from the land of
moonrakers, and he and his colleagues were the Reformers of
to-day and the Tories of to-morrow. And they said to the
people, " Behold, we are on your side," and at the same time
they were seeking how they might destroy their cause.

Then followed a description of Hyde Park, of the " passing
away " of the rails, of the struggle with the police; and
finally came the supplication: " From having the Park gates
shut against us, save us, good Walpole." Upon the arrival
of the procession at the Beaufort grounds, the speakers of
the day began to give addresses. Mr. Beales declared that
the national movement which commenced in July last in
Trafalgar Square, and at Hyde Park, had been increasing
in volume, in intensity, and in enthusiastic unanimity
throughout the length and breadth of England, Scotland,
and Ireland. He wanted manhood suffrage. A Mr. Green-
ing of Manchester pointed out that the working class could
not expect a righteous verdict from a packed jury of rich
men whose whole interest lay in one direction and who therefore could not do justice to the nation, even if they would.
A Colonel Dickson stated that in France every workingman was enfranchised, that in Italy the case was much
the same, and that even the tyrannical Bismarck was giving
universal suffrage to the Prussians.[1] He said that in the
House of Commons as at present constituted, there were
not above a dozen men who cared a straw for Reform; the

---

[1] *Cf.* chapter i.

members of the House were the nominees of the House of
Lords; many of them were railway directors, lawyers, and
bankers, but scarcely any of them represented the working
classes.   Mr. Leicester, a glassblower, spoke with considerable vehemence: " The question was, would they suffer those
little-minded, decrepit, humped-backed, one-eyed scoundrels
who sat in the House of Commons to rob and defraud them
any longer of their rights. . . . Whether those who had
squandered the people's earnings like water should continue to do so?"   The usual resolutions in favor of registered residential manhood suffrage and the ballot and thanks
to Gladstone, Bright, and Mill were voted.

The following evening a great in-door meeting in connection with the trades' demonstration was held in St.
James' Hall.   Admission was obtained by tickets which
sold for five shillings, three shillings and one shilling; and
the hall was crowded.   Mr. G. Potter,[1] chairman, declared
that he would say once and for all that if the Tory party was
not satisfied with what had already been done, then they
would commence the next year with something which would
be admitted to be sufficient.[2]   Mr. Bright, however, was the
leading speaker.   He asked if anyone wished the workingmen of Great Britain to be driven in defense of their rights
to the course of the Fenians—secret societies, oaths and
drillings, arms and menace, and a threat of violence and
insurrection, and declared that the Parliament of landowners
and rich men either were wholly ignorant of or they wholly
despised that great national opinion which had been exhibited
during the last three or four months; that they were resisting " until the discontent which is now so general shall become universal, and that which is now only a great exhibition
of opinion may become necessarily and inevitably a great
and menacing exhibition of force."

[1] Mr. Potter, editor of the *Beehive*, was influential in trade union affairs.
[2] The *Times*, December 5, 1866.

Significant as was the display of interest by the workingmen despite many obstacles — the state of the weather, the
time of the year, the necessity of the loss of a day's work
to all those attending, the threatened discharge of em-
ployees by several large firms employing thousands of workmen if they attended the demonstration (a threat which
was reported to the committees as having been carried out
in many instances) [1] — even more significant was the fact
that this was the first time the trades' societies of London
had taken part in a political movement.   Mr. Bright tells
us [2] that he had warned workingmen eight years before
that the time had come or would soon come when it
would be their duty to make use of the organization of
trade and friendly societies " to bear upon the Government
the united power of a just demand "; that " one year only
of the united action of the working classes, through their
existing organization, would wholly change the aspect of the
Reform question."   Already the trade societies had taken
part in some of the demonstrations outside the metropolis
and were now according to plans made some months previous,[3] active in London. The *Times* stood against the unions
as a political power, claiming that it would excite still more
the jealousy of the middle classes " by the prospect of a vast
organization for political control against which they themselves would have no power unless they resorted in turn to
combinations unknown in our Constitutional history "; that
the chief cause of the postponement of Reform from year to
year had been the tacit fear felt by the middle class of this
very organization of the artisans.[4]   It attacked Bright in no
undecisive manner:

[1] *Vide* letter of Robert Hartwell, secretary of demonstration committee, in the *Times*, December 12, 1866.

[2] In his speech at the trades' Reform meeting, December 4, 1866.

Cf. the *Times*, April 27, 1866, editorial.

[4] The *Times*, December 5, 1866, editorial.

Mr. Bright has taken a step which is rather the last cast of a gambler than the well-considered move of one who would be a statesman. He has invited the Trades' Unions and Friendly Societies to renounce one of their first principles — to throw off what some thought a disguise, and openly assume a political character, with a special view to counterbalancing the influence of land, wealth, and rank. At present the constitution of most of these Societies expressly prohibits political action, not only because politics are not their business, but because it is advisable to welcome all, whatever their opinions.[1]

And the *Times* was not alone in thinking that the mind of a nefarious superbeing had assisted in forming such an organization as the trade unions. It must be remembered that this was a period of strikes and lockouts. In October one [2] of a series of crimes for which Sheffield was notorious, had been committed in New Hereford Street of that city. Such events were so well advertised by press rumors that the isolated cases of violence and intimidation which were limited to certain trades in certain localities, seemed to be to the public, a systematic attempt on the part of trade unions generally to obtain their ends by violence, and "the commercial objection to industrial disputes became confused with the feeling of abhorrence created by the idea of vast combinations of men sticking at neither violence nor murder to achieve their ends. The 'terrorism of Trade unions' became a nightmare." [3]

Such an organization not only was strongly in favor of Reform but was willing to be active in the cause. On December nineteenth a meeting of the trades' council passed this resolution:

[1] The *Times*, December 6, 1866, editorial.

[2] An explosion of gunpowder in the house of a man who was working for a firm against which the saw grinders had struck.

[3] Sidney and Beatrice Webb, *The History of Trade Unionism*, p. 240.

That in the opinion of this delegate meeting of the trades of
London, the House of Commons has, by its treachery to the
cause of Reform, as shown by its defeat of the late Government Bill, and more especially by the cheers and acclamations
which followed the vicious slanders of Messrs. Lowe, Horsman, Elcho, and others equally unscrupulous, lost the confidence of the people, and forced upon the trades' unionists of
Great Britain and Ireland the absolute necessity of assisting
either in their co-operate or individual capacity, as each society
may for itself determine, the present agitation for the enfranchisement of the working classes of this kingdom, now
unjustly excluded by class laws, made by class-elected Parliament; and we hereby declare our sympathy with, and adhesion
to, the principles of the Reform League as the only true basis
of representation, and advise trades' unionists, both in London
and in the provinces, to aid the forthcoming demonstration
under the auspices of the League, to be held in London on
Monday after the opening of the next session of Parliament.
And we further declare that while advising the great bodies
of trades' unionists thus to act, we have no desire to make our
societies channels for political agitation, but to aid in settling
a great question that has so long disturbed the social as well
as the political relations of this country, to the detriment of
its progress and the injury of its people.[1]

The descriptions of the demonstrations during the autumn
and early winter of 1866 bring out three or four facts: with
the exception of the incident at Hyde Park, the crowd had
been orderly and good-natured.   It had been a large crowd,
too,—provided that processions of thirty thousand and
audiences of one hundred and fifty thousand as reported be
considered a large crowd.[2]   The speech-makers had in many
cases pointed out justly defects in the government of the

[1] The *Times*, December 21, 1866. The resolution was proposed by
Mr. Allen of the Amalgamated Engineers.

[2] Stuart J. Reid, *Memoirs of Sir Wemyss Reid* (London, 1905), p. 113,
tells of great crowds at Reform meetings.

country and had suggested certain remedies; a number of the speakers, however, had not been altogether temperate and had urged force to obtain demands. Finally the trade unions, organizations which the middle and upper classes feared, had joined in definite alliance with the Reform League and the Radicals like Bright. Thus stood matters at the opening of the new year. Parliament would meet in February with the Conservatives in office. Popular demand had had little influence on the treatment of the bill of 1866. Were the people now interested in Reform and would the interest thus far shown be a strong enough factor to force those who stood unmoved in the spring of 1866 to bring in a bill? An expression of opinion on the part of many of the leading magazines and newspapers, chosen somewhat at random, is suggestive of the answer.

The *Spectator* gave its opinion:

That puzzle . . . which in August so greatly perplexed the House, whether workmen do or do not desire to enter the Constitution, will be found to have become clear in sleep. In August, every one doubted, in February doubt will be a mark of political incapacity. The workmen do care, care so much that their foes have changed their tone, and instead of charging them with indifference, accuse them of revolutionary fervor and oppressiveness.[1]

In its opinion delay was impossible. *Macmillan's* said:

It has become evident that the demand for reform is more deeply rooted than was at first hastily supposed—that it was not a cry got up by demagogues, nor the fancy of obstinate doctrinaires and fanatics. It cannot be suppressed by a few cynical sneers, nor by the exclamations of those political optimists, who hold the simple faith that whatever is, is right—especially the £10 franchise.[2]

[1] The *Spectator*, February 2, 1867, p. 118.
[2] *Macmillan's*, April, 1867, p. 529.

The *Quarterly Review,* strongly against Reform, pretended in January to believe that the clamor was " the result of the efforts of designing demagogues " [1] but a little later gave a somewhat different version:

There can be no doubt that, as far as those who had no official reasons for passing a Reform Bill were concerned, the one dominant feeling of the present year has been a feverish anxiety to " settle the question." Mr. Henley, with cynical candor, betrayed the ignoble secret, when he acknowledged that a fear lest " the pot should boil over," was the motive that animated his friends. The meetings in the manufacturing towns, and the riots in Hyde Park, had had their effect. The comfortable classes had no stomach for a real struggle. Their hearts misgave them, indeed, about Reform; they saw in it ugly visions of the future—labor giving law to capital, Trades' Union rules supreme, democratic Parliaments contriving a graduated income tax, the poor voting supplies, and the rich finding ways and means. . . . They had beguiled themselves with the belief that it was possible to hold their rights without a struggle; and under that impression they had talked bravely for a time. But when they discovered their mistake, they took their overthrow meekly and gave up at once. All they entreated was that the agitation should be got rid of, and the question settled without delay. And Ministerial speakers boast of it as their great achievement that they have satisfied this one longing. " They have settled the question in a manner so liberal as to leave no room for further agitation." . . . The dullest of their antagonists perfectly understands that they have not yielded to argument or to sentiment; that the apostles of Reform who have the real credit of their conversion are the mobs who beat down the palings of Hyde Park or went out marching with bands and banners in the towns of the North. Any one who reads their organs in the press will be satisfied that there is no mistake among them upon this

[1] *Quarterly Review,* January, 1867, p. 238.

point; and indeed, they would hardly deserve credit for the ordinary sagacity of Englishmen if there was.[1]

The *Fortnightly Review* declared that " the argument can never be again used that the working classes do not care about Reform." [2]

The view in *Frazer's* varies somewhat from the statements given above; it contended that one couldn't tell just before the opening of the session whether Parliamentary Reform was or was not required by the nation, *i. e.,* whether it was so imperatively required as to compel or justify the immediate introduction of a bill; that there prevailed a vague notion that something must be done; but in the absence of any definite scheme that suited either of the great parties, it was a mooted point whether the question could not be advantageously postponed; " whether the House of Commons, having just turned out one Government for meddling with it in the most dainty fashion, would turn out another for not meddling with it at all." [3]

Blackwood's in discussing the subject used such arguments as would justify the actions of the Conservative party. In the December number it was remarked that Reform must be dealt with soon, that within the last month matters had a good deal changed their aspect:

The feelings of the multitude are easily worked upon by such eloquence as has of late been addressed to them; and though the better informed among them may see that much of what was said is false, and a great deal more the merest clap-trap, still a residue abides of power enough to stir them into that state of dogged determination which leads to violence.[4]

---

[1] *Ibid.*, October, 1867, pp. 555 and 556.

[2] *Fortnightly Review*, January, 1867, p. 104.

[3] *Frazer's*, November, 1867, pp. 658 and 659.

[4] *Blackwood's*, December, 1866, p. 783.

Blackwood's, of course, had no use for the Reform League, declaring that it was a fungus of yesterday's growth, and though very noxious, would have been harmless but for the recent adhesion to its views and principles of another body— the trade unions.[1] These had been converted by the management of their paid secretaries into political engines.[2] They were making common cause with the Reform League, and were walking in procession as well as meeting to hear speeches in support of manhood suffrage and vote by ballot. The transformation of trade unions into political leagues had thoroughly alarmed the middle classes.[3] The blame must rest entirely with the three allied powers,—the Whigs, the Reform League, and the trade unions; the first by inciting the two latter to come forward; the two latter by the ostentatious display of physical force. It said that the meetings held were little short of rebellion if directed to overawe Parliament while in session, and advised that the same treatment should be given to Beales and Potter as had been given to O'Conner.[4] The March issue claimed that shirking the question was impossible; that you might postpone Reform for a session,[5]

But what will the people say out of doors? It would be ridiculous to affirm now that the working classes are indifferent on the subject of Parliamentary Reform. Very many among them may wish that it had never been mooted; very many more may regret that they allowed themselves to be duped into joining the League. There they are, however; and whether they like it or not, the chiefs of the party will insist upon their going through with the work. To postpone legis-

---

[1] *Ibid.,* January, 1867, p. 116.

[2] *Ibid.,* January, 1867, p. 125.

[3] *Ibid.,* p. 131.

[4] *Ibid.,* p. 132.

[5] *Blackwood's,* March, 1867, p. 379.

lation, therefore, . . . would be tantamount to challenging the masses to do their worst.[1]

Finally in the May issue there was given a summary of the whole popular movement:

Derby had not been a week in office, before the broadest possible indications were given, that whatever his own disposition might be, the people were determined to have a change in the electoral system of the country. The formation of the Reform League, . . . the Hyde Park riot, all showed in what direction the wind was setting. Then came the recess, and with it Mr. Bright's progresses, Mr. Forster's announcements, Mr. Beales's proclamations, and the coalition, under Mr. Potter's guidance, of Trades-unions with the Reform League. It was impossible to believe, with this evidence before them, that the country was not in earnest in demanding a settlement of the Reform question. . . . The single point demanding attention was, How far shall we go?[2]

The *Westminster Review* agreed that Reform was necessary:

Since the advent of Lord Derby to power the duties of Reformers have been greatly simplified. The apathy for which the mass of the nation was formerly mocked has given place to an excitement far too intense to be allayed by palliatives. We do not blame the handicraftsmen for the energy they have displayed, nor are we astonished at the vehement language in which they express their feelings, and to which they give an attentive ear. That there should have been more appeals to argument and fewer threats about physical force would have pleased us better. . . . The agitation which now convulses England, the demonstrations which appal the timid without gratifying the brave and wise, are the legitimate fruits of the con-

[1] *Ibid.*, p. 387.
[2] *Ibid.*, May, 1867.

duct and the speeches in which the dominant class has indulged during the past few years.[1]

It also stated that " friends of the present ministry are
satisfied that if it does not propose a measure it will be compelled to resign." [2]

Finally, the *Times,* at the opening of Parliament, gave
editorially its opinion upon the coming of Reform:

We are willing to admit that if the House of Commons could
have the needful protection, and did not consist of gentlemen
bound to tell how they vote, it would probably shelve the subject very soon. We are ready to admit that neither the landed
nor the moneyed aristocracy wants Reform; that the middle
class is indifferent to it; that the so-called working class only
want it in order to strengthen their hands against their employers, and that the vast mass of agricultural and unskilled
labor no more want to see Parliament reformed than to see
the circle squared. . . . But the question is not going by argument. . . . The real state of the case is that we are on the
eve of a battle, not of a controversy. . . . We are threatened
with an immense combination of the Trades' Unions that shall
rule the political as well as the industrial action of every
member.[3]

But, it added—the cause is a good one.

Thus, from the consensus of opinions, it is apparent that
the Conservatives were forced to take up the Reform question in the session of 1867. What had already taken place
had scared the upper and middle classes, but these little acts,
they were told, were merely dress rehearsals.[4] The Con-

[1] *Westminster Review,* January, 1867, p. 185.

[2] *Ibid.,* p. 187.

[3] The *Times,* February 5, 1867, editorial.

[4] *Cf.* letter of Robert Hartwell, secretary of the demonstration committee, in the *Times,* December 12, 1866.

servatives, refusing to deal with the question, could have
resigned, but such action would have been playing into the
hands of the Liberals.   Hence the royal speech at the opening of Parliament mentioned that the state of the representation of the people would receive attention.[1]

Public opinion made it necessary that the Reform question
be taken up again and at once.   The influence of the Reform
League and kindred associations upon the legislation passed
is quite a different question.   In one sense that influence was
very great; it marked any bill less liberal than the bill of
1866 as unsatisfactory; but had the franchise been given to
those paying £5 in the towns, many of the Liberal leaders in
the associations would have been willing to repeat John
Bright's statement concerning the bill of 1866: " The Bill
is an honest Bill; and if it is the least the Government could
offer, it may be that it is the greatest which the Government
could carry through Parliament."   Whether those who
wanted the whole loaf would have been able to keep the agitation going after some of the popular leaders had dropped
out is, of course, doubtful.   As it was, Disraeli did give pretty
much the whole loaf but it cannot be said with certainty that
he was forced to do so.   Mr. Potter, speaking to Gladstone
in behalf of a deputation of workingmen representing various organizations of London artisans, said that the London
workingmen and their friends in the country called for a residential and registered manhood suffrage, but they did not
feel bound to stick by that demand if such concessions were
made to them as would permit their class being represented.[2]
Another speaker said the working classes were willing to
allow their claims for a residential and registered manhood
suffrage to fall into abeyance for a time if lodger qualifications of, say four or five shillings a week, were adopted—

[1] *Annual Register*, 1867, p. 4.
[2] *Cf.* the *Times*, March 25, 1867.

a concession which was necessary inasmuch as it was next
to impossible for workingmen in London to become householders.   It was also said that the workingmen did not want
to keep up the agitation, and many agreed that here was no
necessity for the secret ballot—that it would burden the bill.
Gladstone himself was strongly in favor of substituting a
£5 rating franchise for the borough in place of household
suffrage.[1] But such a proposition was not regarded as
favorable to the working class.[2]   Mr. Lucraft,[3] speaking in
July, complained that Mr. Bright and Mr. Gladstone and
the Manchester party had been trying to do all they could
to trip up the Government and make the bill one which
would not enfranchise half those it now would—that the
bill went too far for Mr. Bright and Mr. Gladstone who
wanted the hard line, which would keep the people from the
franchise.   He said he would sooner depend upon a Tory
Government than upon the Manchester party.[4]   Another
speaker at the meeting said that he never had any faith in
Mr. Bright, who had never said a word in favor of household suffrage; others disagreed with this sentiment, claiming that Bright had helped them,—in every speech since 1859
had always stood for household suffrage.

On the other hand, the Reform League in February, when
denouncing the Government scheme, had declared they were
afraid the Liberals would accept halfway measures, in
which case they would not stop the present agitation; that
the country was behind them and they were prepared to
fight not only the Government but the House of Commons
itself.[5]   In fact, the meetings which went on during the

---

[1] *Vide infra*, pp. 206-7.

[2] *Cf.* Mr. Taylor's speech at the National Reform Union meeting, May
10, as given in the *Times*, May 11, 1867.

[3] *Vide supra*, p. 101.

[4] The *Times*, July 4, 1867.

[5] *Cf.* the *Times*, February 28, 1867.

spring of 1867 as formerly were very decided in their
criticisms of the bill.   They probably did much to educate
the Tory party.   At the Reform League demonstration in
London, February 11, where many thousands were present,
the usual resolutions in favor of residential and registered
manhood suffrage and the secret ballot were passed.[1]
O'Donoghue, head of the Irish Reform League, said he had
just come from the House of Commons and according to
the impression left on his mind by Mr. Disraeli's speech, the
Tory party intended, if they could, to smuggle a Reform bill
through the House of Commons without consulting the
people, whereupon his audience cried, " We shall turn them
out." [2]   He also showed the necessity for the people of England and Ireland to unite in their efforts for Reform.   As
for the resolutions [3] which the Conservative Government
offered early in the session, these were called by a Birmingham Reform meeting an insult to the country, were spoken
of by delegates of the Reform League as wholly unsuited
to meet the exigencies of the present crisis, and by the
Working Men's Association as a mockery and an insult.[4]
At a Reform demonstration in Trafalgar Square (March
2, 1867) Mr. Potter declared that they would have a meeting every Saturday for some weeks to come.   In the course
of his speech he said that the Tory *Standard* advised the
Government to consent to a measure and

When they found the Tory press advising household suffrage
it showed that the working classes had screwed the Tory Government up pretty tightly. . . . They would hold a few more
of these meetings, and then, if they found that did not do, he
thought they would have to suggest to the whole of the work-

[1] The *Times*, February 12, 1867.
[2] *Annual Register*, 1867, chronicle, p. 22.
[3] *Vide infra*, p. 193.
[4] This sentiment was echoed at many meetings.

ing classes throughout the country a week's cessation from
business and . . . then he should advise all the working men
to walk about the streets of this great metropolis day after
day, and stop all the traffic, and stop all business, and in fact,
render themselves a public nuisance. . . . He did not advocate physical force, but after the money which had been ex-
pended, and the sacrifices which the working classes had made,
to prove that they were earnest in their demands, and to show
the justice of their being entitled to the franchise, delay was
dangerous.[1]

The Reformers at Bradford thought the entire conduct of
the Government on the question of Reform deserving of
the strongest reprobation and urged the Liberal party to
bring about the downfall of the present ministry.[2]

The Conservatives on the eighteenth of March finally
brought in a bill based on household suffrage but with many
fancy franchises appended and Mr. Potter at Trafalgar
Square on the nineteenth of March called the bill political
jugglery.[3]   Here a resolution was passed " that in the opinion of this meeting the Government Reform bill is a mockery and insult to the people, so bad and vicious in principle
as to be incapable of being satisfactorily amended in committee; this meeting, therefore, trusts it will not be allowed
to pass a second reading, as to do so would be so much
time thrown away."   At a meeting at Birmingham [4] the
recognition of household suffrage as the basis of the franchise in the boroughs was accepted with great satisfaction;
but it was pointed out that the advantages were neutralized
by the condition which limited the right of voting to those
occupiers who paid local rates directly, and by the unwise

[1] The *Times*, March 4, 1867.
[2] The *Times*, March 4, 1867.
[3] *Ibid.*, March 20, 1867.
[4] On March 22; *cf.* the *Times* of March 23, 1867.

innovation of dual voting. Many were the protests, too, against the residence clause.[1] The London Working Men's Association pledged itself (April 16) in the event of the bill passing through Parliament in its present shape—requiring a personal payment of rates and a residential qualification of two years, with the omission of a lodger franchise—to a continued and increased agitation until personal payment of rates should be abolished, the term of residence reduced, and the principles of residential and registered manhood suffrage, protected by the ballot, be acknowledged by the Legislature.[2] It also was firmly against the £5 rating amendment which Gladstone upheld. At a great Reform demonstration at Birmingham (April 22) a resolution stated that while the meeting desired to maintain peace, law, and order in the country, it did believe that the continued obstructions to Reform, and the treachery of the House of Commons in reference to the great constitutional question, would tend to exasperate a loyal and industrious people and, if persevered in, would ultimately lead to anarchy and revolution.[3]

The Reformers, however, showed their pleasure at the changes made in the bill which were favorable to them. At the Hyde Park meeting of May 6, O'Donoghue moved the following resolutions:

That this meeting, whilst still adhering to registered and residential manhood suffrage, protected by the ballot, as the only really efficient measure of Reform in the representation of the people, hails with satisfaction the withdrawal . . . of Lord Grosvenor's proposed amendment,[4] and the majority of 81

[1] Six months was wanted instead of two years; *cf. infra*, p. 200.

[2] The *Times*, April 17, 1867.

[3] The *Times*, April 23, 1867.

[4] Earl Grosvenor had given notice of an amendment to substitute a £5 rating for household suffrage.

on the same evening against the two years' residence clause in the Government bill, and earnestly calls upon the House of Commons to make that bill a more full and honest measure for the execution of the franchise by expunging from it the rate-paying clauses, equalizing the borough and country franchises on the principle of household suffrage, and introducing a provision giving a vote to lodgers, or else to reject that bill altogether.[1]

This meeting, however, is more important for the history of the rights of public meetings than for the history of Reform. The Government, after warning the Reformers not to use Hyde Park as a meeting place, decided that it had taken a wrong position, and, although arrangements had been made that nearly five thousand of the metropolitan police massed together in the park should prevent a second Hyde Park episode, did permit the meeting. Colonel Dickson addressed his "fellow-trespassers," but not on the subject of Reform; he was positively sick of the subject. He thought the game was in their hands now. "You have done the trick. Don't undo it. Be steady and be orderly. Give the lie to your traducers." And the well-attended meeting did go off quietly.

On the seventeenth of May, an amendment to the bill which did away with the compound householder[2] was ac-

[1] The *Times*, May 7, 1867.

[2] Compound householders (comprising more than a third of the entire number of householders) were those who made an agreement with their landlord by which their rates were paid to the landlord. The latter, for the trouble of collecting, was given a percentage off by the authorities and, therefore, charged his tenants not the full rate but a reduced (*i. e.*, a composition) rate. The tenants who compounded, however, did not usually have their names on the register and could not vote, and Disraeli with his cry of "personal payment of rates" had found no convenient method of enfranchising them except by agreeing to the amendment which abolished compounding and had all pay rates "personally" and thus put on the register.

cepted by the Conservative Government and a great obstruction to real household suffrage had gone. Shortly afterwards the *Times* awoke to the knowledge that the nation was at the foot of a precipice;[1] how the descent had been made it knew not; nor, indeed, was it entirely sure that the nation had not received any hurts; only one thing was certain—the nation was at the foot of the precipice.

The Reform League was, of course, quite willing to recognize its own importance in this victory for the Reformers. Mr. Beales said "it was the greatest farce for Mr. Disraeli to say there would be a Reform Bill of any kind but for the agitation of the Reform League. The Reform League were the real authors of the Bill."[2] Others, too, were impressed with the League's influence. Goldwin Smith in writing to the Secretary of the League said:

It is impossible to doubt that the popular movement, so effectively and, at the same time, so legally and peacefully conducted by the two combined associations has been the main instrument in turning the present holders of power from the opponents of the limited Reform Bill of last Session into the advocates of household suffrage and something more. I say of something more, because the lodger franchise plainly interdicts and must in the end break up the restrictive principles of the present Bill.[3]

Disraeli was not keen to acknowledge the influence of an association many of whose leading members were affiliated with the Liberal party. Rather was it to his interests to have the Conservative party recognized as the important factor in granting the franchise. That some of the workingmen were grateful to him for the part he had played was

[1] The *Times*, May 30, 1867, editorial.
[2] Report of League meeting in the *Times* of May 30, 1867.
[3] Given in the *Times*, June 17, 1867.

proved by the deputation of artisans to the Government on
the eighth of June, which expressed itself as opposed to
the Reform League but " hoped that artisans would show
their gratitude to the Government which had enfranchised
them." [1]   Already a Conservative League had been formed [2]
and a deputation had assured [3] Disraeli that Conservative
feeling was spreading throughout the country—a fact of
which he had convincing proof in connection with seventeen
associations which the workingmen of Yorkshire had joined
because they felt that his party was the true and only friend
of the working classes.   Goldwin Smith saw the head of
the Tory Government " decoying the workingmen, who
a few months ago were being reviled amid the vociferous
cheers of the Tory party, into an alliance with the Tory
oligarchy against the middle and commercial classes."

It was, of course, recognized that the suffrage was desired
as a means to an end. [4] Many speeches already quoted tend
to show this. It was felt that a reformed House would do
away, in part, with class government, or would at least give
the working class an opportunity to have its grievances
heard; that some serious " social maladies " would be helped
or cured; that the economic conditions due to the acts of
the middle and upper classes would be improved. Class
government and many of the social evils could have been
and were complained of during most of the preceding years
of the nineteenth century. The terrible economic distress
causing suffering and irritation had been brought in great
part by the panic of May, 1866, the effects of which were
very patent during the autumn of 1866 and the whole of
1867.

[1] The *Times*, June 10, 1867.

[2] Notice in the *Times*, April 30, 1867; *cf.* also *News of the World*,
May 5, 1867.

[3] *Cf.* the *Times*, May 1, 1867.

[4] *Cf.* editorial of the *Times*, June 17, 1867.

Complaints against class government were frequent. That it was unjust[1] to refuse to labor the tribunals given so freely to capital, unjust not to legalize and regulate trade unions as unions of apothecaries, surgeons and barristers were legalized and regulated, was the feeling of many. It was said[2] that probably a reformed Parliament would take a little more pains to help on the improvements of the dwellings of the lower class, and a little less to compensate landowners for the cattle plague.[3] "Even their (*i. e.*, the Liberals') most advanced politician, John Bright," wrote an artisan to the *Times,* "cannot so far forget his class and the class that vote for him as to propose the repeal of the Master and Servant Act and will probably vote for an Adullamite amendment instead of repeal."[4] To many, the words of the pamphleteer sounded like an axiom: "We have the germs of a representative Government, and we know that this, like truth brought to light, will always represent itself, and advance the interests, and the interests only, that it represents."[5]

Complaints against other "social sores" were not few in number. The state of the great cities and of the laborers' homes therein was described[6] as heart-rending: in many of the towns and especially in the metropolis, the number of persons who herded together in habitations scarcely ventilated, drained imperfectely or not at all, with no water supply and, in reference to the filth, indecency, and pestilential condition of which, no language can be too unmeasured, had to be reckoned by hundreds of thousands. In the rural

[1] *Cf.* the *Spectator,* January 19, 1867.

[2] *Macmillan's,* April, 1867, p. 533.

[3] *Vide supra,* p. 65.

[4] The *Times,* August 29, 1866.

[5] W. F. Stanley, *Proposition for a New Reform Bill,* p. 7.

[6] *Cf. Fortnightly Review,* vol. vii, pp. 269 *et seq.*

districts the great proportion lived in hovels. Landowners in these sections were unwilling to allow cottages to be built upon their property lest the rates be increased; in the cities the workingmen had not money with which to buy land for dwellings.[1] In any case the government did nothing.

The deficiencies of the educational system were mentioned time and again.[2] The *North British Review* in a discussion of the subject said:

The notorious facts cannot be gainsaid,—that our agricultural population is for the most part uninstructed mentally, and undeveloped even to stupidity; that a very large proportion of our town population never go near a school, and grow up in absolute brutality; that not one-half of the children of fitting age are to be found under instruction, and that of those who do attend or have attended school with tolerable regularity, a large proportion have their education cut short at an age which leaves little prospect of their retaining what they have acquired, and that these have few opportunities of supplementing their deficiencies in later years. In short, among the working classes, taking the country through, a fair and useful degree of *instructedness* . . . is the exception and not the rule, while the mass, reckoning them by the millions, is deplorably and disgracefully without the rudiments of culture.[3]

Pauperism, too, was a great crying evil. One tenth of our revenue, one twentieth of the population—said one writer [4]—sink in the abyss. Bright declared that the ruling classes in England had miserably failed; there were 1,200,000 paupers in the country.[5] And the winter of 1866 and 1867,

[1] The *North British Review*, new series, vol. viii (1867), pp. 514 and 515.

[2] *Cf. Fortnightly Review*, September 15, 1866; *Frazer's*, November, 1866.

[3] The *North British Review*, new series, vol. viii (1867), "The Social Sores of Great Britain," pp. 512 and 513.

[4] Frederic Harrison in the *Fortnightly Review*, vol. vii, p. 271.

[5] John Bright, *Speeches on Parliamentary Reform* (London, 1866), speech at Glasgow, p. 32.

it will be remembered, was a time when pauperism was increasing greatly in comparison with the winter of the preceding year. The increase was felt to be due to the financial panic.[1] Indeed, added to those " social maladies " which a reformed House would partially or completely cure, were those ailments vaguely called economic, which this same reformed House must relieve.

What, in summary, can be said as to the influence of popular demand upon the Reform movement? In the early 'sixties, it has been pointed out, there was no agitation. But events happening at home and abroad were not unfavorable to Reform; at home a more liberal ministry came into power with the death of Palmerston in 1865; in America, a democratic North sympathized with by the English workingmen, had conquered an aristocratic South; Italy was well on the way to unification under a somewhat liberal government; in Germany, it was said, Bismarck was granting an extensive suffrage. There were those who thought that England should grant privileges to her working classes. The Reform League, formed in 1865, tried by the help of such orators at John Bright, W. E. Forster and other radical Liberals to start an agitation. The attempt was not very successful, however, and only once—during the Easter recess of 1866—did it appear as if the country had been stirred. The agitation, such as it was, soon diminished, and the House of Commons seemed to be quite unmoved. But with the defeat of the bill of 1866, numerous Reform meetings again were held. The arguments of Lowe, applicable against any extension of the suffrage, aroused the working classes; distress and discontent with the economic condition followed the commercial panic in May; the Hyde Park inci-

---

[1] *Vide*, for instance, in the *Times*, January 14, 1867, the letter of W. M. Bullivant; *vide*, also, the *Times*, January 22, 1867.

dent advertised the Reform question throughout the land in a most striking manner. The Reform League, having gained an advantage at Hyde Park, followed up this success by calling together the workingmen in orderly but monster Reform meetings during the autumn of 1866. On most occasions John Bright was the chief speaker. The press already alarmed for the welfare of the country because of the activity of the Fenians, thought the nation had cause to worry when the trade unions came out strongly for Reform. The Conservative Government, reading "the signs of the times" found it necessary to introduce a new Reform bill. Bright had written to Disraeli telling him that a Tory Reform bill must be acceptable to the Commons and the Reform associations. A bill containing a £5 borough and a £10 or £12 county franchise clause, he thought, would be acceptable to both. Disraeli, who, to stop the agitation, had to grant at least these conditions, did follow much more closely the various requests and demands of Reform speakers. The various reasons assigned for his actions will be discussed later. Any history of the Reform bill of 1867 which fails to take into account the influence of the agitation of the working class and especially of that part of the working class represented by the trade unions is incomplete.

CHAPTER IV

THE OFFICIAL ATTITUDE TOWARD REFORM

As opposed to the popular attitude toward Reform there must be taken into consideration the official attitude toward the question. By *official attitude* is meant not only the attitude of those men chosen to carry on the Government of the country, but the attitude of all the members of the House of Commons either as individuals or as combined in parties. Inasmuch as there was little popular pressure during the period that the Reform bill of 1866 was under consideration, a study of the action of the parties and of the arguments used for and against Reform on that occasion may well serve to show what official England thought of the Reform question.

It has already been pointed out that Palmerston, the head of the Government during the early 'sixties, was against any extension of the suffrage. He was a statesman of the old English aristocratic type, and stood for liberalism on the Continent but against any democratic government for England. The two great parties as a whole backed up his administration; they said that they were for a " well-considered measure of reform," as " opposed to any revolutionary change," but at the same time declared it useless to take up the question so long as the public was not interested. It was a period when there prevailed so great a harmony of tone between Whig and Tory that one could scarcely distinguish them.[1] As the *Annual Register* said:

[1] The *Westminster Review*, " Parliament and Reform," April, 1865, p. 503; *Quarterly Review*, " The Six Year Old Parliament," July, 1865.

The spirit of party . . . appeared to have lost nearly all its acrimony, and even a large share of its vitality, both in Parliament and in the country at large; it seemed as if few questions remained to divide in any material degree the opinions of the different sections of politicians. Some of the prominent men on either side of the House of Commons did not hesitate openly to avow their indifference to party bonds and watchwords.[1]

The Government, moreover, enjoyed to a great degree, public confidence.

But with the death of Palmerston in October, 1865, there came a change. It was the opinion of the *Annual Register* that none of his colleagues, however powerful in intellect or mature in experience, was likely to equal the departed chief in that address and tact so necessary to hold together the somewhat diverse elements of the Liberal party in the House of Commons.[2] And, where, indeed, would be found the statesman who could remove the fears or conciliate the support of the Opposition, for the Conservative party, in spite of its attempt at Reform in 1859, was strongly against any radical change!

Earl Russell, head of the new ministry, was, it was said, by birth, by education, by family traditions and political connection a Whig of the usual conviction, believing that the real Constitution of England was an oligarchical Constitution.[3] It is true that he had stood for Reform many times since 1832, but too often he had not been over-energetic in the cause. Besides he was growing old and would need much assistance from Gladstone, the Chancellor of the Ex-

---

[1] *Annual Register*, 1864, p. 3.

[2] *Annual Register*, 1865, p. 159.

[3] *Vide Blackwood's*, "The New Ministry," August, 1866, p. 262. On characteristics of Russell, *cf.* Walpole, *Life of Lord John Russell*, vol. ii, p. 409.

chequer. Gladstone was, indeed, the man on whom much hinged. Entering Parliament as a Tory he had gone over to the Liberal side, not, as he said,[1] by any arbitrary act, but by the slow and resistless forces of conviction. Since his suffrage speech of 1864[2] the Conservatives had become very suspicious of him, and many of the Radicals had pretended to see in him a convert.[3] The *Quarterly Review* in writing on the situation said:

The real and pressing danger of Mr. Gladstone's leadership will undoubtedly be his newly-formed views upon Reform. Or rather, to put it more generally, there will be the dangers arising from any Liberal majority when once the restraining influence of Lord Palmerston is taken away. It must not be forgotten that the Liberal party differs from the Conservative party in this, that it is not a homogeneous body. In the Conservative party there may be here and there individual eccentricities. . . . It is an old remark that the Whigs and the Radicals differ more from each other, in point of political opinion, than the Whigs and the Conservatives.[4]

Indeed, it would be more in accordance with the facts to make a threefold division of the Liberal party rather than the mentioned twofold division of Radicals and Whigs. There were the Liberals proper, following party bonds and party creeds, whipped into line under Gladstone. There was a conservative element, opposed upon principle to any extension of the suffrage. Finally the Radical party, to which reference has been made before, stood strongly for a change in the franchise qualifications.

[1] *Hansard*, vol. clxxxiii, p. 130, debate of April 27, 1866.

[2] *Cf. supra*, p. 37.

[3] Morley, *Life of Gladstone*, vol. ii, pp. 127 *et seq.*; *vide*, also, *Quarterly Review*, July, 1865.

[4] *Quarterly Review*, July, 1865, p. 291.

Robert Lowe, member for Calne, came during the sessions of 1866 and 1867, to be the great leader of the conservative element in the Liberal party.   Although he had been a member of the ministry of 1860, when Lord Russell introduced a Reform bill, his hostility to the 1866 bill was based on an anti-democratic principle.   Back of him were to stand about forty Liberals,[1]—enough to defeat the bill and turn out the ministry.   Their attitude caused Bright to write of the " forty thieves " and the " forty traitors "[2] and to them was applied generally the name " Adullamites." [3]

John Bright was the leader of the Radicals. " Radical " as applied to Bright must be used with quotations since, in some important respects, he was not progressive.   For instance, he was willing enough to confess to his opposition to factory legislation for adults, male and female.   But he was a non-conformist and he had joined Cobden in the fight against the Corn Laws.   The term " Radical," however, was applied because he was doing all in his power to procure the franchise for the working class—a matter in which Cobden did not display unusual activity.   His work during the 'fifties was important and when the bill of 1866 was brought in, he was willing to accept it as the best the Government could give at that time.

Such were the factions which Gladstone must keep together if he were to pass a Reform bill.   According to the Grey Papers,[4] Gladstone, in talking with the Speaker of the House of Commons, admitted that there was no strong feeling for Reform among his constituents, but his majority of

[1] For list *vide* Harris, *History of the Radical Party in Parliament*, pp. 471 and 473.

[2] Trevelyan, *Life of John Bright*, p. 356.

[3] For origin of term *vide infra*, p. 147.

[4] October 22, 1865; quoted from Morley, *Life of Gladstone*, vol. ii, pp. 198 and 199.

eighty bothered him. "They," he said, "will expect some action;"—to which the Speaker answered:

No doubt a majority of eighty, agreed on any point, would expect action. At the time of the first Reform bill, when the whole party was for the bill, the course was clear. But is the party agreed now? The point it was agreed upon was to support Lord Palmerston's government. But was that in order to pass a strong measure of reform? Suppose that the country is satisfied with the foreign policy, and the home policy, and the financial policy, and wants to maintain these and their authors, and does not want great changes of any kind?

Whatever Gladstone may have believed about the popular attitude, the Government of which he was the conspicuous figure, brought in a Reform bill on March 12, 1866. Friends said that his action was due to firm conviction that the working class was not represented in any proportion to their numbers and in accordance with their share of the income of the country;[1] by others it was declared that he was led on by Russell who felt he must take up the question or be guilty of forfeiting a pledge.[2] Enemies of the administration suggested that political advantages had become an important factor.[3] The Radicals had gained[4] somewhat at the election of 1865, and though yet a small minority, they were[5] an energetic and resolute party who were making the Reform question their platform. The Liberals, after the death of Palmerston, needed some added strength.

[1] *Cf.* statement of *Quarterly Review*, July, 1866, p. 265.

[2] *Cf. Frazer's*, January, 1866, p. 6, and William Rathbone, *The Rock Ahead* (Edinburgh and London, 1867), p. 5.

[3] *Quarterly Review*, July, 1866, p. 266.

[4] James Howard Harris Malmesbury, *Memoirs of an Ex-Minister; an Autobiography*, 2 vols. (London, 1884), vol. ii, p. 340.

[5] *Frazer's*, August, 1865, p. 136.

Therefore, said the Opposition press, they surrendered to the Radicals and appointed Mr. Goschen and Mr. Forster to the Government.[1] As for the bill they brought in,—that was but the great game of twenty-five years ago played over again [2]—an attempt to keep the influence of the party from waning by handing out the franchise little by little to grateful constituents.   Mr. Forster, however, at a Reform meeting at Bradford, in November, 1865, gave a summary of his opinion on internal politics and Reform, and, of course, did not make mention of any advantages which might accrue to those passing the bill.   He considered Reform in the ascendent because: (1) Palmerston was no longer Premier; (2) Russell was the head of the Government; (3) Gladstone was leader of the House of Commons and had been rejected by Oxford; (4) a large majority of the new House of Commons had actually pledged themselves to Reform in their election addresses; (5) a new Parliament and a new ministry was ready for work, and " there is more hope in the new than in the old. of which indeed, there was no hope." [3]   On the other hand there were certain signs of opposition; there were many waverers in the Liberal ranks. Many did not want Reform though ready to vote for it, if necessary.   All were afraid of being sent adrift by the bill and of losing their dearly bought seats after one or two years of unquiet possession.

The bill was brought in on March twelfth.   After that portion of the Queen's speech which referred to Reform had been read by the clerk, the Chancellor of the Exchequer rose in a House crowded with curious members and strangers

[1] *Quarterly Review*, January, 1866, pp. 252-253; *vide* also J. H. Murchison, *The Conservatives and " Liberals."* p. xii.

[2] *Blackwood's*, February, 1866, pp. 144 *et seq.*

[3] As discussed in an editorial of the *Times*, November 25, 1865; for the speech, *vide* the *Times*, November 24, 1865.

to state its provisions. Few ministers — said he [1] — have risen in recent years to address this House under greater difficulties than those which at this moment attend my own position and present task.   Although the difficulties be concentrated in their greatest weight upon us, yet, they are not ours alone.   The interest in the successful solution of this problem is an interest common to the whole House of Commons, and to every party, and every section of a party that sits within these walls.   By no less than five administrations, and in no less than five Queen's speeches before that of the present year, the House of Commons has been acquainted by the sovereign, under the advice of her constitutionally appointed ministers, that the time, in their judgment, had arrived when the representation of the people ought to undergo revision.   The election of a new Parliament naturally made the Government feel that the time had arrived when it was right that the sense of representatives of the people should again be taken in regard to the laws which regulated the electoral system.   The duty of the Government in this respect was a very plain one.   Hence they had taken measures to obtain information which could throw light on the case.   The statistics obtained showed that the working class, which ought, owing to its advance in education, in social conduct, in self-command and power of endurance, and avidity for knowledge, to have borne an increasing and growing proportion has borne a dwindling and diminishing proportion to the whole number of the town constituency.

As to the measure itself—was it to be complete? Would it deal with the franchise in England and in Wales, in Scotland, and in Ireland?   Would it take into consideration that whole group of questions included in the common phrase, "redistribution of seats?"   Would it treat of the question

[1] *Cf. Hansard,* vol. clxxxii, pp. 19 *et seq.*

of the boundary of boroughs? Would it concern itself with
the corrupt practises at elections and with the administra-
tive machinery for registration and for the holding of elections? Inasmuch as time and space are not yet annihilated,
declared the Chancellor of the Exchequer, such a measure
cannot now be discussed. He thought it quite impossible to
do more than to look at what came first in the order of importance, the electoral franchise. According to his proposal the occupation franchise in the counties was to be
reduced from £50 to £14. This was an occupation franchise,
not of land alone but of a house with land. It was calculated that 172,000 voters would be added, but from the middle class, since the number of persons properly belonging to
the working classes who had a £14 rental franchise would
be so very small as not to be worth taking into calcula-
tion. Copyholders and leaseholders having property within
limits of boroughs were to be allowed to vote in the county
within which it lay under the same condition as freeholders.[1]
By a savings-bank franchise for adult male depositors of
£50 who possessed that deposit for two years, 10,000 to
15,000 persons were to be added. Such a special franchise
would have its principal operation in the counties. In the
town constituencies some 60,000 persons above the £10 line
were to be enfranchised by abolishing the law allowing landlords by arrangement with the parish officers to pay rates for
rate-paying householders, by new provisions causing the
compound householders to be treated like rate-paying householders, and by putting lodgers who occupied rooms of the
clear annual value of £10 on the same footing as those holding tenements. For enfranchisement below the line the clear
annual value as determined by the gross estimated rental
was taken as the basis.[2] Because a £6 rental would give

[1] Freeholders in boroughs who did not occupy their property could
vote in the county in which the borough was situated.

[2] The gross estimated rental is defined by the 25 and 26 Vict., c. 103

242,000 new voters and would place the working class in a
majority, a proposal to use such a figure, thought the
Chancellor of Exchequer, would not be agreeable to Parliament. Hence a clear annual value of £7 was chosen as the
dividing line. By such a provision 144,000 would be enfranchised, who, taken with those of the working class now
voting, 126,000, and those to be added above the £10 line,
60,000, would make a total of 330,000 voters belonging to
the working class as against 362,000 voters of classes other
than the working class. The bill in itself would enfranchise
204,000 persons in the towns, and 172,000 in the counties,
not including about 24,000 added by clauses relating to the
copyhold, leasehold, and savings-bank franchises, or 400,000
altogether.[1] Apropos of the proportion of the new constituency to the total householders, it was said that the actual
constituency represented 36 per cent of the male occupiers,
that the proposed constituency would represent 51 per cent
of those male occupiers, and that of the working classes
there would be in the towns 330,000 enfranchised against
588,000 unenfranchised. A clause disqualifying from voting, persons employed in the government yards while so employed, was also promised.

In conclusion the Chancellor of the Exchequer said:

If issue is taken adversely upon this Bill, I hope it will be
above all a plain and direct issue. I trust it will be taken
upon the question whether there is or is not to be an enfranchisement downwards, if it is to be taken at all. . . . We can-

to be "the rent at which the hereditament might reasonably be expected
to let from year to year, free of all usual tenants' rates and taxes, and
tithe commutation rent charge, if any;" a rateable value was obtained
from the gross estimated rental by making various deductions (which
varied extremely in different places).

[1] There was much disagreement over Gladstone's statistics. Many
members of the House of Commons thought the proportion of workingmen greater than shown, others much less.

not consent to look upon this large addition, considerable although it may be, to the political power of the working classes of this country as if it were an addition fraught with mischief and with danger. We cannot look, and we hope no man will look, upon it as upon some Trojan horse approaching the walls of the sacred city, and filled with armed men, bent upon ruin, plunder, and conflagration. We cannot join in comparing it with that *monstrum infelix*—we cannot say—

> " —scandit fatalis machina muros,
> Foeta armis: mediaeque minans illabitur urbi."

I believe that those persons whom we ask you to enfranchise ought rather to be welcomed as you would welcome recruits to your army or children to your family.

The reception of the measure on the first night could not have been gratifying to the ministry. Mr. Laing, usually a supporter of the Government, was opposed to reopening a question which he thought had been settled long since, and at a period of the session when there was not time to give full and fair consideration to the whole subject.[1] He had thought it advisable to express the opinions he had, because he believed they were held by many of the moderate Liberal party and he felt bound to express his deep disappointment that the Government had resolved to deal with the matter piecemeal, and not by one comprehensive measure. The House was asked to support the bill on pledges given some years ago. For himself he had given no pledge on entering Parliament but a promise generally to support Lord Palmerston's administration, and he did not feel disposed to violate that pledge, either in the letter or the spirit. Would Lord Palmerston have consented, in the face of the returns recently presented to the House, to introduce a measure proposing to lower the franchise without redistributing the seats, to reopen an agitation the issue of which none

---

[1] *Hansard*, vol. clxxxii, pp. 75 *et seq.*

could foresee, to offer them a Reform bill which was not final and contained no element of security?

On the same evening, Mr. Horsman also showed the attitude of the conservative faction of the Liberal party. He attacked the bill as the work of Bright—it was, in short, the old battle revived—the Member for Birmingham and Lord Russell against the majority of the Cabinet and the country. Judging Bright by his political principles, he was not an Englishman but an alien, not a believer in the British Constitution, but as ardent a Republican as President Johnson himself.[1] Bright, however, proved himself able during the following debates to retort effectively to any and all slurs. On the thirteenth of March Mr. Lowe in a well prepared speech showed himself to be in harmony with Mr. Horsman and Mr. Laing. He spoke against any extension of the franchise. Seldom in the nineteenth century was any speaker to utter in Parliament words more significant of opposition to thorough-going democracy than these spoken by Lowe on this occasion:

Let any Gentleman consider the constituencies he has had the honor to be concerned with. If you want venality, if you want ignorance, if you want drunkenness and facility for being intimidated; or if, on the other hand, you want impulsive, unreflecting, and violent people, where do you look for them in the constituencies? Do you go to the top or to the bottom? It is ridiculous for us to allege that since the Reform Bill the sins of the constituencies or the voters are mainly comprised between £20 and £10. But, then, it has been said the £10 shopkeepers, and lodginghouse keepers, and beerhouse keepers, are an indifferent class of people; but get to the artizan, and there you will see the difference. It is a sort of theory the ancients had about the north wind. The ancients observed that as they went further to the north the

[1] *Hansard*, vol. clxxxii, pp. 90-114.

wind got colder. Colder and colder it got the further they
went, just as the constituencies get worse and worse the
nearer you approach £10. They reasoned in this way—If it
is so cold when you are in front of the north wind, how very
warm it would be if you could only get behind it. And, therefore, they imagined for themselves a blessed land we have all
read of, where the people, called the Hyperboreans, were
always perfectly warm, happy and virtuous, because they had
got to the other side of the north wind. It is the same view
that my right honorable Friend takes with respect to the £10
franchise—if you go a little lower you get into the virtuous
stratum. We know what those persons are who live in small
houses—we have had experience of them under the name of
" freemen " — and no better law, I think, could have been
passed than that which disfranchised them altogether.[1]

Such words quoted as a whole or in part by opponents of
Lowe became far more effective as a means of stirring up
the working classes than as any obstacle to democratic tendencies.[2]

The members of the Radical wing were of course not any
too pleased with the actions and words of the dissenters.
Mr. Fawcett referred to Mr. Horsman as an " honorable
gentleman who sits on the Liberal benches, and is always enthusiastically cheered by the Conservatives who sit on the
opposite side of the House." [3]   Bright suggested that Lowe
was resentful because out of office:

> " For who, to dumb forgetfulness a prey,
>   That pleasing, anxious office e'er resigned,
>   Left the warm precincts of the Treasury,
>   Nor cast one longing, lingering look behind? " [4]

As for Horsman:

[1] *Hansard*, vol. clxxxii, pp. 147-148.
[2] *Cf. supra*, p. 100.
[3] *Hansard*, vol. clxxxii (March 13), p. 200.
[4] *Hansard*, vol. clxxxii, p. 219.

The right honorable Gentleman is the first of the new party who has expressed his great grief by his actions—who has retired into what may be called his political cave of Adullam— and he has called about him every one that was in distress and every one that was discontented. The right honorable Gentleman has been long anxious to form a party in this House. There is scarcely at this side of the House any one who is able to address the House with effect or to take much part in our debates that he has not tried to bring over to his party or cabal—and lastly, the right honorable Gentleman has succeeded in hooking the right honorable Gentleman the member for Calne (Mr. Lowe). I know there was an opinion expressed many years ago by a member of the Treasury Bench and of the Cabinet, that two men would make a party. When a party is formed of two men so amiable and so disinterested as the two right honorable Gentlemen, we may hope to see for the first time in Parliament a party perfectly harmonious and distinguished by mutual and unbroken trust. But there is one difficulty which it is impossible to remove. This party of two is like the Scotch terrier that was so covered with hair that you could not tell which was the head and which was the tail.[1]

The reference to the cave of Adullam [2] was at once made use of. Those of the Liberals who opposed the bill and joined forces with Lowe, Horsman and Laing were given the name of Adullamites [3]—a name which lasted until a

[1] *Ibid.*, vol. clxxxii, pp. 219-220.

[2] 1 Samuel 22: 1-2 reads:

" David therefore departed thence, and escaped to the cave Adullam : and when his brethren and all his father's house heard it, they went down thither to him.

"And everyone that was in distress, and every one that was in debt, and everyone that was discontented, gathered themselves unto him; and he became a captain over them: and there were with him about four hundred men."

[3] J. F. Rhodes, in the *History of the United States*, vol. iv, p. 464, relates how in 1864 Lincoln when told by a friend of the nomination of Frémont for president by a few hundred men, opened his Bible and read the passage just quoted (1 Sam. 22:2).

Reform bill had been passed. Apropos of the bill, Bright said that he was not able to find a point in it which he had recommended; that he believed in a household franchise for the boroughs; that he was not for a £14 franchise in the county and not for a savings-bank franchise and that he did not trust Gladstone's statistics concerning the number of workingmen on the register. He did not think the bill sufficient but gave it his support. This gentle censure of the Chancellor of the Exchequer seemed to Viscount Cranborne to give the House an exhibition of a lover's quarrel.[1] At the close of the evening's debate (March 13), the bill was presented and read the first time.

But the great contest of the session commenced on the twelfth of April. The debates characterized by so conspicuous a display of Parliamentary oratory as perhaps no occasion in recent times had produced,[2] were continued for eight nights. On the first day the Chancellor of the Exchequer moved the second reading. He promised to present bills upon the Scotch and Irish franchise and upon the redistribution of seats before going into committee upon this bill. Earl Grosvenor, Adullamite, moved an amendment to the effect that a bill for reducing the franchise could not be discussed until the entire scheme contemplated by the Government for the amendment of the representation of the people was presented. The Government, he thought, put itself open, upon this question, to the charge of deserting its party, when in bringing forward a measure of Reform it consulted mainly and in the first instance, the feelings and wishes of the Radicals.

The debaters had considerable to say upon the amendment but devoted much more time to a consideration of the whole question of Reform.[3] Lord Stanley, Conservative,

---

[1] *Hansard*, vol. clxxxii, p. 225.

[2] Opinion of *Annual Register*, 1866, p. 117.

[3] *Vide infra* for arguments for and against Reform.

in seconding the amendment, spoke in favor of suspending the entire question until 1867, when it might be taken up at the very beginning of the session.[1]   The objections of the Adullamites and Conservatives were many.   They claimed that, by bringing forward only part of the measure, the Government asked the House to put trust in them while they refused to put trust in the House; that they saw " the House of Commons managed as pious missionaries manage their savage converts, not telling them too much for fear of embarrassing their simple minds ";[2] that the House when called upon to vote for a measure which depended on another measure was really asked to resign its functions as a deliberative assembly, and to place a blind confidence in ministers.   It was to ask the assembly to jump at once to the *ultimatum* to which universal suffrage would finally lead it; namely, the separate and independent dictation of the Executive.   Arguments were used against legislation by " piecemeal," as an unusual and unconstitutional procedure. Besides, taking up the franchise before the redistribution of seats would make the absurdity and anomaly of the small boroughs more glaring.   And, it was said, there was no certainty that there would be the same ministry in office next year to complete the measure, should the franchise bill pass this session.

The Liberals, of course, gave reply to the objections and were not slow to point out [3] that whereas the amendment was for a more nearly complete measure, many arguments used were against Reform.   Mr. Forster declared that most of those speaking against the amendment had discussed the merits of the bill, although the amendment expressly stated

---

[1] *Hansard,* vol. clxxxii, p. 1169.

[2] Mr. Gregory, *Hansard,* vol. clxxxii, p. 1799.

[3] In addition to speeches given, *vide* Mr. W. E. Baxter's speech, *Hansard,* vol. clxxxii, pp. 1227-1237.

that it was inexpedient to do so till the whole bill was before the House.[1] They had shown why the franchise should not be reduced, or why it should not be reduced in the manner proposed in the bill. What they should have done, therefore, was to propose an amendment, declaring that it was inexpedient for the House to pass the bill. But they knew that it would not have answered their purpose to meet the question in this direct way. Mr. Bright declared that the bill that was not before them was made an excuse and weapon for destroying the bill that was before them,[2] and Mr. Layard [3] pointed out that the country at large was feeling that the real issue at stake was, not whether the bill proposed by the Government or any other bill should pass, but whether the question of Reform should be entertained at all [4] — a statement of fact which corresponds closely with the evidence of the leading speakers and writers out of doors.

In addition to the time needed for the speeches for and against the bill, and for and against the amendment, much attention was given to the opinions, the inconsistencies of thought and action, and the conduct of individual members. John Bright, because of his prominence in the Reform question and because it was assumed that he had influenced the Government to bring in the single-barrelled bill, came in for so much attention that one [5] of the members declared he must speak of Bright lest he be open to the accusation of having neglected a form, the constant observance of which by preceding speakers led him to conclude that it was one of courtesy and etiquette. Lord Elcho, an Adullamite, made [6]

[1] *Hansard*, vol. clxxxii (April 16, 1866), p. 1387.
[4] *Hansard*, vol. clxxxii (April 23, 1866), p. 1876.
[3] Under Secretary of State for Foreign Affairs.
[2] *Hansard*, vol. clxxxii (April 16, 1866), p. 1424.
[5] Captain Grosvenor, *Hansard*, vol. clxxxiii, p. 29.
[6] *Hansard*, vol. clxxxii (April 19), p. 1674.

a speech against the tyranny of the Saul on the Treasury Benches,[1] and his armor-bearer.[2]   That was the motive which drove him and his colleagues into the Cave where they were, he assured the House, a most happy family daily increasing in number and strength, and whence they should go forth to deliver Israel from oppression.   When he told the Liberals that many of them were going to vote for the Government against what they knew to be right, he provoked the retort [3] that he was a noble Lord who after going along the benches with a lantern in search of what it seems he could not find, turned the full blaze of its light upon himself and there discovered his honest man.

Toward the close of the debates Mr. Lowe, loudly cheered by the Opposition, spoke with great effect against the conduct of the ministry, and against democracy.[4]   To him it seemed that the measure was calculated to destroy those institutions which had secured for England an amount of happiness and prosperity which no country had ever reached, or was ever likely to attain.   On the following day, Disraeli declared that even if the noble Lord, the Member for Chester (Earl Grosvenor), had not come forward to oppose the bill, somebody on the Conservative benches must have done so; for while they were perfectly willing to consider a complete measure of Reform, and had shown their readiness to do so, they must still oppose this measure on account of objections to the county franchise.[5]   Gladstone in a noteworthy speech delivered just before the division on the twenty-seventh of April declared that the point to be decided was whether the House would vote by a majority for the

[1] Gladstone.

[2] Bright.

[3] By Mr. Coleridge, *Hansard*, vol. clxxxii, p. 1831.

[4] *Hansard*, vol. clxxxii (April 26), p. 2118.

[5] *Hansard*, vol. clxxxiii, pp. 94 *et seq.*

second reading of the bill—" that is to say, for a measure
affirming the reduction of the franchise in the counties, and
especially in towns." [1]   In bidding for the support of the
Opposition he warned them that by resisting great measures,
as civil disabilities on account of religious belief, the first
Reform Act, the repeal of the Corn Laws, they had given the
power five out of every six years to the Liberals, and had
reduced their influence in the country.   When he sat down,
the Speaker, writes a spectator,[2] put the question on the
amendment in the dry technical form so puzzling to those
unfamiliar with the proceedings.   Strangers withdrew and
members went to their respective lobbies.   As the members
returned to the seats on the floor or in the galleries great
excitement began to manifest itself, and when finally the
tellers walked up the floor, the House—says the writer—was
charged as with electricity.   Strangers in the galleries rose
in their seats—Conservative M. P.'s sat upon the edges of
benches—the Royal princes leaned forward in their incon-
venient standing place and the officers of the House, partici-
pating in the universal excitement, had no eyes or ears for
any breach of rule or order.   Hardly had the ominous
words, ayes to the right, 318, noes to the left, 313, been
uttered than there arose a wild, raging shout from floor and
gallery.   Dozens of Tories hurrahed at the very top of their
voices.   Strangers in both galleries clapped their hands.   The
Adullamites cheered as loudly as any.   And Lowe, the prince
of the revolt, the instigator and prime mover of the conspir-
acy, stood up in the excitement of the movement—flushed,
triumphant, and avenged.   "'Who would have thought there
was so much in Bob Lowe?' said one member to another;
' why, he was one of the cleverest men in Lord Palmerston's
Government!'"   "'All this comes of Lord Russell's send-

[1] *Hansard*, vol. clxxxiii, p. 140.
[2] *Vide Annals of our Time.*

ing for Goschen!' was the reply. 'Disraeli did not half so
signally avenge himself against Peel' interposed another;
'Lowe has very nearly broken up the Liberal party.'"
There he stood, that usually cold, undemonstrative, intellec-
tual, venerable-looking individual, shouting himself hoarse
like the ringleader of school boys at a successful barring out!
The Government had been saved from downright defeat by
only five votes, but the bill was read a second time. As the
members stepped out into New Palace Yard the twilight of
that long-to-be-remembered night was brightening into day.
Early as was the hour some three hundred persons were
assembled to see them come out, and cheer the friends of
the bill.

On the thirtieth of April the Chancellor of the Exchequer expressed determination to go on with the bill.[1]   The
Government understood the situation to be this—one moiety
of the House was prepared to accede to the proposal of the
Government to enter upon the consideration of the franchise bill, upon the understanding that they would introduce
a bill relating to the redistribution of seats and bills relating
to the subject of Reform in Scotland and Ireland; the
other moiety, that the House must have the whole intention
of the Government with respect to Reform.

On the seventh of May Gladstone produced the bill for
the redistribution of seats.[2]   By this no constituency was
disenfranchised, but some constituencies returning two members were deprived of one of them, and no less than forty-
one small boroughs were grouped together according to
their geographical relation in sixteen groups, returning one
or two members each according to population. Of the
forty-nine seats obtained by these arrangements it was pro-

---

[1] *Hansard*, vol. clxxxiii, pp. 163-166.

[2] *Hansard*, vol. clxxxiii, pp. 486-507.

posed to distribute twenty-six among populous counties, to
give a third member to Liverpool, Manchester, Birmingham,
and Leeds, and a second to Salford, to divide the Tower
Hamlets into two divisions, with two members each, to
create six new electoral boroughs with one member each
and one with two, to give a seat to the University of London,
and seven seats to Scotland. As to the boundaries, whatever enlargements should take place, the Parliamentary
borough should follow the enlargement made for local purposes. Finally, the Government would not advise a prorogation of Parliament until the question of the franchise
and redistribution had been disposed of. Leave was given
to bring in the bill. The *Times* thought it simple in concep-
tion, practical in details and just in principles,[1] although so
far as the parties were concerned, it would throw a certain
amount of political weight to the Liberal side.[2] This, it
said, would be the probable effect of the lower franchise in
towns, still more of the lower franchise in counties, and of
the transference of seats from small towns to large ones and
populous counties. On the same day the Scotch and Irish
Reform bills were also introduced.

The second reading of the Redistribution bill was moved
by Gladstone on the fourteenth of May. During the evening Disraeli attacked the manner in which it was proposed
to deal with small boroughs as a scheme to disenfranchise
the boroughs which had returned to the House representatives of the commercial, financial, colonial, and Indian interests. He advised the Government to withdraw the bill,
prepare careful electoral statistics of the borough and county
franchise, and in the next session give a good measure. Mr.
Cardwell,[3] on behalf of the Government, refused to accept

[1] The *Times*, May 8, 1866, editorial.
[2] Opinion of the *Times*, May 9, 1866, editorial.
[3] Secretary of State for the Colonies.

this advice, claiming the object was to postpone Reform indefinitely. In reply to a question as to whether the Government would assent to having the bill referred to the same committee as that on the Representation of the People bill, with a view to the amalgamation of the two, the Chancellor of the Exchequer gave assent to the proposal, and then the bill was read a second time.

On the twenty-eighth of May the order for committee was read. After a motion for the fusion of the two bills had been agreed to, it was moved " That it be an instruction to the committee that they have power to make provision for the better prevention of bribery and corruption at elections." The Chancellor of the Exchequer objected to the motion, saying that the subject was one that amply merited separate discussion but could hardly be discussed to advantage in connection with a bill for the redistribution of seats or a bill relating to the franchise, and that additional information was needed.[1] Mr. Osborne [2] upheld the motion, declaring this a point which required reform even more than the franchise or the redistribution of seats. The Attorney General [3] pointed out that this was not a proper time to consider the question and that the motion was a good one only as one means of throwing over all Reform in the present session. Mr. Bright also condemned the motion as really aimed at the destruction of the bill. Nevertheless it was carried against the Government by 248 as against 238 votes,—Disraeli and Lowe voting with the majority. The announcement was the occasion for great cheering on the part of the Opposition. The Chancellor of the Exchequer moved that the Speaker leave the chair, saying that the Government would give a dispassionate considera-

[1] *Hansard*, vol. clxxxiii, p. 1322.
[2] R. Bernal Osborne was an Independent Liberal.
[3] Sir Roundell Palmer.

tion to clauses on bribery but would hold to their purpose to go on with the bill. Captain Hayter [1] moved that the redistribution scheme be considered an unsatisfactory measure.

Thereupon the debate continued for four nights. In addition to many details upon redistribution, many of the arguments of the second reading were repeated.[2] Sir George Grey, Secretary of State for the Home Department, attacked the motion as one, which, if carried, would involve the whole bill,[3] and as a " mode resorted to by the right honorable Gentleman to get rid of the bill altogether." To this speech Sir Hugh Cairns, a Conservative, replied that the Government did not answer criticisms and objections, and did not try to promote a free discussion of the question that the House was anxious to have sifted.[4] He thought those out of doors would judge of the course which had been taken in this debate. Sir John Pakington [5] wanted to have the question settled, but the Government—he thought—had rendered that impossible by having precipitately produced a vague and immature measure. During the course of the debates John Stuart Mill spoke for the representation of minorities [6] and Mr. Lowe made use of a chance again to plead against trying anything like democracy:

To our hands at this moment is intrusted the noble and sacred future of free and self-determined Government all over the world. We are about to surrender certain good for more than doubtful change; we are about to barter maxims and traditions that have never failed, for theories and doctrines that have never succeeded. Democracy you may have at any

[1] Captain Hayter was elected as a Liberal in 1865.

[2] *Cf. infra*, pp. 160 *et seq.*

[3] *Hansard*, vol. clxxxiii, p. 1402.

[4] *Hansard*, vol. clxxxiii, p. 1403.

[5] A Conservative.

[6] *Vide* chapter v.

time. Night and day the gate is open that leads to that bare
and level plain, where every ant's nest is a mountain and
every thistle a forest tree. But a Government such as England has, a Government, the work of no human hand, but
which has grown up the imperceptible aggregation of centuries—this is a thing which we only can enjoy, which we cannot impart to others, and which, once lost, we cannot recover
for ourselves.[1]

The Attorney General in reply declared Lowe's motto to be:
" Move an inch from that point (the £10 franchise) and you
are lost—you are on the high road to ruin;"[2] and, he added,
" When he implores and entreats us to defer this bill for another year, I will tell my right honorable Friend the year to
which he wishes us to defer the consideration of this subject—it is the millennium." Of course, many whose seats
were to be taken away, spoke against the bill. On the other
hand, Earl Grosvenor, now that the Redistribution bill had
been brought in, supported the Government upon the
ground that no resignation should be forced because of the
state of affairs in Europe and because of the financial crisis.[3]
He said that some of the Opposition were prepared to compromise with the Government to get the measure through.
Disraeli, however, declared the measure ill-advised and ill-
prepared and hoped that the good sense of the House would
allow the question to be adjourned until next session.[4]
Gladstone said that even if the grounds against the bill for
the redistribution of seats were good grounds, they were
totally insufficient to justify a vote against going into
committee upon the bill.[5] Captain Hayter by this time

[1] *Hansard*, vol. clxxxiii, p. 1650.
[2] *Hansard*, vol. clxxxiii, p. 1651.
[3] *Hansard*, vol. clxxxiii (June 4), pp. 1812-1813.
[4] *Hansard*, vol. clxxxiii, pp. 1912-1913.
[5] *Hansard*, vol. clxxxiii (June 4), p. 1889.

" feeling certain that the measure would not be proceeded with in its present form in the present session " withdrew his amendment.

The House then went into committee, at which stage every clause was discussed in detail—and fought point by point with great earnestness and pertinacity on both sides.[1] Mr. Walpole, a Conservative, proposed a £20 instead of the £14 county occupation franchise. This change the Chancellor of the Exchequer strongly opposed and the amendment was beaten 297 to 283. During the debates on this amendment, Lord Stanley [2] proposed that the clause be postponed, hoping to have the redistribution settled before the franchise clauses, lest the ministry play the trick of dropping the Redistribution bill altogether. Bright denounced this action as another attempt to delay the bill and Gladstone congratulated the " honorable Gentlemen opposite upon their perfect mastery of the arts of ambush." [3]   On a division the motion was rejected.

The next controversy took place on the basis of value to be used in fixing the franchise. In place of the rental as the standard adopted by the Government, Mr. Hunt [4] proposed,[5] in respect to the county franchise, to change the standard by adding to the clause the words—" such clear yearly value being rateable value of the premises as ascertained for the purpose of the Poor Rate." Those for the amendment pointed out [6] the advantage of making the rate book the register and the security against collusion; those against it, the fact that the rating varied in different places and was not a good test. The motion was rejected.

[1] *Annual Register*, 1866, p. 151.
[2] A Conservative.
[3] *Hansard*, vol. clxxxiii, p. 2068.
[4] Mr. G. W. Hunt was a Conservative.
[5] This was on June 11, 1867.
[6] *Cf. Annual Register*, 1866, pp. 153-154.

But Lord Dunkellin,[1] on the eighteenth of June, moved an amendment referring to the borough franchise, similar to Mr. Hunt's motion.   He proposed to leave out of the clause the words " clear yearly " in order to insert the word " rateable."   It was argued on the one side that the rating was a convenient, inexpensive, and a constitutional mode of fixing the franchise,[2] that the rating test could be appealed against whereas the rental could not,[3] that as the burden of local taxation was calculated on the rateable value, the advantage of the vote ought to be placed on the same basis; [4] on the other, that even a £5 rating franchise would not admit so many as the present bill, that the rateable value was a test merely for local taxation which was borne by property, and had nothing to do with an occupation franchise, that inequalities in rateable value must always be greater than in the gross estimated rental, that many, as owners of mines, were not rated at all and would be disfranchised.[5] According to Bright the object was to substitute £9 for £7; and many argued that the real object of the amendment was to get rid of the bill and the Government.   The Chancellor of the Exchequer declared, " it is in my judgment an Amendment striking at the plan of enfranchisement proposed by the Government.   So viewing it, I cannot enter into any engagement that we will accept an adverse vote, or regard it as otherwise than incompatible with the progress of the Bill." [6]   The question was put, that the words " clear yearly " stand.   The result of the vote came—ayes 304;

[1] Lord Dunkellin had been elected in 1865 as a Liberal.

[2] Lord Dunkellin, *Hansard*, vol. clxxxiv, p. 540.

[3] Mr. Henley, *Hansard*, vol. clxxxiv, p. 568.

[4] Sir Hugh Cairns, *Hansard*, vol. clxxxiv, pp. 616 *et seq.*

[5] Gladstone, *Hansard*, vol. clxxxiv, pp. 550 *et seq.*

[6] *Hansard*, vol. clxxxiv, pp. 637-639.

noes 315; majority against the Government, eleven. Once again there was occasion for a great demonstration of joy by the Adullamites and the Conservatives; the defeat of the Government produced a frantic enthusiasm unequalled by any of the frequent divisions of the session.[1]

The bill had failed to pass. A part of the Liberals plus the Conservatives had defeated a measure not itself so liberal but regarded by popular opinion as an advance in the right direction. Thus Parliament stood in June, 1866, opposed to Reform, not that all who voted against the bill professed an aversion to Reform, but it could not escape notice that many of the most telling speeches were against any democratic tendencies.

Among the many arguments used against the bill the following summary presents a number of the most important. In the first place there were the arguments against the bill itself. It was said that the bill was not wanted—that if there had been any great necessity for it or any desire for it on the part of the country, instead of the question being before the country for fourteen years there would not have been fourteen months of agitation upon it.[2] The question of Reform had been agitated under the most favorable circumstances from 1852 to 1865.

It had been taken up by every Administration, and supported and recommended by every prominent public man. It has had three-fourths of the press as the partisans of one side or the other writing in its favor. It had public meetings innumerable, and an active agitation founded on the undisputed fact of 5,000,000 of unenfranchised operatives. Yet these cabinets were all defeated, the ministers more or less discredited, the bills all rejected; the agitation a failure: and the

[1] *Vide Annals of Our Time* and the *Annual Register.*
[2] Lord Elcho (an Adullamite), vol. clxxxii (April 19), p. 1664.

more the question was stirred, the more vividly apparent it became that the projected changes were not suited to the wants
and temper of the times, and that the country — watching,
listening, reading, and judging—was brought slowly, but surely
to the conviction that these changes were not founded in
reason, that they were opposed to justice, that they were fatal
to the growth of liberty—that they were the creed of a small
and noisy section of politicians of extreme opinions, who had
gained an accidental and mischievous importance from the
fact that the two great political parties in the State were so
evenly balanced that rival chiefs vied with one another in
bidding for the support of that extreme minority; but that
the general thought and education of the country—the morality, the statesmanship, the patriotism of every class, from the
highest to the lowest—clung with instinctive fervor to the institutions which they saw approached with an unfriendly hand,
and with one will and one voice forbade that that old tree of
English liberty which had been the slow growth of ages and
the admiration of nations should be transformed into the
brazen image of ignorance and intolerance which the worship-
pers of Trans-Atlantic equality wanted to set up.[1]

It was said that the old £10 formed a line giving a precedent
and a principle. " It afforded a precedent, because it formed
part of a great historical settlement which had worked well
and done admirable service for thirty-five years. It constituted a principle, and one recognized throughout the
whole of our English Constitution, that the franchise was
a trust and not a right." [2]

Besides, the electoral statistics upon which the bill was
based, were not satisfactory, said Viscount Cranborne.[3]
It should be known who the new masters were to be, before the House of Commons was asked to transfer the power

[1] Mr. Horsman (Adullamite), *Hansard*, vol. clxxxii, pp. 98-99.
[2] Mr. Laing (Adullamite), *Hansard*, vol. clxxxii (March 12), p. 81.
[3] Conservative, *Hansard*, vol. clxxxii (March 23), p. 876.

over the legislation, the taxation, and the finances of the country from that section of the community holding it to another section. The question of the number to be enfranchised should be carefully studied especially since a great increase in that number would result from having the £5 and £6 houses changed to houses to be rented at £7.[1] Another defect of the bill was that it would suppress the agricultural interests, especially by permitting the city voters not within the limits of the represented boroughs and those from the numerous towns which were unrepresented to inundate the county constituencies with urban and trading votes of £14 rental.[2]

The bill was going to enfranchise under a new name one class of men who had been disfranchised heretofore—the " freemen "—a class in which Mr. Lowe and the Adullamites had no confidence.[3] One member [4] opposed the bill as a scheme on the part of the North of England which had grown important by the rise of the great manufacturing towns, to get more power in the body politic than it had hitherto possessed.

One of the chief sources of opposition was due to the fact that it was only a franchise bill. And when this defect was remedied,[5] the additional provisions were denounced as lacking that care, deliberation, and foresight which ought to have been exercised by the Government.[6] The principle

---

[1] Lord Elcho, quoting from letter, *Hansard,* vol. clxxxii (March 23), p. 863.

[2] Mr. Adderley (Conservative), *Hansard*, vol. clxxxii (April 16), p. 1414.

[3] *Hansard*, vol. clxxxii (March 13), p. 148.

[4] *Cf.* Mr. Beresford Hope (Independent Conservative), *Hansard,* vol. clxxxii (April 19), p. 1695.

[5] *Cf. supra*, p. 153.

[6] Sir John Pakington (Conservative), *Hansard*, vol. clxxxiii, p. 1573.

of equal electoral districts, or an approximation to such districts, was attacked as the wrong principle upon which a
redistribution bill ought to be based,[1] and the anomalies
created by the bill were declared to be worse than those
existing.[2] The granting of three members to counties [3] was
to Lowe the mere worship of numbers.[4] As it seemed to
him, every member had two separate and distinct duties to
perform.   He was the representative of the borough which
sent him to Parliament, and he had to look after its local
interests to the best of his power.   That was a small and,
in the mild and just times in which he was living, generally
a comparatively easy duty, but his greater and more pre-
eminent duty was to look after the affairs of the Empire.
Sir Hugh Cairns objected to the grouping, saying that there
was no harmony in the boroughs put together, that bribery
would go on in the grouped boroughs because the telegraph
had done away with the advantage of having polling places
twenty or thirty miles apart, that large constituencies were
expensive because elections were sure to be contested, that
Scotland had no claim to more members inasmuch as its
population, wealth, and interests were not increasing in
proportion to England's, and that the bill should have given
special attention to boundaries.[5]

Finally, a motive for opposing the bill—a motive which
may have influenced a number of the Adullamites—was well
expressed by Lord Elcho.   He dreaded the bill not only on
account of the provisions which it contained, but because
it met " with support from persons who have hitherto been

[1] Mr. Lowe, *Hansard*, vol. clxxxiii, p. 1627.

[2] *Ibid.*, p. 1635.

[3] As was done to some extent by the Redistribution of Seats bill.

[4] *Hansard*, vol. clxxxiii, p. 1639.

[5] A Conservative, *Hansard*, vol. clxxxiii (June 1), pp. 1698 *et seq.*

in favor of the very widest possible extension of the franchise." [1]

In addition to the arguments against the bill itself there were arguments against the present Government dealing with the question of Reform. Mr. Horsman suggested that the Government was not strong enough to deal with it.[2] It was said that Reform was again brought up to excite popular feeling on behalf of a weak Government.[3] The faults of the bill were attributed to the fact that it had been drawn not so much with regard to the wants and requirements of the case as to satisfy the requirements of particular constituencies and to ensure the support of certain politicians.[4]

But arguments of far greater interest than these given, are the ones against any Reform. Sometimes they took the shape of a denial of the need for Reform, sometimes they were a portrayal of democracy and the evils thereof, sometimes an appeal to patriotism—a plea that the Constitution, of glorious origin and history, of happy influence upon a great nation, be not ruined by the acceptance of the American doctrine of representation according to numbers.

As to the first of these arguments—it was said that there was nothing to be done by a reformed or a new Parliament. Mr. Laing declared that

Previous to 1832 the Conservative element so far preponderated that the country was brought into great danger; it was impossible to effect salutary changes in time, and, consequently, matters were brought to a point where a choice had

[1] *Hansard*, vol. clxxxii (April 19), p. 1672.

[2] *Hansard*, vol. clxxxii (March 12), p. 100.

[3] *Cf.* Viscount Royston (Conservative), vol. clxxxii, p. 2130, and Horsman, vol. clxxxii, p. 92.

[4] Mr. Doulton (Conservative), *Hansard*, vol. clxxxii (April 19), p. 1711.

to be made between the alternative of Reform or revolution. But since the Reform Act of 1832, could any one fairly and justly say that the Conservative element had unduly preponderated in the political representation of this country? Had not abuse after abuse been reformed until at last we had no practical abuses left? ("Oh.") He repeated that deliberately. Improvement had been carried to such an extent that it was no longer possible for the public opinion of the country to declare, "There is something which ought to be done, and the Parliament of the country will not do it." There were no longer any great questions upon which the opinion of the country was not in entire accordance with the opinions represented in the House. The existing system worked admirably, yet Parliament was asked to re-open most exciting questions.[1]

It was affirmed that the object of government is to construct the best machinery for the purpose to which it is to be applied, and that the present government was the best possible![2]

Reform was not needed because it was no more necessary for workingmen to be represented by workingmen than it was necessary for clergymen to be represented by clergymen.[3] Besides, how could the real workingman who lived by his own labor sit in Parliament unless provided with the means to do so? The middle class, "which goes upwards into the highest extreme of society, and penetrates into the lowest, was the class of all others that could exercise the best influence on the policy and the government of the country."[4]

[1] *Hansard*, vol. clxxxii (March 12), pp. 79-80; *cf.*, also, Mr. Lowe, *Hansard*, vol. clxxxii (March 13), p. 161, and Mr. Meller (Conservative), *ibid.*, p. 187.

[2] *Cf.* Mr. Adderley, *Hansard*, vol. clxxxii (April 16), p. 1421, and Mr. Lowe, *Hansard*, vol. clxxxii (March 13), p. 154.

[3] Mr. Gathorne Hardy (Conservative), *Hansard*, vol. clxxxii (April 19), p. 1741.

[4] Mr. Gregory (Adullamite), *Hansard*, vol. clxxxii (April 20), p. 1795.

Change in the electoral laws was unnecessary because higher rents and higher wages—due to the discovery of gold in California and Australia, emigration, the vast extension in trade and commerce, the increasing demand for labor—had caused enfranchisement by a gradual process.[1] And the proportion of the working classes now, instead of being so insignificant as had been supposed, amounted to 26 per cent of the whole number of the borough electors; so far from being rigid and inelastic that number was steadily and rapidly rising.[2] If one excluded from one's calculations on the increase of the number of workingmen enjoying the franchise since 1833 the scot and lot voters, who were dying out, that increase would be seen to be almost double the number usually given. Finally Mr. Lowe told the House that if the working class had only 128,000 in the present constituencies, it was very much their own fault, because many more of them had the means if they chose to live in £10 houses.

Furthermore the working class should not be represented in proportion to numbers, because according to the principle of the Constitution, Parliament was a mirror—a representation of every class—not according to heads, not according to numbers, but according to everything which gives weight and importance in the world without, so that the various classes of the country might be heard, and their views expressed fairly in the House of Commons without the possibility of any one class outnumbering and reducing to silence all the other classes in the kingdom.[3] If you corrected the anomaly by which numbers were excluded from the Constitution, you had to correct also the anomaly by which wealth was excluded.[4]

[1] Mr. Lowe, *Hansard*, vol. clxxxii (March 13), pp. 146 and 147.
[2] Mr. Laing, *Hansard*, vol. clxxxii (March 12), pp. 76 and 77.
[3] Sir Hugh Cairns, *Hansard*, vol. clxxxii (April 16), p. 1463.
[4] Viscount Cranborne, *Hansard*, vol. clxxxii (March 13), pp. 230-231.

Again, it was said that those who really desired Reform
were those who wished to bring the country to the lowest
level of democracy;[1] that the proposition for the extension
of the franchise was simply a rule of thumb change, a lowering without modification or check. It was placing the
franchise on an incline, where once placed, it had an inevitable tendency to reach the bottom.[2] The same necessity
now alleged to justify the lowering of the franchise from
£10 to £7 would under the same pressure take it down from
£7 to £4 or even to 4s.[3] As to the argument that the urban
working class had been admitted to a fourth share of the
suffrage without danger, that they had been admitted without Parliament's realizing the fact, and that, therefore,
there could be no danger in giving them a half share upon
a principle which must soon give them a preponderant
majority—such an argument reminded Sir E. Bulwer-Lytton
of the Irishman's bull: " If one quince can give so good a
flavor to an apple pie, how wonderfully good must be an
apple pie that is all quinces." [4] Democracy seemed to him
to be essentially the government that belonged to societies
in their youth when the habits of men, even more than their
laws, produced a certain equality of manners and education.[5]
Said he:

If there be a country in the world in which democracy would
be a ruinous experiment, it is surely a country like England,
with a very limited area of soil compared to the pressure of

[1] Mr. Marsh (Adullamite), *Hansard*, vol. clxxxii (March 12), pp. 61-62.

[2] Mr. G. Hardy, *Hansard*, vol. clxxxii (April 19), p. 1746.

[3] Mr. Horsman, *Hansard*, vol. clxxxii (April 20), p. 1844.

[4] Sir E. Bulwer-Lytton (a Conservative by this time although he had
stood for the Reform bill of 1832), *Hansard*, vol. clxxxii (April 13),
p. 1243.

[5] *Ibid.*, p. 1244.

its population, with a commerce so based upon credit and national prestige, that it would perish for ever if by any neglect of democratic economy, or, what is more probable, any adventure of democratic rashness, our naval power were destroyed; and with differences of religious sects so serious that we should find it impossible to precede democracy by that universal and generous system of education without which it would be madness to make the working class the sovereign constituency of a Legislative Assembly.

Mr. Lowe had learned at Oxford that democracy was a form of government in which the poor, being very many, governed the whole country, including the rich, who were few, and for the benefit of the poor, and he feared a government of the rich by the poor.[1]

Moreover, many other evils resulting from democracy were depicted. Bribery would be greatly increased.[2] To those who said that enlarging the number of voters would tend to do away with bribery, Mr. Lowe gave answer that such a remedy was like turning one hundred sound cattle among half a dozen diseased ones with the hope of doing good to the latter. The sound ones were very apt to be infected, he thought.[3] Again, adding a large number of persons to the constituencies would increase the expenses of candidates, and it would enormously increase the expenses of the management of elections, even supposing that everything was conducted in a legitimate and fair manner.[4] It would weaken the executive, "because the moment you have universal suffrage it always happens that the man who

[1] *Hansard*, vol. clxxxii (April 26), p. 2095.

[2] Mr. Gregory, *Hansard*, vol. clxxxii (April 20), p. 1792.

[3] *Hansard*, vol. clxxxii (April 26), p. 2107.

[4] Mr. Lowe, *Hansard*, vol. clxxxii (March 13), pp. 148-149; Mr. Laing, *Hansard*, vol. clxxxii (March 12), p. 83.

elects despises the elected." [1]   It compelled a limitation to
the powers and authority of the representative chamber as
was shown in America and France where the popular
chamber had not the same voice in foreign affairs and in
peace and war. [2]   Democracies were for war and against
free trade. [3]

Mr. Lowe was not the only member of Parliament who
could not trust the working classes.   Others [4] there were,
who could not place implicit trust in the workingman in boroughs and for this reason : he was always engaged in strikes
and would be the cause of sending capital and business to
foreign countries; and he would believe almost everything
told him by his leaders.   As to the representatives of the
workingmen,—one could see in America, where the people
had undisputed power, that they did not send honest, hard-
working men to represent them in Congress, but traffickers
in office, bankrupts, men who had lost their character and
had been driven from every respectable way of life, and
who had taken up politics as a last resort. [5]   And as to
their laws—

Under the democratic institutions of America they had such
legislation as the Maine Liquor Law: [6] and in this country,

[1] Disraeli, *Hansard*, vol. clxxxiii (April 27), p. 93.

[2] Bulwer-Lytton, *Hansard*, vol. clxxxii (April 13), pp. 1248-9.

[3] Lowe, *Hansard*, vol. clxxxii (April 26), p. 2105.

[4] *Cf.*, for instance, the words of Mr. Banks Stanhope (Conservative)
in *Hansard*, vol. clxxxii (April 12), p. 1217.

[5] An observation which Mr. Lowe made, *Hansard*, vol. clxxxii (April
26), p. 2107.

[6] The first state prohibitory law in Maine was passed in 1851, and,
since its enactment, has been amended somewhat during almost every
session.   Under this " Maine law" the manufacture and sale of intoxicating liquors, except the sale for medicinal purposes, *etc.*, were
prohibited, but the enforcement of the law devolved upon the county
attorney and the sheriff and his deputies.   For medical purposes, an

where trades unions legislated for their fellow-workmen, the result was that the houses and workshops of those who did not assent to the legislation of those unions were blown up by gunpowder. In Australia the influence of trades unions was more extensive than here; there they operated on Parliament with a view to give their measures the force of law, and a deputation from trades unions had urged on the government there the propriety of introducing an eight hours labor bill.[1]

The franchise should not be indiscriminately lowered, but rather given to the working classes as a reward for good conduct and provident habits. It was evident[2] that the present working-class ten-pound householders were superior men of their class. But if the franchise were indiscriminately lowered there would be admitted to the privilege of voting those of not so high a character and those who had not been so provident and careful to lodge their families in comfortable houses. The franchise was not given as a right but as a trust for the benefit of the country, and in the selection of the trustees, they must consider who were the best qualified to hold it.[3] The moral aspect of the question must be considered.

agency, authorized by municipal officers, was established. Opponents of the law have claimed it has been either a dead letter or a license rather than a prohibitory law, and that widespread corruption has come from its pretended enforcement. They became so strong in numbers that in 1911 prohibition was saved by only a few hundred votes, and even as late as 1914-1916 the enforcement of the law was very lax. In 1917, however, the legislature gave the executive the machinery for absolute enforcement and the law can no longer be called a " dead letter." *Vide* William MacDonald, *The Government of Maine* (London, 1902), pp. 159-161, and for the most recent account (by a partisan of prohibition) and a bibliography, Ernest Gordon, *The Maine Law* (New York, 1919).

[1] Mr. Marsh, *Hansard*, vol. clxxxii (March 12), p. 62.

[2] Mr. Laing, *Hansard*, vol. clxxxii (March 12), p. 83.

[3] Mr. Horsfall (Conservative), *Hansard*, vol. clxxxii (April 12), p. 1186.

Enfranchising a number of the workingmen would not be enfranchising that great number of minds all independently turned upon the same questions from different points of view, which the widening of the franchise would be in other portions of the social polity. It would be merely performing a multiplication sum, and developing the same single instincts, single prejudices, single desires, and single opinions influenced by one newspaper and one set of ideas. There might be expected, therefore, further claims as soon as this bill was passed.[1] And when once the workingmen have found themselves in a full majority of the whole consituency, they

will awake to a full sense of their power. They will say, " we can do better for ourselves. Do not let us any longer be cajoled at elections. Let us set up shop for ourselves. We have objects to serve as well as our neighbors, and let us unite to carry those objects. We have machinery; we have our trades unions; we have our leaders all ready. We have the power of combination, as we have shown over and over again; and when we have a prize to fight for we will bring it to bear with tenfold more force than ever before." [2]

They might be expected most warmly to support those extreme Reformers who wished to substitute direct taxation for all indirect taxation and would then become perfectly indifferent to the amount of the public expenditure.[3] They might be expected to have great influence in those questions between labor and capital, between manufacturer and mechanic, between supply and demand, upon which the very existence of this commercial England depended.[4]

[1] Mr. Beresford Hope, *Hansard*, vol. clxxxii (April 19), p. 1688, and *vide*, also, Viscount Cranborne, *Hansard*, vol. clxxxii (March 13), p. 234, and Sir Hugh Cairns, *Hansard*, vol. clxxxii (April 16), p. 1474.

[2] Lowe, *Hansard*, vol. clxxxii (March 13), pp. 148-149.

[3] Gen. Peel (Conservative), *Hansard*, vol. clxxxii (April 12), p. 1207.

[4] Bulwer-Lytton, *Hansard*, vol. clxxxii (April 13), p. 1248.

But should the bill pass, by what special course of legislation [1] was the poor man's daughter to be enabled to view the
face of nature as a consequence of Parliamentary Reform? [2]
As for the rate of wages—that depended on " the inflexible
laws of supply and demand." It was not the duty of the
Legislature to house and feed the people, or to look after
such things as adulterated food or industrial diseases.[3] The
working classes could not succeed in the attainment of
these objects which were so much in violation of the truths
of political economy, but the attempt to do so might be
more disastrous than the success of the measures themselves.
The very fact that the men whom they trusted as their
speakers and delegates at political meetings urged such subjects on the notice of their hearers, ought to be sufficient to
warn of the danger of entering the course which proposed
to give the working classes entire and undisputed control
over the policy of Parliament.

In addition to the arguments given, were those characterized by vagueness but nevertheless often effective upon an
audience: " We are opposed to a measure of this nature,
which unsettles everything and settles nothing." [4]   Then,.
too, one must not forget the influence of oratory. What
now seems at times to be a platitude, was of great effectiveness, as the editorials of the newspapers bear witness, when
uttered by a Robert Lowe, a John Bright, or a Gladstone.

Refutations, of course, played an important part in the
debates. In reply to Gladstone's plea that those to be en-

[1] *Cf. supra*, pp. 98-99, a reply to Mr. Odger's speech; note also the
amount of harm which a reformed House might do, although no good
could be expected of it.

[2] Cranborne, *Hansard*, vol. clxxxii (March 13), p. 233.

[3] *Vide* speech of Mr. Gregory, *Hansard*, vol. clxxxii (April 20),
pp. 1794-1795.

[4] Mr. Whiteside (Conservative), *Hansard*, vol. clxxxii (March 13),.
p. 192.

franchised should not be treated as an invading army but
as their own flesh and blood and fellow Christians, it was
suggested [1] that Gladstone, according to the bill, looked upon
the £7 voters as real flesh and blood but those below as only
gradual flesh and blood, and that if this fellow-Christian
theory were pushed to the utmost, should not the five millions
of adult women in the country be considered? [2]

Gladstone's arguments that the working classes deserved
more representation because of their share of taxation was
retorted to in several ways. Even admitting the taxation
of the working classes to be three-sevenths, said one,[3] by
far the greater portion of that was paid on articles of spirits,
beer, and tobacco. Certainly it was most extraordinary in
estimating the fitness of persons for the franchise, to maintain that a class is entitled to a larger share in the representation in exact proportion to the larger quantity of beer and
spirits which its members consume. Another [4] saw a fallacy in the income argument because the income of the
workingmen was payment for their labor from the capital
of others; another,[5] because the figures on the income referred to all members of the working class, whereas the bill
would not admit all.

Against the speeches of Bright to the effect that something should be done in time before the working classes
became excited, the opponents talked about yielding to
intimidation.[6]

As for fulfilling the pledges—a subject of so much dis-

---

[1] Bulwer-Lytton, *Hansard*, vol. clxxxii (April 13), p. 1246.

[2] Mr. Banks Stanhope, *Hansard*, vol. clxxxii (April 12), p. 1217.

[3] Mr. Laing, *Hansard*, vol. clxxxii (April 13), p. 1320.

[4] Mr. Banks Stanhope, *Hansard*, vol. clxxxii (April 12), p. 1217.

[5] Lowe, *Hansard*, vol. clxxxii (April 26), pp. 2092-2093.

[6] *Vide*, for instance, Bulwer-Lytton, *Hansard*, vol. clxxxii (April 13),
p. 1244.

cussion — Disraeli said that no Parliament could be bound
by the acts of its predecessors, except so far as they had
taken the forms of law; and such forms Parliament had the
power to revise.[1]

The Liberals being the authors of the bill, found themselves quite often on the defensive.   Among their speeches
are to be found replies to most of the important arguments
of the Adullamites and the Conservatives.   For instance, in
defense of the bill, they declared that there *was* agitation
for Reform but it was of a peaceful and orderly character;[2]
that what excitement there was on the bill, was for it;[3] that
a feeling prevailed, universally throughout the country, that
the whole number of electors was much too small to afford
a satisfactory representation of the people, and that the
largest class in the country, that class which, most of all,
made the nation, was specially excluded.[4]   It was predicted
that there might not always be the same political calm in
the country as was now happily prevailing; and that if any
great disasters should happen to the people, and in the midst
of their misery they should also be goaded by a sense of
wrong. they would not appeal to the House in a calm and
moderate tone.[5]   Besides it had often been alleged against
the settlement of other great questions that the change was
not required because not demanded; the Opposition main-
taining that the people did not want Reform, because they
were so quiet and orderly, led one to the conclusion from this
kind of argument that if the people did desire it, they would
have to resort to other than constitutional means to obtain

[1] *Hansard*, vol. clxxxiii (April 27), p. 75.

[2] Captain Grosvenor, *Hansard*, vol. clxxxii (March 12), p. 88.

[3] The Attorney General, *Hansard*, vol. clxxxiii (May 31), p. 1659.

[4] Mr. Bright, *Hansard*, vol. clxxxii (April 23), p. 1883.

[5] Mr. Maguire, *Hansard*, vol. clxxxii (April 16), p. 1374, and Mr.
Baines, *Hansard*, vol. clxxxiii (April 27), p. 59.

it.[1]   Also it was said that citizenship together with its accompanying privileges was an inducement for laborers to go to the colonies, so that England was losing strong and skillful arms.[2]   As to the virtue of the sacred £10 line,—£7 was held to be as safe a point now as £10 was in 1832.[3] According to the great progress in education, in prudential habits, as shown by the savings banks' returns, and in various other respects, which had been made by the working class, the bill of 1832 was not fitted for 1866.[4]

Inasmuch as there were found in the constituencies at the present moment a large number of workingmen whom honorable members opposite did not suspect to be there, Mr. Goschen thought minutely exact electoral statistics not so important;[5] Gladstone complained that the Opposition in dealing with the statistics acted as if they were engaged in ascertaining the numbers of an invading army.[6]   In reply to the cry that the bill was suppressing the agricultural interests,—where, it was asked,[7] would the landowners be if influence in elections were merely proportionate to numbers!

The bill, of course, was only a franchise bill, but it was declared to be distinct, clear, without any tricks—without semblance of giving something in one clause, and then withdrawing that something in the clause that followed.[8]   The Reform question had been one of franchise more than redis-

---

[1] Mr. Villiers, *Hansard*, vol. clxxxii (March 13), pp. 176-177.

[2] Mr. Fawcett, *Hansard*, vol. clxxxii (March 13), p. 208.

[3] Mr. Young, Solicitor General for Scotland, *Hansard*, vol. clxxxii (April 20), p. 1809.

[4] Sir Francis Crossley, *Hansard*, vol. clxxxii (March 12), p. 70.

[5] *Hansard*, vol. clxxxii (March 23), p. 878.

[6] *Hansard*, vol. clxxxii (March 23), p. 873.

[7] Sir Francis Goldsmid, *Hansard*, vol. clxxxii (April 13), p. 1278.

[8] Mr. Bright, *Hansard*, vol. clxxxii (March 13), p. 209.

tribution all along.[1]   The extension of the franchise affected
a particular portion of the population; the redistribution
of seats did not; it affected all.   Derby's Government in
1859 had regarded the question of the franchise as the more
important.[2]   Gladstone pointed out that of the one hundred
and seventeen borough members who entered into particulars on the subject of Reform before their constituents, no
more than sixteen referred to the redistribution of seats,
and of those sixteen all were willing to vote for the bill.[3]
The Redistribution bill, when added, Gladstone defended as
not creating a single anomaly but only reproducing a much
milder form of the old anomalies.[4]   He defended the grouping by pointing out that the system worked well in Wales,
and in general answered the objections of the Opposition.[5]
The Radicals supported the measure not because it was adequate but because it was good to some extent and because
they preferred such a bill to force.[6]

In defense of the Government the point was made that it
was far better situated to pass the bill than the coalition
was to defeat it, since such a combination of Conservatives
and moderate Liberals would fall to pieces at the moment
of victory.[7]

The arguments set forth by the opponents of the bill,
which may be classed as arguments against any further Reform acts, were often well met.   It was shown that many
of the same arguments used against this bill were used

[1] Mr. Bright, *Hansard*, vol. clxxxii (April 23), pp. 1879-1880.

[2] Mr. Bright, *Hansard*, vol. clxxxii (April 23), p. 1887.

[3] *Hansard*, vol. clxxxiii (April 27), p. 133.

[4] *Hansard*, vol. clxxxiii (June 4), pp. 1879 *et seq.*

[5] *Cf.* long speech on June 4.

[6] Mr. Bright, *Hansard*, vol. clxxxii (March 13), pp. 222-223 and elsewhere.

[7] Mr. Childers, *Hansard*, vol. clxxxii (April 26), p. 2171.

against the bill of 1832 which now was so reverently upheld.[1]
Even if, according to the electoral statistics, the working
class now had 25 per cent of the votes, they did not have
25 per cent of the representation to the House.[2]   Reform
was needed because there were abuses to be done away with:
a larger representation of the working class would have a
happy effect in bringing about an early settlement of some
important questions affecting capital and labor.[3]   The working classes indeed had many grievances of which they had
a right to complain.[4]   While they were laboring for themselves, and working out their own ideas, how had the Legislature helped them?   For instance, had it housed, fed, or
educated them?   There was the question of arbitration
courts, as connected with the labor problem, which had been
handed backwards and forwards, sometimes in one House
and sometimes in another.   Then there was the question of
the Master and Workmen's Acts; the question of the workhouse infirmaries; the question of dangerous and unwhole-
some trades.   Would any one who looked at this subject
fairly and dispassionately say that if the class upon whom
these interests pressed—who worked in these workshops and
lived in these hovels—had been fairly represented, their condition would not have been improved?   As an instance of
the want of sympathy on the part of the House with the
working class, there might be mentioned the existing laws
regulating the sale of alcoholic drinks; for though a very
large majority of the working class complained of them as
throwing temptations to insobriety in their way, the only
answer they got from Parliament was that they ought to

---

[1] *Ibid.*, pp. 2168 *et seq.*

[2] Mr. Goschen, *Hansard*, vol. clxxxii (April 23), p. 1967.

[3] Mr. Baxter, *Hansard*, vol. clxxxii (April 13), p. 1237.

[4] Mr. Thomas Hughes, *Hansard*, vol. clxxxii (April 19), pp. 1707 *et seq.*

have resolution enough to resist those temptations. Another [1] asked, if there were no practical abuses in the year of grace, 1866, would Ireland be in her present condition? Would there be a rampant church in this country? Would the old land question remain unsettled? Would the enormous and profligate expenditure still be going on to the same extent as was declaimed against in 1859 by the Chancellor of the Exchequer, when he said he could not answer for the consequences if such an enormous outlay were continued? The best thing that could happen in this country would be a healthy admixture of the artisan class among the members of this House. Concerning the argument that the present government was the best possible and that the electoral system was all that could be desired, Mr. Baines pointed out that in 1830 the Duke of Wellington affirmed that no conceivable form of representation could excel in excellence and adaptation to its ends the then existing system, that the Reform Act of 1832 was declared by the Conservative party in Parliament to be nothing less than a revolution calculated to subject the intelligence and education of the country to the ascendency of the uneducated classes and the mobocracy of the country.[2] Many practical grievances which existed before 1832 had been removed in consequence of that very infusion into the House of the popular element which Conservative members declared at the time to be a revolution. He believed that there were good grounds for expecting a further measure in the same direction to be attended with the like beneficial effects.—Moreover, in a case of great emergency, it would not be well to have large sections of the people feel that they had no sphere in the government of the country.[3]

[1] Mr. Osborne, *Hansard*, vol. clxxxiii (June 9), p. 1819.

[2] *Hansard*, vol. clxxxii (March 12), pp. 84-85.

[3] Mr. Villiers, *Hansard*, vol. clxxxii (March 13), pp. 175 and 176.

Indeed, Reform was needed in order to allow the workingman to be represented by members of his social class. What, it was asked, do [1] members of the House know about the workingman's view of trade unions, strikes, and apprenticeships? Every man and every class has erroneous opinions to be checked up only by contact with others. The questions, which are likely each year to assume a greater importance in this House, are questions affecting capital and labor, and many gentlemen who now consider themselves the representatives of the working class are notably capitalists, and on such questions are more likely to sympathize with their order than with labor.[2] John Bright, for instance, had always been opposed to the operatives on the question of factory legislation. While much was said of the danger and impropriety of giving the working classes a predominance in Parliament, it was the complaint of one member that he had heard nothing of the impropriety of the opposite course—the predominance of the middle classes—" indeed the working classes being in a minority seems to be accepted as of perfectly unquestionable right." [3] Another [4] complained:

I find that 217 of this House's Members are either directly connected with or are actual members of the aristocracy. Talk of trade unions! Why, is not this House a trades union to a certain extent? (Mr. Bright: " Hear, Hear! ") Have we not 217 members who constitute to all intents and purposes a trades union? But it is said, do they all give their votes on one side? No; like the Trade unions, they differ in their political sentiments. I find, on referring to Mr. Sandford's *History of Great Families*, that there are no less than 1,500

[1] J. S. Mill, *Hansard*, vol. clxxxii (April 13), pp. 1259-1260.

[2] Mr. Fawcett, *Hansard*, vol. clxxxii (March 13), p. 206.

[3] Mr. Graham, *Hansard*, vol. clxxxii (April 19), p. 1653.

[4] Mr. Osborne, *Hansard*, vol. clxxxiii (June 4), pp. 1818-1819.

members of great families who constitute the whole of the Upper Chamber, and one-third of this House, and yet we hear honorable Gentlemen talk of the necessity of keeping out the artizan class.

It was denied that the enfranchisement of the working classes was actually in course of being effected by a natural process.[1]   No proof was to be found for the statement that there was a rapid growth of the working classes among the ten-pound householders.   When the first register was made up after 1832, it was found that the proportion of electors to male adults in England and Wales was one in five—that one out of every five male adults had a vote—and that proportion was still continuing in 1865.[2]   Only a small portion of the working class could hope to receive income enough to reach the ten-pound line.[3]   And, although many artisans had risen to wealth and eminence from the humblest walks of life and were deserving of much credit, they were not representative men of their class.[4]

The Constitution would not be endangered by gradual changes made in time or wise concessions gracefully given but by a policy of determined resistance to all changes, and the persistent refusal to grant reasonable popular demands.[5]   Gladstone thought the noble Constitution of England had struck deep roots in the soil and was fixed there in a manner to defy the harmful effects of such a slight change as would result from a £3 reduction in the franchise qualifications.[6]

[1] Gladstone, *Hansard*, vol. clxxxii (April 12), p. 1142.

[2] Mr. Milner Gibson, *Hansard*, vol. clxxxii (April 19), p. 1726.

[3] Gladstone, *Hansard*, vol. clxxxii (March 12), p. 54.

[4] Mr. Thomas Hughes, *Hansard*, vol. clxxxii (April 19), p. 1706.

[5] Mr. Baxter, *Hansard*, vol. clxxxii (April 13), p. 1230.

[6] *Hansard*, vol. clxxxiii (April 27), p. 123.

Of those who alleged to see in the bill an inevitable tendency towards democracy on the ground that the franchise was being placed on an incline, Bright asked:

Did any honorable Gentleman sitting in this House ever vote upon any measure of arrangement and organization like this one, and could confidently assure himself that the measure would be final? He must have a very poor notion of what our children will be if he thinks them less competent to decide such questions for themselves than we are at present to decide them.[1]

And, though this bill gave nothing like democracy, what were the great evils which were supposed to come with any tendency in that direction? Large masses could not be so easily bribed as a few people.[2] Besides, said Mr. Layard,[3] "You have no right to throw it in the teeth of the workingmen that they are unfit to exercise the franchise because they are corrupt, whilst you (*i. e.*, Members of the House) are their corruptors. (Great confusion and interruptions from the Opposition.)" The workingmen would not be anxious for war, for with their property they had interest in taxes.[4] Look at the colonies where they had the right of voting.[5] The financial condition was good; there was a liberal provision for public worship; the votes for public education would shame this House; they tended to their own defense; and their protectionist members were returned largely by the agricultural constituencies, not by the working class. In Australia, said Mr. Fawcett, property is as secure, law is as justly administered, as here;

[1] *Hansard*, vol. clxxxii (March 13), p. 213.
[2] Mr. Baxter, *Hansard*, vol. clxxxii (April 13), p. 1236.
[3] *Hansard*, vol. clxxxii (April 16), p. 1449.
[4] Mr. Layard, *Hansard*, vol. clxxxii, p. 1447.
[5] Mr. Childers, *Hansard*, vol. clxxxii (April 26), pp. 2158-9.

" and they at least have not, as we have, a burden of destitution constantly reminding our statesmen that they have
left their highest mission unfulfilled, and that is to wage successful war against pauperism."[1] Mr. Goschen thought
it of little use to argue from conditions in the colonies and
America inasmuch as there was a difference in the relative
position of labor and capital in those countries as compared with England.[2] No constituencies in England, however, in which the working class had the decided influence
now were returning demagogues as their representatives.[3]

To assume that the working class would vote *en masse*
was no more right than to assume that the middle class or
the upper class would do so.[4] Workingmen followed their
own opinions,[5] not those of their leaders as could be seen
from their disagreement with Cobden on the subject of the
Russian war. No political union could be arranged between the miners of Cornwall, the masons of London, and
the mill hands of the North, unless a real bond of union
should be given by keeping them, as wage receivers, from
the franchise. And if excluded too long they might at
last be induced to make their trade unions a political en-
gine. But if this bill passed it would be final for their
political lives, because it was not easy to get up a political
agitation. The workingmen did not find it easy to leave
work and lose wages for the purpose of attending political
meetings.

The Liberals had, of course, a good argument when they
mentioned the advance in general intelligence of the work-

[1] *Hansard*, vol. clxxxii (March 13), p. 204.

[2] *Hansard*, vol. clxxxii (April 23), p. 1966.

[3] Mr. Layard, *Hansard*, vol. clxxxii (April 16), p. 1449.

[4] Mr. Fawcett, *Hansard*, vol. clxxxii (March 13), pp. 205-6.

[5] W. E. Forster, *Hansard*, vol. clxxxii (April 16), pp. 1391-3.

ing class since 1832. Mr. Baines, a member in whose
statistics the House had a degree of confidence, stated that
in 1865 there were 3,100,000 scholars in day schools compared with 1,250,000 in 1832. In 1831 the number of
copies of newspapers circulating in England was 38,000,000;
in 1864 the number had increased to 546,000,000. The
circulation of the magazines and serials, weekly and
monthly, literary, scientific, religious, and moral, had increased in the same time from 400,000 copies a month to
6,000,000 a month—an increase for which the working
class was in no small degree responsible.[1] They were able
to carry on successfully such organizations as the Amalgamated Society of Engineers;[2] they were successful with
their co-operative societies;[3] they were interested in librar-
ies.[4] Besides they had shown a most commendable patience
and fortitude in Lancashire during the cotton famine which
was the theme for much praise. As a class, too, the workingmen needed representation. John Stuart Mill championed them:

While so many classes, comparatively insignificant in numbers, and not supposed to be freer from class partialities or
interests than their neighbors, are represented, some of them,
I venture to say, greatly over-represented in this House, there
is a class, more numerous than all the others, and therefore,
as a mere matter of human feeling, entitled to more consideration—weak as yet, and therefore, needing representation
the more, but daily becoming stronger, and more capable of
making its claims good — and this class is not represented.
We claim, then, a large and liberal representation of the working classes, on the conservative theory of the Constitution.

[1] *Hansard*, vol. clxxxiii (April 27), pp. 57-58.

[2] *Vide* Mr. Thomas Hughes, *Hansard*, vol. clxxxii (April 19), p. 1705.

[3] *Vide* Mr. Baxter, *Hansard*, vol. clxxxii (April 13), p. 1235.

[4] *Vide* Gladstone, *Hansard*, vol. clxxxii (April 12), p. 1132.

We demand that they be represented as a class, if represented they cannot be as human beings.[1]

In conclusion it may be stated that the belief of the working class that the majority of the members of the House of Commons stood against Reform was not without foundation. Arguments against any extension of the suffrage had been boldly spoken; the Conservatives and Adullamites had tried to have the bill put off, had tried to cast it aside through various amendments, had tried to make it even less liberal than it was, and had finally defeated it. One can argue that the Conservatives may have been more opposed to the bill and its authors than to Reform itself; but certain it is that the bill of 1866 contained more promising material from which could have been constructed a good bill than the platitudes put forth by Disraeli in the following session, which were changed by a House under pressure into one of the most important measures of the century. And if the Conservatives as a party were anxious to grant electoral Reform their past history gave no evidence of the desire. At least the working class expressed itself more than once in 1866 as seeing in the men of the Conservative and Adullamite faith—men elected to represent England—strong opponents to Reform.

[1] *Hansard*, vol. clxxxii (April 13), pp. 1255-1256.

CHAPTER V

DISRAELI'S SUCCESS WITH REFORM IN 1867

THE Adullamites and the Conservatives had given the Liberal Government an adverse vote in passing Lord Dunkellin's amendment to the Reform bill for the rateable value instead of the gross estimated rental as the basis of the franchise. Resignation was the natural method of procedure for Gladstone and his colleagues. They might have demanded dissolution but Mr. Brand, the whip, thought that such a course would be unpopular with the Liberals on account of election expenses.[1] Moreover, an appeal to the country on the Reform question would have had the effect of breaking up the party by causing the Palmerstonian Liberals to go to the Opposition at a time when the country itself was more or less apathetic. They might have gone on with the bill, trusting to reverse the vote on report or they might have taken shelter under a general vote of confidence. However, at a cabinet meeting on June 25, 1866, resignation was agreed upon. Gladstone himself was glad to have the matter near its close.[2] The Queen, when informed of her ministers' intentions expressed opposition to change because of the critical situation on the Continent.[3] But Russell and Gladstone after an interview with Her Majesty and a consultation with Brand and the cabinet decided finally (June 26) on resignation. " At six," writes

[1] *Cf.* Morley, *Life of Gladstone*, vol. ii, pp. 207 *et seq.*
[2] *Ibid.*, p. 209.
[3] The Seven Weeks' War had broken out on June 18.

Gladstone, " I went down and made my explanation for the
government. I kept to facts without epithets, but I thought
as I went on that some of the words were scorching. A
crowd and great enthusiasm in Palace Yard on departure."

Although Gladstone's speech on this occasion may not
strike a reader of to-day as being especially " scorching "
under the circumstances, he cannot help noticing that it is
a clear and definite statement of the attitude taken by the
Government on the situation. The Chancellor of the Exchequer showed that Dunkellin's motion was absolutely un-
acceptable because there was no form or figure of enfranchisement founded on mere relation to rateable value
which would express faithfully and exactly the scale of
enfranchisement best suited, in the Government's opinion,
to the public interest. In 16 boroughs the adoption of a
franchise founded on a rateable value of above £6 would enfranchise a number at least equal to the number the bill
proposed to enfranchise. But in 39 boroughs a rateable
value of £6, in 112 boroughs a rateable value of £5, in 21
boroughs a rateable value of £4, and in 5 boroughs a rateable value of less than £4, would be necessary in order to
enfranchise those to whom the franchise would be given by a
£7 rental. Moreover, owing to the differences of rating
which frequently prevailed in different parts of the
same town, there would be inequalities in the operation of
a rating franchise in the same borough. The ministry, however, had tendered resignation of their offices not only because of the effect of this motion but also because of the
attitude of members during the previous divisions and debates. Patent to all had been the attempt to overweight
the measure by an inclusion of bribery and corruption
clauses, the attempt, without giving public notice, to postpone the clauses of enfranchisement for the clauses affecting the redistribution of seats, the attempt to raise the

franchise when already the bill had been framed to conciliate those members who were timid or fastidious on the
subject of Reform at the expense of those by whom Reform was ardently supported.[1]

Earl Russell announced in the House of Lords that the
resignations had been accepted. While taking occasion to
give a history of the Reform movement during the last
seven years, he justified the measure which had just been
rejected as a fair and moderate one which had been opposed
with a view of putting off Reform,[2] and attacked Lord
Derby because of speeches made in condemnation of the
measure. Lord Derby in reply criticized the hasty and
inconsiderate conduct of the Government, and pointed out
that the amendments from the ministerial side of the House
had caused more trouble than any of his speeches.

Lord Derby himself was destined to worry over Reform
before the passing of many months. To him, as leader of
the Conservatives, was given the task of forming an administration.

Inasmuch as the Adullamites had been a party to the overthrow of the Russell-Gladstone ministry, it was but natural
that their co-operation should be sought in the formation
of a new ministry. Their terms, however, could not be
accepted by the Conservatives;[3] and after an attempt to
utilize Lord Shaftesbury, Palmerstonian, philanthropist, and
friend of the working classes, had failed, Derby had to give

[1] Speech of June 26, *Hansard*, vol. clxxxiv, pp. 684-692.

[2] *Cf. Annual Register*, 1866, p. 159.

[3] *Vide* George Saintsbury, *The Earl of Derby* (New York, 1892), p. 170,
where the statement is made that the Adullamites would have been willing to join a Government under Lord Stanley, son of Lord Derby.
Stanley was known as a very liberal Conservative and had been offered
office in 1855 by Palmerston. In the *Life of Disraeli*, vol. iv, pp. 439
et seq., Monypenny and Buckle declare, however, that the Adullamites
wanted the premiership to go to a Whig.

up the idea of making a Government on an enlarged basis.
He chose Disraeli as his foremost man. The latter, after
several unsuccessful attempts to enter Parliament—on the
first occasion as a Radical—finally had been elected in 1837
under Tory auspices. Certain political ideas as expressed
by pamphlets and by his novels *Coningsby* (1844) dealing
with political conditions, and *Sybil* (1845) descriptive of
the social relation between rich and poor, became the tenets
of a considerable number of Tory followers. The passing
of the Whig oligarchy in 1832 had made it possible,
Disraeli believed, for the Crown and the old noble families
to do something for the mass of the people, in which kind
of activity the Liberals had been negligent. He had failed
to follow Peel in the latter's espousal of the repeal of the
Corn Laws and had caused a split in the Conservative
party. When he became, in a short time, leader of the Conservatives in the House of Commons, he gave up, however,
ideas of a sudden return to protectionist principles. He
was successful as Chancellor of the Exchequer under Derby
in 1852 and again in 1858 in the second Derby ministry.
In the following year he tried to pass the Reform measure
of 1859, but, as has been noted, failed. Brilliant, clever,
and able, nevertheless as son of an apostate Jew he was
looked at askance by British society. He now again became Chancellor of the Exchequer and as Derby's assistant
probably had much to do with the selection of men and
the distribution of offices. Stanley [1] became Foreign Secretary, General Peel Secretary of War, Walpole [2] Secretary
of State for the Home Department, Lord Cranborne [3] Secre-

---

[1] Stanley had been Colonial Secretary in 1858 and subsequently President of the Board of Control.

[2] Walpole had occupied the same position in 1852 and 1858.

[3] Later Lord Salisbury, leader of the Conservatives after Disraeli's
death; at this time he was an independent Conservative.

tary for India, the Earl of Carnarvon [1] Colonial Secretary, and Sir Stafford Northcote and Gathorne Hardy,[2] two men of talent in Disraeli's opinion, President of the Board of Trade and President of the Poor Law Board respectively. According to an authority it was a strong combination with very few weak spots—" a proof, in itself alone, of the success with which Disraeli had built up the Conservative party out of the ruins of the late 'forties, and had attracted to the service of the cause a goodly proportion of the intellect of the country."[3]

As for Reform—a discussion of the subject was not renewed in Parliament during the remainder of the session. Lord Derby, in his ministerial statement on accession to office, touched most guardedly on the subject.[4] He reserved to himself the most entire liberty as to whether the Government should or should not undertake to bring in a measure for the amendment of the representation of the people but promised that if there was " no reasonable prospect of passing a sound and satisfactory measure," the session would not be spent in the wasteful contest over a Reform bill.[5]

Disraeli, too, in his hustings speech on re-election declined to pledge himself to introduce a Reform bill in the following session. And he assured his constituents

if we deal with the question at any time, we will deal with it in the spirit of the English Constitution. We shall not attempt to fashion or remodel the institutions of this country on any

---

[1] According to Monypenny and Buckle, Carnarvon was appointed through the influence of Derby.

[2] Hardy had defeated Gladstone at Oxford.

[3] Monypenny and Buckle, *Life of Disraeli*, vol. iv, p. 445. *Cf.*, also, George Saintsbury, *The Earl of Derby*, p. 170.

[4] *Cf.* opinion of the *Edinburgh Review*, January, 1867, p. 287.

[5] *Hansard*, vol. clxxxiv, p. 740.

foreign type whatever, whether they be American or whether
they be French . . . we (who opposed the Liberal Reform
bill) did not recognize that the rights of man should prevail
in legislation, or that a numerical majority should dictate to
an ancient nation of various political orders and classes.[1]

But of the qualifications of himself and of his friends to
deal with Reform—of that he expressed himself in almost
sanguine terms.[2]—Yet the royal speech at the prorogation
of Parliament on the tenth of August did not touch the
subject of " the Representation of the People."

Would the Conservatives bring in a bill during the 1867
session? That was a question asked and answered by almost every newspaper and magazine in the country during
the autumn and early winter of 1866.[3] Some of them
thought that the people had spoken decisively in the Hyde
Park episode; others began to realize the state of public
mind only with the meetings held rather regularly in the
northern towns. Before the opening of Parliament, however, not only did the newspapers and the magazines agree
as to the necessity for action but the pamphleteer concurred
with their opinions:

There is enough of anxiety to have the question settled; the
timid fear prolonged agitation, and the man of business sees
it hurts trade; the man of pleasure feels the subject a bore, and
all grow weary of it. One party sees an opportunity to snatch
advantages that may not soon occur again; and another fears,
perhaps, that whatever bargain can be made now, there is
small hope of making better hereafter.[4]

[1] The *Times*, July 14, 1866.

[2] *Vide Edinburgh Review*, January, 1867, p. 287.

[3] *Cf. supra*, chapter iii.

[4] William Rathbone, *Soundings in Political Waters* (Edinburgh, 1867),
p. 30.

What did Disraeli and Derby think of the necessity for
action?—Strange as it may seem, it was Derby rather than
Disraeli who first saw that there was a genuine call for Reform.[1] It is true that Disraeli suggested on the twenty-
ninth of July, shortly after the "famous Reform riot," that
a modified form of Gladstone's bill be rushed through Parliament to stop agitation and " dish " Gladstone.   When this
suggestion was not accepted he seems to have been very slow
to perceive the signs of the times.   He was opposed to
Derby's opinion expressed in writing on the sixteenth of
September that the Conservatives would have to deal with
Reform and might proceed by resolutions.   He was impatient with the Queen, who, becoming anxious that the question be settled, wanted to urge Gladstone and Russell, by a
personal appeal, to aid the ministers in finding terms of
agreement.   Even in November he wrote to Derby, giving
as his opinion that any dealing with the Reform question
should take place by resolutions " which, though laying down
a complete scheme, should end in a Royal Commission."
He must have realized that very little could be accomplished
during the coming session by such a method of procedure.
In a letter to Lord Cranborne, dated December 26, he
wrote:[2]

I have throughout been against legislation, and continue so.
Lord Derby, about the time you were here, thought it inevitable, but, as you know, his views are now modified.

It's a difficult affair, but I think we shall pull through; the
Whigs are very unanimous in wishing the question " settled "
—but you and I are not Whigs.

Yet, as his biographer points out, his opinion gradually

[1] Documents for this statement quoted in Monypenny and Buckle, *Life
of Disraeli*, vol. iv, pp. 453-454. The Queen even before Derby seems
to have recognized the need of a real settlement. *Ibid.*, p. 561.

[2] *Ibid.*, p. 463.

changed, for by mid-winter he permitted his Reform speeches to be published and on the third of January wrote to Derby saying that the Reform question was paramount. By this time the ministers of the realm as well as the journalists and magazine writers may be said to have felt the pulse of the country. The financial crisis, the Hyde Park riot, the popular demonstrations in various parts of the country had contributed to produce a feeling of insecurity and distrust. Something must be done.

Hence the royal speech on the opening of Parliament on February 5, 1867, expressed a desire for moderate diliberations on the state of the representation of the people in Parliament.[1] In the comments on the speech Earl Russell, speaking for the Liberals in the House of Lords, promised to consider upon its merits any bill which the Government should propose and said that he would rejoice to support one which should confer the franchise upon a large body of the artisans of the country who were well qualified to possess it. Any delusive attempt to deal with the question he denounced as only tending to foster agitation for manhood suffrage, which few members of either House of Parliament at present were disposed to support. In the House of Commons Gladstone said that the interests of the country demanded a speedy settlement of the question; it was the duty of Parliament to accept an adequate measure.

On the eleventh of February the Chancellor of the Exchequer in telling of the manner of proceeding declared that the question ought not to be an affair of party — that the House of Commons had incurred responsibility in the matter and that, therefore, in order to get the view of the House, proceeding should be by resolution. Procedure by resolutions, as has been mentioned, had been advised by Derby in September as well as at a somewhat later period.[2]

[1] *Annual Register*, 1867, p. 4.
[2] *Vide* Monypenny and Buckle, *Life of Disraeli*, chap. xiii.

Disraeli also had thought this manner of preceeding very desirable.[1] The resolutions, however, as brought forth were so vague as to please no one. Of the thirteen, the first stated that the number of electors for counties and boroughs ought to be increased; the second, that such increase might best be effected both by reducing the value of the qualifying tenement in counties and boroughs and by adding other franchises not dependent on such value; the third, that while it was desirable that a more direct representation should be given to the laboring class, it was contrary to the Constitution of the realm to give to any one class or interest a predominating power over the rest of the community; the fourth, that the occupation franchise in counties and boroughs should be based upon the principle of rating; the fifth, that the principle of plurality of votes would facilitate the settlement of the borough franchise on an extensive basis; the sixth, that it was expedient to revise the existing distribution of seats. Such platitudes caused the press, in a body, to express disappointment.[2] Members of the House, unable to curb their curiosity, questioned the Chancellor of the Exchequer as to the extent of change. In vain did they put their questions, for he refused to promise explanation of the proposed resolutions before the twenty-fifth of February. In fact, Disraeli had good reasons for refusing to give information. He himself was not sure of the measure to be proposed. The cabinet was finding agreement almost impossible.

The disagreement among the cabinet members, in fact, led to the application of the principles of the resolutions (February 25) in a scheme known as the Ten-Minutes bill. The explanation of the origin of the name given to this scheme and the circumstances making necessary its intro-

[1] *Ibid.*, p. 459; resolutions had been of use in 1858 in the India bill.
[2] *Cf.* Malmesbury, *Memoirs of an Ex-Minister*, vol. ii, p. 365.

duction are as follows:[1] General Peel, Secretary of State
for War, had announced on the sixteenth of February his
inability[2] to sanction any reduction of the franchise and
his intended resignation; later at the urging of his colleagues
and the desire of the Queen he agreed to conform to the
general opinion.   The cabinet then decided to bring in a
bill with household suffrage as a basis but with personal payment of rates and a residence qualification, *etc.,* as checks.
The discussion was settled agreeably at the cabinet meeting on Saturday, the twenty-third of February.   " The
Cabinet unanimous for the great plan " wrote Disraeli to
his private secretary.   He had promised to explain the
plans to the House of Commons on Monday, the twenty-
fifth.   But on Sunday Lord Cranborne examined more
closely the scheme, and concluded that its effect would be to
throw the small boroughs almost entirely into the hands of
voters of less than the £10 qualification.   Such proceeding
he did not think to be for the interest of the country.   Carnarvon, Colonial Secretary, agreed with him.   Hence on
Monday morning, Disraeli and Derby had threats of the
resignation of two of their colleagues.   The cabinet, hastily
summoned, could not be brought together much before half-
past one, and by the time the situation was explained, it was
after two.   At two-thirty[3] Derby had to address the party;
at four-thirty Disraeli was to address the House.   Literally,
the cabinet did not have " more than ten minutes in which
to make up their minds " on their course.[4]   They determined,

[1] The Beaconsfield papers, the addresses of Lord Derby to the House
of Lords and of Sir John Pakington to his constituents in his reëlection
speech and various memoirs, give data.

[2] For a full account in the Beaconsfield papers, *vide* Monypenny and
Buckle, vol. iv, pp. 495 *et seq.*

[3] Pakington says at two o'clock.

[4] The speech of Pakington is given in the *Times,* March 14, 1867.

in that brief time, to take up a milder scheme which had
previously been drawn up in an attempt to please Peel.[1]
This was the scheme Disraeli with no enthusiasm explained
on the twenty-fifth.

Rising in a House crowded with many distinguished
strangers, the Chancellor of the Exchequer, in the first
place, took occasion to point out that since 1832 the middle
class had governed the country, but that it now seemed proper that the working class should be granted some of the rights
they desired.   He then proceeded to an explanation of the
proposed resolutions: there were to be some new or fancy
franchises—those in boroughs, who could meet a certain
educational requirement, about 10,000 in number, those who
were depositors in savings banks, about 35,000, those who
had £50 in public funds, about 7,000, and those who paid
20 s. in direct taxes, about 30,000, were to have a vote.
The principle of plurality (*i. e.*, the principle that a person
who had a right to vote for a member of Parliament should
vote in addition under any one new franchise which he might
possess), however, would not be insisted upon.   A £6 rating
in the boroughs, as the occupiers' qualification, would give
130,000 voters and a £20 rating in the counties together with
the fancy franchises would add 187,500 county voters.   In
all there would be an addition of some 400,000 voters.[2]
There was to be a slight redistribution of seats.   If the
House liked the resolutions, as interpreted in this scheme
(the Ten-Minutes " bill "), a moderate bill based on them
would be brought in.

The House immediately showed that it did not like the
resolutions.   Lowe of the Adullamites asked the Government to do away with such ambiguous and abstract resolu-

---

[1] *Vide* Monypenny and Buckle, vol. iv, p. 500.

[2] By the bill of 1866, the total number of new voters would have
been 400,000.

tions and bring in a bill.   He intimated that they were now
playing to keep in office, that they were willing for the House
to " say what you like to us, only, for God's sake leave us
our places."   But " why are they to have the mark of
Cain set upon them, that nobody may kill them?"   Mr.
Bright said that discussion of the resolutions would be a
mere waste of time.   He asked for and in fact promised
to support a measure which should be big enough to do away
with agitation during his life.   Mr. Laing of the Adullamites thought that the scheme did not have finality. He would
prefer household suffrage.   Even friends of the Government were not favorably inclined.[1]   Further consideration
of the resolutions was put off until the twenty-eighth of
February.

In the meantime, two hundred and eighty-nine of the
Liberals met at Gladstone's house on the twenty-sixth and
resolved to support an amendment urging the Government
to bring in a bill.[2]   But Disraeli was ahead of them.   Realizing that his proposals were not pleasing to those who
wanted no Reform and that they were too moderate for
those who did want Reform, the Chancellor of the Exchequer
determined not to go on with the resolutions.   Hence at
the meeting of the House that evening he announced the
Government's intention of bringing in a bill.   He explained
that the chief object of the resolutions had been accomplished in that the proposals had been given a fair and candid
consideration.

Disraeli could not at once bring in a bill.   He had first to
consider whether he should adhere to the Ten-Minutes
" bill " and keep a cabinet intact or whether he should bring
in a bill based on household suffrage—*i, e.,* the scheme

[1] *Cf.* the ministerial explanation of Lord Derby in the House of Lords,
Hansard, vol. clxxxv, pp. 1284-1289.

[2] *Annual Register*, 1867, p. 29, and *News of the World*, March 3, 1867.

originally settled upon, the twenty-third of February—and lose Cranborne, Carnarvon and Peel. Which plan would his own party favor; what attitude would the Radicals take; how would the Liberals manœuver; with what action would the country be pleased?—these were some of the questions over which Disraeli had to ponder.

That a number of his own party stood for the bolder course, Disraeli soon became aware. Henley, one of the Conservative leaders,[1] had declared in favor of household suffrage in 1859,[2] and would support such a plan. Members[3] of the Carlton Club[4] gave their support to the movement. A feeling that the party should settle the question, was growing rapidly among the Tories, Monypenny and Buckle declare,[5] as was also the feeling that " a generous extension to a new and respectable class, the rate-paying householders, might well inure to the benefit of a party which claimed to be national, and dethrone one which was still largely oligarchical." [6] And when, three days before the bill was to be brought in, the more liberal plan was explained at a meeting at Derby's almost all of the 195 present approved. That the Radicals could be counted on for the greater change was also well known to Disraeli. Bright had promised, in the open, to accept the bill which would

[1] Henley was not, however, a minister. For his attitude toward the suffrage question, *vide* Roundell Palmer, 1st Earl of Selborne, *Memorials,* 4 vols. (London, 1896-1898), vol. i, pt. ii, p. 64.

[2] *Hansard,* vol. clii, pp. 1064 *et seq.,* and vol. cliii, p. 1217.

[3] *I. e.,* a majority.

[4] The leading Conservative political club of London, founded in 1832 by the Duke of Wellington.

[5] Vol. iv, p. 508; the *Times,* March 11, 1867, expresses a similar opinion in an editorial.

[6] But Stanley declared in the ministerial explanations of the fifth of March that he could conceive no circumstances which would cause the Government to " reduce the franchise to an almost unlimited extent." *Hansard,* vol. clxxxv, p. 1364.

settle the question for a given period, and promised, in private, to the Chancellor of the Exchequer to do all he could fairly to help a bill through if the right thing were done.[1] Gladstone recognized that Bright would help the Conservatives if they gave him his demands. Writing from Rome to Brand in October, 1866, he said: "We have no claim upon him (Bright), more than the government have on us; and I imagine he will part company the moment he sees his way to more than we would give him."[2] That Gladstone would go further than the Ten-Minutes "bill" and hence get the country back of him had to be taken into consideration by the Conservative leaders. Writing confidentially to Lord Derby on the twenty-sixth of February, Disraeli said:

I dined alone with Walpole, who thinks that our fall now is only an affair of a little time, assuming that, in our present feeble position, all the sections will reunite for a vote against which it would be absurd to appeal to the country. *That,* he thinks, is Gladstone's tactic: to play with us until we are contemptible. As Sir Lawrence Palk says, "Till he comes in with household suffrage, which is getting riper every minute."[3]

Writing to Lord Derby on the twenty-seventh he expressed the opinion that Gladstone would go slowly but by the time the bill was in committee would be "prepared to try five against six" and would probably succeed in passing an amendment calling for such a substitution.[4] That the country would be much better pleased with a larger bill, Disraeli knew from the Reform meetings. And when the larger bill was brought in, the Reform meeting at Birming-

[1] Trevelyan, *Life of Bright*, pp. 370 and 371.
[2] Morley, *Life of Gladstone*, vol. ii, p. 223.
[3] Monypenny and Buckle, vol. iv, p. 504.
[4] *Ibid.*, p. 506.

ham on March 22 accepted " with great satisfaction the
recognition of household suffrage as the basis of the franchise in the boroughs," although, of course, opinion was
against the checks.[1]   That even a number of the Adullamites
thought household suffrage a good basis was made known
to Disraeli.[2]   Hence influenced by various considerations,
he determined to take the bolder course.   The cabinet decided to revert to the plan of the twenty-third of February.
On the fourth of March it became known that Cranborne,
Carnarvon, and Peel had resigned.   Lord Derby expressed
to the House of Lords the regret he felt at parting with three
of his most important and most valued colleagues but promised to put before Parliament in a very short time the
measure which the majority of the cabinet had in the first instance considered the more desirable.   Lord Carnarvon
explained his resignation by declaring that he was unable to
sanction the innovations contemplated by the Government.
On the following day, Peel and Cranborne gave their reasons
for withdrawing.   Lord Cranborne imparted the following
information to the House of Commons: on the sixteenth of
February he first heard of the more nearly radical proposition.   He stated at once that the proposition was inad-
missible and thought that it had been abandoned.   But on
the nineteenth the proposition was revived with the statement of certain statistics, not at that time complete.   When
he had time to investigate the complete figures carefully,
after the cabinet meeting on the twenty-third, he concluded
that though the figures stated in block, had had fair seem-
ing, when looked at in actual working they would operate
in a very large number of boroughs by giving practically
household suffrage.[3]

[1] The *Times*, March 23, 1867.
[2] *Cf.* Monypenny and Buckle, *Life of Disraeli*, vol. iv, p. 508.
[3] *Hansard*, vol. clxxxv, pp. 1348-1349.

Whether or not the ministry was actually to blame for the vacillations of the last few weeks, due, as it is sometimes stated,[1] to a lack of consideration and study upon the bill introduced, it caused the country and the House of Commons to become impatient at its irresolution. " The Conservative leaders were in the position of a stage manager who, when the audience are assembled and the time for raising the curtain had arrived, has not resolved what piece he will put upon the stage." [2] With a ministry in which Cranborne had been succeeded by Northcote, Peel by Pakington, and Carnarvon by the Duke of Buckingham,[3] Disraeli proceeded to bring in the original scheme.

On the eighteenth of March, this Reform bill was explained to a crowded House.[4] The Chancellor of the Exchequer first stated the Government's object, namely, to strengthen the character and functions of that House, and to establish them on a broad and popular basis. But popular privileges and democratic rights were not identical. Nay, they were contradictory; he hoped that it would never be the fate of this country to live under a democracy, and this bill had no tendency in that direction. This bill followed out the plan of Lord Dunkellin's motion of last year, in that rating was made the basis of valuation. Every householder paying his own rates and meeting a two-years residence qualification should be admitted to vote. This provision would admit 237,000 men living in houses under £10.[5]

[1] *Vide* Homersham Cox, *A History of the Reform Bills of 1866 and 1867* (London, 1868), p. 104.

[2] *Ibid.*

[3] He had been Lord President, probably through the influence of Disraeli, whose friend he was.

[4] *Vide Annual Register,* 1867, pp. 40 *et seq.*

[5] Cox, pp. 108 *et seq.*, shows that Disraeli's figures are too high. He concludes that the net number of electors will be fifty per cent less than the gross number of rated occupiers.

Every facility would be given to have the 486,000 unenfranchised householders [1] not paying their own rates (*i. e.*, compound householders), make payment of their own rates, that the right of voting might be obtained. The bill would confer the franchise on payers of 20 *s.* direct taxes. Householders in towns paying this tax would have the dual vote and such a right would add more than 200,000. It also would contain an education franchise which would admit 35,000, and would give votes to the extent of 70,000 to holders of savings banks' deposits and funded property of £50. In all more than 1,000,000 would be added to the borough constituency. In the counties a £15 rating would take the place of the £50 rental. By this reduction 171,000 would be added to county constituencies and the lateral franchises would bring the total to more than 300,000. Cumulative voting and three-cornered constituencies did not meet with the favor of the Government. According to the redistribution scheme, thirty seats would be affected. New boroughs would be given fourteen, counties would be given fifteen, the London University would be given one.

As soon as the Chancellor of the Exchequer had finished explaining his bill, Gladstone rose and in one of his most brilliant speeches attacked the scheme. He objected to the estimates of the Government, declaring that only 140,000 would be admitted by extending the franchise to all who personally paid their rates. Rating would leave the franchise at the direction of the vestry; the practise with regard to compounders varied in almost every parish. hence many anomalies would arise. Moreover, a principle had been set up only to be knocked down again by the use of checks. Additions to the bill would have to be introduced—a lodger

---

[1] Cox, *A History of the Reform Bills*, p. 113, complains that this is not done in the original bill. Studying the statistics carefully he comes to the conclusion that the original bill of 1867 would have added a smaller number of voters in the boroughs than the franchise bill of 1866.

franchise, for instance, was needed. Some of the Conservatives, too, showed opposition. Mr. Beresford Hope spoke on the Conservatives outbidding Liberals in a Liberal market. Lord Cranborne declared that they soon would have household suffrage, for the checks must go. To this statement Disraeli replied that the Government would never introduce household suffrage pure and simple. Leave was then given to bring in the bill and the second reading moved for the twenty-fifth of March. Before that date, a meeting of the Liberals was held at Gladstone's house (March 21) to consider their course toward the bill. Although Gladstone himself was opposed [1] to the second reading he did not think that the general disposition of the meeting would bear him out in his opposition.[2] But if the ministers would not abandon the dual voting and equalise the privileges and facilities of the enfranchised in all cases, however the qualification arose, then the measure, he thought, should not be permitted to go into committee. Bright took about the same attitude as Gladstone.

The debate on the second reading of the bill lasted two nights. Gladstone opened the discussion. Many alterations [3] were needed on this bill:[4] a lodger franchise must be inserted; means to stop traffic in votes must be found; distinction between different classes of ratepaying householders must be abolished;[5] the taxpaying franchise and dual vote

[1] *Vide Blackwood's*, May, 1867, p. 643.

[2] *Cf.* Cox, *A History of the Reform Bills*, p. 133.

[3] *Cf.* Cox, p. 134, who says these alterations were actually made through Gladstone.

[4] *Hansard*, vol. clxxxvi, pp. 472-504.

[5] Gladstone's exact words are: "It seems to me we must do away with the vexatious distinctions that now exist between compound householders in a condition of life and society that are recognized by law as fitting them for the franchise, and those persons of the very same condition not being compound householders."

must be abandoned; the redistribution part must be enlarged,
the county franchise reduced and voting papers [1] dropped.
For himself he was sorry that the £6 rating had been given
up and thought a definite line in rating desirable.   Hardy
attempted to answer Gladstone.   The Government believed
in mutual concession and forbearance, but if, as Mr. Gladstone had said, every leading provision of the bill required
revision, then the division ought to take place at this stage.[2]
After combating the arguments of the Opposition leader,
he repeated that the Government declined to accept Mr.
Gladstone's dictum.   They wished for discussion and would
not show themselves unreasonable, if met in a reasonable
spirit.   They did intend, however, to stand by the main
principle of accompanying a free enfranchisement by judi-
cious limitations.

Mr. Bright, like Mr. Gladstone, found much to criticise
in the bill.   It had the marks upon it of being the product,
not of the friends, but of the enemies of Reform.   It gave
nothing to the workingmen, for to the few enfranchised
there was the set-off of a vote to 200,000 of a higher class.
Hence the dissatisfaction throughout the country would not
cease.   For himself, he would give the warmest support to
a fair and honest measure, but it was impossible to assist a
Government which would not tell frankly what it intended,
what it stood by, what it would get rid of.

To Gladstone and Bright the Chancellor of the Exchequer
replied in one of his noteworthy speeches.[3]   The tone and
manner of Mr. Gladstone had not been pleasing but the
Government was willing to make many changes in the bill.
They had never had the idea that much consideration would
not be required in committee.   They would have to con-

---

[1] Clause 29 dealt with voting papers.

[2] *Hansard*, vol. clxxxvi, pp. 506-507.

[3] *Hansard*, vol. clxxxvi, pp. 642-664.

sider, as Mr. Gladstone had suggested, the lodger franchise. He declared himself to be the father of this suffrage, and thought that the House would adopt it if satisfactory arguments should be urged in its favor in committee. Mr. Gladstone, last year, however, had thought its effect would not be great, and the other objections, he promised, would also receive consideration in committee. He defended the principle of personal rating as against the £5 rating—the rigid line for which Gladstone was contending. The Government was laying down a principle, and had not cared so much about the numbers to be admitted. The dual vote which Mr. Bright had opposed so warmly would not be insisted upon. He again asked the co-operation of the House in passing a bill; the ministry was convinced that their duty was not to desert their posts until this question had been settled; and he entreated the House:

Act with us cordially and candidly, assist us to carry this measure. We will not shrink from deferring to your suggestions so long as they are consistent with the main object of this Bill which we have never concealed from you, and which is to preserve the representative character of the House of Commons. Act with us, I say, cordially and candidly, you will find on our side complete reciprocity of feeling. Pass the Bill, and then change the Ministry if you like.

This "reasonable and attractive appeal" is to Monypenny and Buckle a turning point of the session: "it practically secured the carrying of a Reform bill under the conduct of the Government." [1]

To the *Annual Register* his speech gave the impression that the Government would yield to pressure and would discard obnoxious and impracticable provisions, thus taking

[1] *Vide* Monypenny and Buckle, vol. iv, pp. 526 and 527, where is given additional material upon the effect of this important speech.

a course which would lead " to the ultimate acceptance of the measure." [1]

From this time it was felt that the probabilities of a settlement of the question before the termination of the Session were much increased; the only material doubt that remained depending on the power of the leader of the Conservative party in the House of Commons to carry his supporters along with him in that course of concession for which it was quite evident that he was individually prepared.[2]

The *Spectator,* too, was influenced by the speech and suggested that Disraeli really felt that the country needed a bill, and, having passed it, would resign.[3] Lord Derby was much pleased with the success of Disraeli and wrote to him to that effect.[4] Now, for the first time, he announced to the Queen a sanguine hope of carrying a bill through in the course of the present session. The House of Commons, for its part, passed the second reading without a division.

Before the House went into Committee on the eighth of April disagreement in the Liberal party had tended to strengthen the position of the Conservatives. Gladstone tried to strike at the bill through the compound householder. A large proportion of occupiers under £10, not paying their own rates, but giving their proportion to the landlord who paid the assessment for all the occupiers, would be excluded, according to the terms of the bill, from the franchise. If they did choose to pay the rates directly, their assessment would need to be larger since they or the landlord would have to make up a discount formerly received by him for pay-

---

[1] *Annual Register*, p. 53.

[2] *Ibid.*

[3] The *Spectator*, March 30, 1867.

[4] Monypenny and Buckle, *Life of Disraeli*, vol. iv, p. 527.

ing his tenants' rates in a lump; the increased assessment was referred to by certain members as a fine placed upon the working class.[1]   Gladstone, making this point the issue with the Government, called together a meeting of the Liberals at his house on the fifth of April.   There were present 259 members of the House of Commons.   He proposed an amendment which the party agreed to:

That it be an instruction to the Committee that they have power to alter the law of rating; and to provide that in every Parliamentary borough the occupiers of tenements below a given ratable value be relieved from liability to personal rating, with a view to fix a line for the borough franchise, at and above which all occupiers shall be entered on the rate-book, and shall have equal facilities for the enjoyment of such franchise as a residential occupation franchise.[2]

Gladstone wished in fact to substitute a £5 rating franchise for the borough franchise of the Government but neither the public nor the radical element in the Liberal party agreed with him.[3]   The *Times* saw the strange sight of " an attempt made by the Liberal party to repress the enfranchising zeal of a Conservative Administration." [4]   The London Working Men's Association at its (adjourned) annual meeting expressed its strong opposition to the drawing of any arbitrary line of rating—whether £5 or any other sum —below which householders should not be admitted to the franchise, and suggested that Gladstone devote his energies to obtaining a reduction in the residential term of qualification, and the insertion of a lodger franchise.[5]   The dis-

---

[1]Cox, *A History of the Reform Bills of 1866 and 1867*, pp. 113-116.

[2]*Annual Register,* 1867, p. 55.

[3]*Vide* the *Times*, April 6, 1867.

[4]*Ibid.*

[5] The *Times*, April 17, 1867.

satisfied Liberals held a meeting in the Tea-room of the
House of Commons and resolved not to support the amendment, and hence the motion had to be withdrawn.[1] In Sir
Robert Phillimore's Journal under the date of April 9 is
found the following summary of the situation:[2] " Entire
collapse of Gladstone's attack on government yesterday.
Tea-room schism of Liberal members, including the House
of Commons Russell. Disraeli's insolent triumph." This
first breakdown of the Opposition party was justly regarded
by the *Annual Register* " as symptomatic of the disunion
which would render their efforts to dictate the terms of the
bill unavailing." Certain it is that the troubles of the
Liberal leaders contributed not a little to give strength and
confidence to the ministers.[3]

   After considerable debating by various members upon the
bill itself and the actions of the Government, the House
went into committee. And now, once again, Gladstone determined to test the strength of his opponents and proposed an amendment to the effect that the direct and personal
payment of rates by the householder should not be essential
for obtaining the franchise. But the provision was to
apply only to those whose premises were of the yearly value
of £5.[4] Gladstone himself defended his position by saying
that the rates of two-thirds of the houses under £10 value
were compounded for, therefore the working class would
still be without the vote and hence would continue to agitate,
and that too great expenditures of money and of time would
baffle any attempts made by them to pay their own rates.
But the motion, standing as it did " for a hard and fast line,"

[1] *Annals of Our Time*, April 8. There were forty or fifty Liberal
members who dissented from Gladstone's policy.

[2] Quoted from Morley, *Life of Gladstone*, vol. ii, p. 232.

[3] *Annual Register*, 1867, p. 56.

[4] *Cf. Annals of Our Time*, April 11, 1867.

was regarded as being reactionary. Lord Cranborne, for instance, the Conservative who had withdrawn from a too liberal Conservative cabinet, announced that he would support Gladstone. Many of the Liberals, however, refused to follow their leader and when the division was taken, the Government was found to have triumphed by 310 to 289. " The supporters of the Government were found upon the Opposition benches; their opponents sat beside and behind them." [1]   The Government was well pleased with the result; the country gentlemen rushed forward to shake hands with the leader who was said to have betrayed them; " Dizzy " proudly went home to his wife.[2]   Gladstone was so discouraged by this " smash " that it was rumored that he would give up the leadership of the Opposition.

But when the House came together after Easter, Gladstone still remained " at the service of his party." He was backed, too, by Bright who, speaking at Birmingham during the vacation, had declared that the bill had fallen into the hands of enemies by the defeat of the amendment and that the Tories were using the measure for Tory purposes.[3]   Yet Gladstone announced that for the present he would not lead in amending.

After the House had resumed its discussions of the bill in committee on May 2, one [4] of the Radicals proposed a twelve-months instead of the two-years residence requirement. Sir John Pakington, for the Government, said that the amendment could not be adopted. If two years is a proper time, why not apply it to a £10 householder, came the question, and on the division the Government lost by a majority

---

[1] The *Times*, April 13, 1867.   Bright spoke and voted with Gladstone.

[2] T. E. Kebbel, *Lord Beaconsfield and Other Tory Memories* (New York, 1907), pp. 39 and 40.

[3] The *Times*, April 23, 1867.

[4] Mr. Ayrton.

of eighty-one. " They promptly put in practice the readiness
to defer to the opinion of the House which they had repeatedly announced." [1]   In fact, as Malmesbury wrote,[2] the
laissez-aller system was being followed by the Government.
They were trying to make the best they could of the situation, but were constantly yielding something. In this particular case, moreover, Disraeli may have been influenced by
the attitude of the workingmen. At least one deputation [3]
had told him that the bill was good except for the residence
provision. And furthermore, in order to pass *a* bill,[4] the
great Conservative leader would be willing to stretch such
a point as this.

Next it was moved to procure the enfranchisement of
lodgers. The amendment, however, was withdrawn when
the Government promised to embody the lodger franchise
in their bill: lodgings of a clear yearly value, if let un-
furnished, of £10 or upwards plus one year residence became the basis of the qualification.

Then came up again the question of the " compound
householder." Mr. Hibbert, a Liberal, thought that householders under £10 should come in on the same terms as the
compound householders at and above that amount, namely,
by simply paying the amount of composition and not the
full rate, and moved an amendment to that effect. Gladstone, Bright, John Staurt Mill, all spoke for this plan and
against Disraeli's proposal that " a compound occupier claiming to be registered as a voter should be rated as an ordinary
occupier " (*i. e.,* should pay the full rate).[5] Disraeli in the

[1] Monypenny and Buckle, vol. iv, p. 537.

[2] Malmesbury, *Memoirs of an Ex-Minister*, vol. ii, pp. 369-370.

[3] *Vide* the *Times*, May 1, 1867.

[4] *Cf.* comments in Monypenny and Buckle, vol. iv, p. 536, on Stanley's
note to Disraeli.

[5] *Cf.* Cox, *A History of the Reform Bills*, p. 178.

test was able to defeat Hibbert's amendment by a vote of 256 to 322.[1]

But at this point the Chancellor of the Exchequer did the surprising thing. Mr. Hodgkinson, a Liberal, had moved to abolish composition altogether. All those rated for the poor would be given the franchise. In his opposition to the Government, Gladstone defended the motion. If the Reform question was to be settled, if the agitation was to be stopped, such a course must be taken. And then Disraeli spoke! The amendment would really carry out the principle of the bill; the Government having had intentions of using a similar clause earlier had struck it out lest they encumber the ship so much as to imperil the voyage. Therefore, he would offer no opposition to the provision, and if the amendment were withdrawn he would undertake to carry out its object. There was a sensation in the House. Gladstone, who had anticipated the defeat of the motion by a majority of a hundred, wrote long afterwards:

Never have I undergone a stranger emotion of surprise than when, as I was entering the House, our whip met me and stated that Disraeli was about to support Hodgkinson's motion. But so it was, and the proposition was adopted without disturbance, as if it had been an affair of trivial importance.[2]

Bright, we are told,[3] "noted the victory of his cause very quietly:—'Government accepted our demands on Borough Franchise.'" Others of the Radicals showed their great joy at the turn events had taken. Mr. Forster, for instance, was found dancing down the lobby.[4] In the House he

[1] Consult Cox, pp. 179 and 180, on Disraeli's tactics.

[2] Morley, *Life of Gladstone,* vol. ii, pp. 225 and 226.

[3] Trevelyan, *Life of John Bright,* p. 377.

[4] All this happened on the seventeenth of May.

observed that there was a hope of settling the borough franchise in a way that would be satisfactory to the country.
The conservative wing of the Liberals was very bitter. Mr.
Lowe was able to give his usual tirade against the ignorance
and what not of the commonalty; the restrictions had now
been swept away; the Chancellor of the Exchequer had not
shown his supporters his whole plan at once, for they would
have been frightened at it. Among the Conservatives there
was much surprise. Disraeli had made his decision without the advice even of his chief counselor, Gathorne Hardy,
and in a letter to him explains that he had taken his position
because [1] the public mind was ready for the change, because
the Liberals had started the move and would have been able
to make a *coup*,[2] because, without receding from his position and principle of a rating and residential franchise, he
had taken a step " which would destroy the present agitation and extinguish Gladstone and Company." Hardy supported his chief. Later he wrote: " We had so far stepped
in that we could not, on such a point, draw back, but it was
a new proof that a great measure ought not to be in the
hand of a minority, but with those who can mould and resist the moulding of others." [3] In the House, Mr. Henley,
of the Conservatives, backed up the Government: he considered this proposal the most conservative that could be
made, considering how often the question had been mooted
in the House, and how much agitation had been going on out
of doors. Lord Cranborne, on the other hand, was opposed
to such startling changes.

And by accepting the amendment Disraeli so materially

[1] *Vide* letter to Hardy in Monypenny and Buckle, vol. iv, pp. 540-541.

[2] Contrast what Gladstone and Disraeli have to say on this point:
Gladstone expected the amendment to fail; Disraeli says that it would
have carried.

[3] Gathorne Hardy, *A Memoir*, 2 vols. (London, 1910), vol. i, pp. 208-210.

altered the character of the bill that for all practical purposes it became a new measure.[1] All occupiers of tenements, not disqualified by the receipt of parochial relief, change of residence and certain other conditions which affected all classes of electors, were placed upon the electoral lists. Cox estimated that over 300,000 borough voters were added as the effect of Mr. Hodgkinson's amendment.[2] The original bill added over 100,000 voters; so that excluding lodgers, there would be a total increase of over 400,000. " It thus appears that the effect of the momentous amendment was to extend the franchise *almost four times as much as was originally contemplated.*" Inasmuch as there were less than 500,000 borough electors according to the electoral returns of 1865-1866, it follows that the effect of the amendment was nearly to double the borough constituency. The large addition in the number of voters of the working class put England well on the way to democracy.

The question of the county franchise had then to be taken up. By the original clause the occupation franchise had been fixed at a £15 rateable value. Locke King, a Liberal, wished to substitute a £10 rating and when Disraeli showed a willingness to compromise on the £12 line, Gladstone recommended the withdrawal of King's motion.[3]

The clauses on " the fancy franchises " were soon dealt with. One of the members pointed out that since they had

---

[1] Cox, *History of the Reform Bills*, pp. 201 *et seq.*

[2] The statistics of Disraeli and Cox, it will be noted, are by no means identical; the borough voters numbered 488,920 in 1865 (*Accounts and Papers,* 1866, [3626] lvii, 215) ; 1,210,001 in 1868 (*Accounts and Papers,* 1877, [432] lxviii, 318).

[3] After much discussion it was agreed that a man might be a voter for a county, who had an estate in copyhold, or any other tenure, for his life, of the clear yearly value of £5, or was the holder of a lease, for not less than sixty years originally, of lands or tenements of the clear yearly value of £5.

got rid of the dual vote, had established a lodger franchise, and had based the borough franchise on household suffrage, these fancy franchises were entirely unnecessary.[1]   Hence the educational franchise, now supported by Mr. Fawcett alone, was given up, the clause giving the franchise to those who had certain sums in the savings banks or in the public funds, was struck out after a slight protest from Disraeli, and the dual vote was done away with.   That part of the Reform question which related to the franchise and which had caused trouble for so many ministries had finally been completed.

Redistribution now became the subject of discussion. Mr. Laing brought forth a scheme much more extensive than that proposed by the Government.   A population of 10,000 rather than of 7,000 as the Government had fixed it, was to be the minimum for returning two members by any borough.   He also further proposed the grouping of some of the smaller boroughs.   A small addition should be made to the members in the House in order to give Scotland the number of representatives it deserved.[2]   Six towns with a population of 150,000 each, should have their representatives increased from two to three, and four towns with a population exceeding 50,000 which now had one member, should have two members.   Although Disraeli spoke against the proposal,[3] so many of the Conservatives were for it, when Laing gave way on the point of grouping, that it was carried in the test.   And after the Whitsuntide recess, the Chancellor of the Exchequer on the thirteenth of June, gave announcement of the propositions which the Government had to make.   Every borough with a population less than

---

[1] Sir R. Palmer, *Hansard*, vol. clxxxvii, p. 1236.

[2] Mr. Laing represented Wick Burghs, Scotland.

[3] *Vide* Monypenny and Buckle, vol. iv, p. 544, for evidence that Disraeli really wanted this measure passed, although he spoke against it.

10,000 which returned two members, should now return one.
This action together with the disfranchisement of several
corrupt boroughs would give 45 seats for reappropriation.
Of these, nineteen were to be given to boroughs, one to the
University of London and twenty-five to counties.   Mr.
Laing was disappointed that additional representation had
not been given to six or seven large towns and took occasion
to move that additional members be given to them.   Mr.
Gladstone and Mr. Baines stood for the amendment.
Disraeli strongly opposed it.   On the division it was rejected by 247 to 239.   Later, however, the committee did
grant a third member to Birmingham, Manchester, Liverpool, and Leeds, and consequently the number of new
boroughs was correspondingly limited.[1]

Other amendments dealing with various topics were presented at different times.   A motion " of rather singular
character " made by John Stuart Mill, was a proposal to
enable women to vote.   Mill, declaring that taxation and representation should co-exist, first placed this question
seriously before Parliament, but many of his colleagues gave
a jocular character to the discussion.[2]   On the test the
motion was negatived 196 to 73, and although the subject
was brought up often after 1870 it was not favorably acted
upon in the nineteenth century.

A clause of the bill authorizing the use of voting papers
in lieu of personal voting at the polls was attacked especially
by some of the Liberals.   The ballot, demanded by the
Radicals in 1832 and by the Chartists, was still regarded
with hostile eyes by the majority of the official class.   The

[1] Thomas Chisholm Anstey, *Notes upon the Representation of the
People Act, 1867* (London, 1867), conveniently gives the schedules, the
Act of 1867 together with the original bill, and many returns relating
to the franchise and redistribution.

[2] *Annual Register*, 1867, p. 72.

Reform League did not have influence enough to change that majority into a minority. Disraeli himself spoke for the clause but admitted that " there was much to be said on both sides."   The clause was discarded and when the House of Lords added to the bill a motion that " any voter for a county or borough may, in compliance with the provisions hereinafter contained, give his vote by a voting paper instead of personally," the addition was rejected by the Com- mons.[1]

Representation of minorities was another subject on which proposals were made.   Mr. Lowe moved that at any contested election for a county or a borough every voter should be entitled to a number of votes equal to the number of vacant seats, and might give all such votes to one candidate or to many, as he liked.   The minority would thus get representation.   The proposition was not well received in the House of Commons.   Disliked by Gladstone, Bright, and Disraeli, it was defeated by a vote of 314 to 173.   In the House of Lords, however, a minority provision moved by Lord Cairns—that at a contested election for any county or borough represented by three members, no person should vote for more than two candidates[2]—was carried by a majority of 91 and was accepted in the House of Commons by a majority of 49.   The clause had the general effect of causing the election of a member from the party unrepresented heretofore.   In some places, however, it was seen that a careful distribution of votes in such a way that each of the three candidates from the dominant party would receive only the number strictly necessary to obtain the requisite majority at the poll, led to the selection of the three members and the exclusion of any representative from the

[1] For the future of the ballot *vide* chap. vi.

[2] In the City of London which had four seats, an elector was to vote for only three candidates.

minority. The organization which obtained the desired
results by controlling the activity of the electors came to be
known as the Caucus and was an important development in
party electoral machinery.[1] On the whole, the minority provision was not so successful that advocates of Hare's
scheme[2] did not desire change.

After a discussion of the schedules specifying the
boroughs and counties to be affected by the increase or
decrease of members, or the boon of enfranchisement, had
been finished, the bill finally emerged from the committee
" in its amended shape on the ninth of July; when,
amidst considerable cheering, the Preamble, which is always

[1] A. Lawrence Lowell, *The Government of England*, 2 vols. (New
York, 1917, new edition), vol. i, pp. 483 *et seq.*, and M. Ostrogorski,
Democracy and the Organization of Political Parties, 2 vols. (New York,
1902), vol. i, pp. 161 *et seq.*

[2] Thomas Hare (1806-91) was a political reformer who wanted to
secure proportional representation of all classes including minorities.
His views were set forth in his *Treatise on the Election of Representatives, Parliamentary and Municipal* (1st edition, 1859). Much was
written for this system and John Stuart Mill presented the plan in
1867 in an amendment for the representation of minorities. According to
Mill's explanation in the House of Commons votes should be received
in every locality for others than the local candidates, and if there were
found in the whole kingdom other electors, in the proper number, who
fixed their choice on the same person, that person should be declared duly
elected. The number of votes needed to elect would, of course, depend on
the number of members of the House compared with the total number
of electors in the country. Lest a few popular names should get
nearly all the votes and many voters, therefore, lose in reality their
votes, a second name was to be put on the voting paper for whom the
vote could be used if it was not required by the candidate who stood
first. In case this second candidate also should not need the vote, the
voter might add a third, *etc.* The mode of sorting the voting papers
is discussed in detail in Hare's book. Mill pointed out that the scheme
would do away with the danger of having some classes in the nation
swamped by other classes (a fact which would please conservative
persons) and would permit everybody to be represented (a fact pleasing
to democrats). *Cf. Hansard*, vol. clxxxvii, pp. 1347 *et seq.*

considered last, was agreed to, and the bill was ordered to be reported to the House." [1]

Of the amendments now presented, none were of importance.[2]   Finally on the fifteenth of July the motion was made to read the Reform bill a third time.   A last opportunity was presented for a review of the measure itself or of its passage, and several of the leading members took advantage of that opportunity.   Viscount Cranborne, leading seceder from the cabinet, cried out that all the precautions, guaranties, and securities of the second reading had disappeared. "If it be a Conservative triumph," said he, "to have introduced a Bill guarded with precautions and securities, and to have abandoned every one of those precautions and securities at the bidding of your opponents, then in the whole course of your annals I will venture to say the Conservative party has won no triumph so signal as this." [3]   The result of the bill would be that 800,000 would be added as voters and that there would be 1,000,000 workingmen as against 500,000 of the other classes.   But—he was the "champion of a forlorn cause."

And Mr. Lowe also complained—"We are about, on this momentous occasion, to enter upon a new era, when the bag which holds the winds will be untied, and we shall be surrounded by a perpetual whirl of change, alteration, innovation, and revolution." [4]   To him the principle of the bill was the principle of numbers as against wealth and intellect. England now must necessarily turn her attention to the education of the masses.   But another of the Adullamites, Lord Elcho, quite gladly accepted the bill as a satisfactory

[1] *Annual Register*, 1867, p. 87.

[2] One change, however, allowed a holder of certain offices to change to another without vacating his seat.

[3] *Hansard*, vol. clxxxviii (July 15), pp. 1526-1539.

[4] *Hansard*, vol. clxxxviii, p. 1540.

settlement; to go down at once to household suffrage was much safer than to admit merely a portion of the working classes.

Mr. Bright, too, was not sorry that the House had agreed to the bill although it had gone farther than he had expected it to go.   He had always contended, he said, that household suffrage was the best permanent foundation for the franchise even when he had been ready to accept as compromises, propositions falling short of his own views.

The Chancellor of the Exchequer, giving the last of the important speeches, declared that the Government had acted in a consistent manner in every respect; that they had followed out a suggestion of 1859 in basing the borough franchise on household suffrage; that they had never been in agreement with those who advocated the admission of a certain portion of the working classes to serve as a sort of Praetorian guard to the middle classes; that they had done well in offering the resolutions inasmuch as the House had finally accepted the policy on which they were based; that the securities had not been yielded to Mr. Gladstone's imperious dictations but more to the wishes of the Conservative party.   In support of the latter statement he said that out of twenty-six divisions in committee, Gladstone had voted in eighteen against the Government.[1]   He acknowledged the assistance and co-operation of the House and concluded by asserting that he did not believe the country to be in danger.   " I think England is safe " he declared, " in something much more precious than her accumulated capital—her accumulated experience; she is safe in her national character, in her fame, in the tradition of a thousand years, and in that glorious future which I believe awaits her." [2]   The motion was then made and the question

---

[1] Disraeli fails to go into detail in this matter.

[2] *Hansard*, vol. clxxxviii, pp. 1599-1614.

proposed " that the Bill be now read the third time."
" There was a loud and general cry of ' Aye,' " says the
Annual Register, " and only one solitary voice uttered ' No.'
Whereupon the further question ' That the bill do pass ' was
declared, amidst considerable cheering, to be carried." [1]

The House of Lords now had the opportunity to express its opinions on Reform.   Gladstone, writing years
after the passage of the Reform bill of 1867 had become an
event of the past, was of the belief that the Government
counted on the Lords blocking their measure or at least putting in important restrictions on the granting of the franchise.[2]   Public opinion, he thought, made it impossible, however, for the Lords to pursue such a course.   And whether
or not Gladstone's belief was the correct one, the historian of
to-day may assume without much doubt that the upper
House would have been unwilling to accept such a radical
measure without having pressure put upon it, had the
measure come from the hands of the Liberals.[3]   As it was,
there were times during the debates when opposition became strong.   However, Lord Derby got the House fairly
well in hand at the beginning by summoning to a meeting at
his official residence those members whom he regarded as the
supporters of his administration.   There he asked that
the measure should be passed as speedily as possible and
with as few alterations as possible.   Those present agreed
to this request. Many of them may have thought in terms of
their chief when he so well defended the bill with that simple
argument attributed to him: " Don't you see how it has
dished the Whigs? " [4]

[1] *Annual Register,* 1867, p. 91.

[2] *Cf.* Morley, *Life of Gladstone,* vol. ii, p. 226; but *vide* also Monypenny
and Buckle, vol. iv, pp. 550-551.

[3] *Vide* Trevelyan, *Life of John Bright,* p. 379.

[4] *Cf.* Granville's speech in *Hansard,* vol. clxxxviii, pp. 1856-1863, and
also the *Spectator,* August 10, 1867.

In the discussions of the bill and the amendments in the House of Lords the reader will find few arguments which had not been given previously in the House of Commons. A few amendments were adopted; the two of importance dealt with the use of voting papers and the representation of minorities.[1]   On the whole, the Earl of Derby was much pleased with the " spirit of impartiality and consideration " in whic.. the House dealt with the measure.   He acknowledged the experimental character of the bill:

No doubt we are making a great experiment and " taking a leap in the dark," [2] but I have the greatest confidence in the sound sense of my fellow countrymen; and I entertain a strong hope that the extended franchise which we are now conferring upon them will be the means of placing the institutions of this country on a firmer basis, and that the passing of this measure will tend to increase the loyalty and contentment of a great portion of Her Majesty's subjects.[3]

The bill was passed and sent to the Commons.   Disraeli recommended that the amendments of the Lords be adopted. In spite of the opposition of Bright and Gladstone the " restricted vote " proposal as is noted above, was carried; the other amendment, however, was not passed.   The House of Lords accepted the decision of the Commons and on the fifteenth of August " the bill for Amending the Representation of the People " received the royal assent.[4]

---

[1] A clause enacting that Parliament should not henceforth be dissolved on the demise of the Crown, was added by the Lords.

[2] Spencer Walpole in his *History of Twenty-five Years*, vol. ii, p. 193, discusses the origin of this phrase, showing that Cranborne had used it previously in 1867, and that Disraeli had used it in 1866. I find, however, the same expression used in *Vivian Grey* (London, 1881, original edition in 1826-27), p. 87: Grey makes a " leap in the dark" to save all.

[3] *Hansard*, vol. clxxxix, pp. 951-952.

[4] The 30 and 31 Vict., c. 102.

At this point the reader who has followed the account of
the passing of the Reform bill of 1867 may well ask the
questions: "Whose bill, after all, is it?" "Does the
credit for the measure belong to Gladstone as many have
asserted; to Bright as many likewise have asserted; or to
Disraeli?" "And whether or not it is the work of Disraeli,
why did he and the Conservatives pass such a radical
measure, or allow such a measure to pass?"

Was Gladstone the one who changed a measure which at
its introduction was very conservative to a piece of radical
legislation?   Such, indeed, has been the assertion of many
of his contemporaries and of many of the historians.   Viscount Cranborne, one of the seceders from the Government,
declared before the third reading, that the bill was the work
of Gladstone:

My right honorable and gallant Friend near me (General Peel)
said that this was a compound Bill, and that he did not know
to whose authorship it was due.   I cannot help thinking that if
he had referred to the record I have just mentioned—if he had
taken the original scheme of the Government, and had corrected it by the demands of the right honorable Gentleman, the
Member for South Lancashire (Gladstone), he would have
with tolerable exactness the Bill as it now stands.   I mention
this because I see with enormous astonishment that the passing of this Bill is spoken of as a Conservative triumph.   Now,
it is desirable that the paternity of all the strange objects that
come into the world should be properly established; and I
wish to know whether this Bill, as is generally supposed, is
exclusively the offspring of the Government, or whether the
right honorable Gentleman, the Member for South Lancashire,
has not had something to do with it?   If he has, it follows as
an indisputable axiom that it cannot be a Conservative triumph.
Now, I heard the demands which the right honorable Gentleman, the Member for South Lancashire, made on the second
reading of the Bill. . . . They are ten in number: — First, he

demanded the lodger franchise. Well, the lodger franchise has been given. Secondly, and this is the only doubtful one, provisions to prevent traffic in votes. . . The right honorable Gentleman next demanded the abolition of obnoxious distinctions between compounders and non-compounders. Not only have those obnoxious distinctions been abolished, but all distinctions whatever have disappeared. The fourth demand of the right honorable Gentleman was that the taxing franchise should be omitted. It has been omitted. Fifthly, that the dual vote should be omitted. It has been omitted. Sixthly, that the re-distribution of seats must be considerably enlarged. It has been enlarged full fifty per cent. Seventhly, that the county franchise must be reduced. It has been reduced to something like the point at which it stood in the proposal of last year. Eighthly, that the voting papers must be omitted. To my extreme regret, the voting papers have been omitted. The last two demands were that the educational and savings banks' franchises should be omitted. These two franchises have been omitted. . . . No man in this House of Commons can remember a Government who have introduced a Bill of this importance, and who have yielded in Committee Amendments so vitally altering the whole constitution and principle of the Bill as has been done in the present instance.[1]

Lord Elcho on the same evening decided to do as others had been doing—to devote some time " to personal explanations and to Parliamentary condolences and prophecies." He as an Adullamite was not sorry that the question was being settled but he blamed Gladstone for sweeping away the securities.[2]

If we turn from the speeches of the members of Parliament to the writings of the historians of the period we again find it said that the bill was the work of Gladstone. Cox, in the *Whig and Tory Administrations*, writes:

[1] *Hansard*, vol. clxxxviii (July 15), pp. 1526-29.
[2] *Hansard*, vol. clxxxviii, pp. 1574-1576.

The allegation that the Reform Act of 1867 is mainly or substantially the work of the Conservative Government, is one
of the most impudent falsifications of history that was ever
attempted. Neither in form, nor in substance, does the statute
actually passed agree with the measure introduced by Mr. Disraeli.   The Act comprises sixty-one sections, and of them
there are but four (1, 12, 49, 54) which are the work of the
Conservative Ministry.[1]

In *The Reform Bills of* 1866 *and* 1867, Cox states that
Gladstone had early enumerated ten principal defects in the
bill and that an amendment " for every one . . . . except
the second (which involved a proposal that occupiers of
houses below some specified value should be excluded from
the suffrage), has been carried out in the Reform Act now
passed." [2]

Sir Spencer Walpole, in his *History of Twenty-five Years*,
gives this conclusion:

The fact, however, is that, if the first edition of the Reform
Bill of 1867 was the work of Lord Derby, Mr. Disraeli, and
the Conservative Cabinet, the last edition of the measure was
the work of Mr. Gladstone. Mr. Gladstone had, no doubt,
many difficulties to encounter. His party was disorganised;
he was himself regarded by some of his followers with distrust. And cave and tea-room formed convenient refuges for
the discontented to frequent. Yet Mr. Gladstone, in this memorable Session, succeeded in making all the alterations in the
Bill which he declared in the debate on the second reading to
be necessary. And if, therefore, to Mr. Disraeli attaches the
blame of surrendering, one after another, the securities and
safeguards, on which he professed that he relied, to Mr.
Gladstone belongs the credit of carrying the changes which he

[1] Homersham Cox, *Whig and Tory Administrations* (London, 1868),
p. 51.
[2] Cox, *A History of the Reform Bills of 1866 and 1867*, pp. 134-135.

pronounced to be indispensable for the conversion of a bad Bill into a good one.[1]

In spite of the foregoing statements the person who follows the course of the Reform bill is apt to have a suspicion that credit for the bill does not belong to Gladstone.   Whatever influence he may have had on some of the amendments, on the point of making the bill a *democratic measure* Gladstone was not the leader.   Never in his life was he more surprised than when he found that Disraeli had accepted Hodgkinson's amendment to do away with the compound householder,[2] although he stood for that amendment himself, doubtless for political reasons.   He did not want manhood or household suffrage but put forth a great struggle to get a £5 rating as the basis of the franchise.   In a letter to William Horsfall on August 8, 1866, he wrote:[3]

Sir—In reply to your letter of the 6th, I beg respectfully to express my desire that my views respecting Reform in Parliament should be gathered from my own acts, and from my language, in which they have been amply stated.   I do not agree in the demand either for manhood or for household suffrage; while I own with regret that the conduct of the opponents of the Government measure of this year has done much to encourage that demand, which, but for such opposition, would scarcely have been heard of.   You are at liberty to make such use of this letter as you may think fit, and I remain, Sir, your very humble servant.—W. E. Gladstone.

And for his views[4] toward the end of the session of the

[1] Walpole, *History of Twenty-five Years*, vol. ii, p. 196.

[2] *Cf. supra*, p. 210.

[3] To be found in the *Times*, August 11, 1866.

[4] In reply to a deputation of the National Reform Union Gladstone said that the House of Commons was inveigled and tripped into household suffrage when probably not twenty members were in favor of it.   *Cf. News of the World*, May 19, 1867.

following year, the *Fortnightly Review*[1] asserted with a
degree of certainty that he had not apparently swerved a
hair's breath from his last year's views when he never concealed his aversion to household suffrage as the basis of the
franchise.

As a matter of fact, Gladstone's attitude toward the £5
rating caused him some unpopularity among members of
the Reform League.   At the meetings protests[2] were made
against the half-way measure which the Liberals seemed
apt to accept, and Gladstone himself was named[3] by the
London Working Men's Association as one who had attempted to draw an arbitrary line of rating below which
householders should not be admitted to the franchise, and
by a speaker[4] at a Reform meeting as a member of the
Manchester party who had been trying to do all he could
to trip up the Government in order to make the bill less
extensive.   It seems to be a myth, then,—this tradition of
Gladstone as the author of the Reform Bill of 1867.[5]

But what about John Bright and the bill?   The *North*

---

[1] *Fortnightly Review*, vol. vii (June 1, 1867), pp. 755 and 756.

[2] *Cf.* meeting of February 27 (the *Times*, February 28), of March 6,
of the London Working Men's Association at St. Martin's Hall (April
16), *etc.*

[3] The *Times*, April 17, 1867.

[4] Mr. Lucraft; *vide* the *Times*, July 4, 1867.

[5] As a matter of fact, Gladstone himself, toward the middle of the
session, gave the following opinion of his power, when he wrote in
reply to Mr. Crawford, one of the members for the City, as to whether
he intended to persevere in moving the different amendments on the
Reform bill of which he had given notice: " The country can hardly
fail now to be aware that those gentlemen of Liberal opinions whose
convictions allow them to act unitedly upon this question, are not a
majority, but a minority of the existing House of Commons, and that
they have not the power they were supposed to possess of limiting or
directing the action of the Administration, or of shaping the provisions
of the Reform Bill." *Cf. Annals of Our Time*, April 18, 1867.

British Review, for instance, declared that the main outline and the chief provision of the scheme were clearly Mr. Bright's.[1] In the House of Commons Mr. Osborne[2] on the third reading said:

We have heard something tonight about the paternity of this Bill. There is no doubt who is its father. The Chancellor of the Exchequer is no doubt its putative father, but he is not the real father. This offspring is a stolen child; the right honorable Gentleman has stolen it, and then, as the *School for Scandal* has it, he has treated it as the gipsies do stolen children,—he has disfigured it to make it pass for his own. But the real author of this Bill is an honorable Gentleman who sits below me—the honorable Member for Birmingham. I have got a draught of his Bill of 1858, and in that Bill there is this mischievous proposal of household suffrage based upon rating. It is the honorable Gentleman who is the real father of it—he ought to be a right honorable Gentleman and be sitting cheek by jowl with the putative father of the Bill, and why he is not, I do not know. It is all very well to speak of this as a Conservative measure. Why, Sir, the hands that brought in the Bill are the hands of Lord Derby, but the voice was the voice of John Bright. Now, that must be a great consolation to all the Gentlemen on those Benches who for years have been denouncing the honorable Member for Birmingham, and accusing him of Americanizing our institutions—for "Americanizing " was the word. The right honorable Gentleman on the Treasury Bench and his Colleagues are Americanizers, for they share with the honorable Member for Birmingham in the merit of the measure; and the Conservative party are nothing more than votaries and supporters of the honorable Member for Birmingham.[3]

Trevelyan in his *Life of John Bright* points out that Bright

[1] *North British Review*, September, 1867, p. 223.
[2] An Independent Liberal.
[3] *Hansard*, vol. clxxxviii, p. 1583.

in 1858 and 1859 made proposals which with very slight and quite immaterial changes, became the basis of the enfranchising act passed nine years later;[1] that in 1867 Bright sent Disraeli a memorandum suggesting the terms of the bill as passed;[2] that Bright himself declared he was becoming an authority with the Tory party.[3]

To the person who tries to sum up the importance of the various leaders in the Reform discussion, Bright, at least in one respect. does stand out as an important personage.   He had great influence in keeping up the popular agitation. Friends and enemies alike acknowledged this.[4]   Now it was this popular agitation which caused the Conservatives to bring in a bill and apparently had somewhat to do with the terms of that bill.   But when the reader goes through the account of the passing of the bill itself, he will note that Bright all too often kept to his leader Gladstone rather than to the other leading Radicals or to Disraeli.   He spoke for the hard and fast line, not the £5 line of Gladstone. but one at £4 or £3, and even though, as Trevelyan says,[5] he was the prime mover of the Hodgkinson amendment, he had no idea that it would pass.   Bright followed Gladstone so closely as a matter of fact that he fell under the same popular disfavor at times as did Gladstone.[6]

And what can be said for Disraeli?   His own account of the passage of the bill may be read in a speech delivered in Edinburgh at a banquet given in the Corn Exchange by twelve hundred of the leading members of the Conservative

[1] Trevelyan, *Life of John Bright*, p. 271.

[2] *Ibid.*, pp. 371-372.

[3] *Ibid.*, p. 372, on the fourth of March.

[4] *Cf.* the estimate of Bright's work in this respect in T. Wemyss Reid, *Life of the Right Honorable W. E. Forster*, vol. i, pp. 392-396.

[5] Trevelyan, *Life of John Bright*, p. 376.

[6] *Vide supra*, p. 124.

party in Scotland.[1]—Having decided that the Conservatives
had a right to deal with Reform and feeling that they
ought to deal with it, he had for a considerable period
endeavored continuously to lay down the principles upon
which a measure of Parliamentary Reform ought to be
founded.   He and those of his opinions had to prepare the
mind of the country—" to educate, if it be not arrogant to
use such a phrase '"—to educate his party on this subject of
Reform.   These were the points which he tried to impress
upon the conscience and conviction of the country: first that
the measure be a complete and comprehensive one, lest they
be seduced into dealing with the question in detail.   " And
for this simple reason, that if you deal with it in detail you
may indeed establish a democratic constitution." [2]   In the
second place, no proposal for grouping boroughs could be
sanctioned,[3] and in the third place, there should be a *bona
fide* boundary commission.[4]   A fourth point was that added
representation must be given to the counties, and a fifth was
that the principle of rating should be the basis of the
borough franchise.   When there was a change of Government, the Conservatives had come into power.   " We
brought in a Reform Bill; we passed a Reform Bill; and
now we ask you to consider, were the five points that during
these seven years . . . I impressed upon Parliament and
the country, were they obtained or not? "   These points
formed, of course, Disraeli indicates, the main outline of
the bill as passed.   He then goes on—

[1] *The Chancellor of the Exchequer in Scotland, being Two Speeches
Delivered by Him in the City of Edinburgh* (Edinburgh and London,
1867).

[2] *Ibid.*, pp. 11 and 12—*i. e.*, Disraeli explains, the borough and county
franchises and redistribution must be taken up together to keep " political equilibrium."

You must get a certain class of boroughs, by appealing to their
patriotism, to spare you one of their members.

[4] To see that borough occupiers should not become county electors, *etc.*

and then I am told, when measures recommended to the country during seven years have been so triumphantly carried into effect, that we have done nothing, that it is our opponents who have suggested the Bill. I can only say this, that if you had seen the countenance of the gentleman [1] who recently made a speech in this city when we did carry that Bill, you would not have read in those lineaments that triumph of the Liberal party after a toil of seventy years of which we have heard so much. I must say I never saw such a command over the exultation peculiar to man when he succeeds in an object dear to his heart and his friends.[2]

Monypenny and Buckle, too, contend that the bill was the work of Disraeli:

When Disraeli did finally acknowledge that decisive action was necessary, he was prompt, in conjunction with Derby, in sweeping aside temporary expedients, and founding himself upon an abiding principle. There is no evidence to show whether the definite acceptance of rating household suffrage is due rather to Disraeli or to Derby; both based themselves upon it in January, 1867. Both, too, cordially accepted the only method by which a settlement could be affected — the policy of welcoming, and deferring to, the co-operation of the House of Commons in the application of the principle adopted. But Derby was not so quick as Disraeli to see that the frank acceptance of this method could hardly fail to involve the disappearance of checks and securities to which he originally attached importance. The actual determination of what amendments should be accepted and what resisted necessarily devolved mainly on the leader of the House of Commons; and for the shape in which the Bill emerged from Committee—for

[1] Reference to Mr. James Moncreiff (Liberal), member for Edinburgh.

[2] Much of interest is to be found in the remaining sections of this speech. Disraeli states that the Tories caused him to give up plural voting, the two-years residence clause, *etc.*, and that when the Liberals asked that the compound householder be done away with, it was the very proposal he desired, to carry out his principle.

the fact, indeed, that it emerged with safety at all—Disraeli was almost solely responsible.[1]

In fact the student who goes carefully over the history of the passing of the Reform bill of 1867 may be expected to agree with Derby who said [2] that it was mainly due to Disraeli's tact, temper, and judgment, that the arduous undertaking in which they were engaged had not resulted, instead of a triumphant success, in disastrous failure. For although Disraeli consulted the House, apparently he kept the upper hand. With his principle [3] of personal rating [4] as against an artificial line he withstood the attacks of the Liberals. He accepted the Hodgkinson amendment and by his very acceptance led the Conservative party to accept it. This act of leading the Conservative party to household suffrage is remarkable, whether or not, as Cox suggests, Disraeli was forced to do so, when he came to realize that his principle as applied in the original intent would enfranchise communities in a most haphazard manner according to a very capricious distribution of the compound householding system.[5] Here as at other times Disraeli with almost

[1] Monypenny and Buckle, *Life of Disraeli*, vol. iv, p. 562.

[2] Monypenny and Buckle, vol. iv, p. 554.

[3] Cox, *A History of the Reform Bills of 1866 and 1867*, pp. 122 *et seq.*, points out that either test—the payment of rates, or the possession of houses of a particular value—is artificial. " Both criteria are imperfect, and only in rough imperfect ways serve to eliminate the drunkard, the spendthrift, the sluggard, the vagrant, and the profligate."

[4] *Ibid.*, pp. 169 *et seq.*, Cox says: The principle of personal *payment* " is not in the Reform Act, it never had a place in any edition of the Reform Bill." *Public Opinion*, December 7, 1867, discusses legal decisions on payments of rates. Quoting the *Manchester Examiner* it states that " payment of rates by agent is for all intents and purposes the same as payment by the principal."

[5] *Ibid.*, pp. 197 *et seq. Vide* also Monypenny and Buckle, vol. iv, p. 563, where is to be found an acknowledgement of this fact. *Vide* Cox's further statement (pp. 206 *et seq.*) on Disraeli's attempts to neutralize the effects of Hodgkinson's amendment.

superhuman cleverness, extricated himself easily from an
embarrassing situation and made his blunders contribute to
his success.[1] On the other hand those who like to find
consistency in a man, may well point out that in the debates on the 1866 bill Disraeli had stood for lateral rather
than vertical extension of the suffrage. With even greater
effect can they point out that after the passage of the bill,
Disraeli was not anxious to regard it as a democratic
measure. He himself was unwilling to accept praise (or
blame) for that which calls forth to-day our laudation. In
the House of Commons he said:

There are 4,500,000 inhabited houses in England. I do not
pretend to speak with severe statistical accuracy, but I think I
do not make much of a mistake. Not more than a moiety of
these, even if the Bill passes, will be inhabited by persons
qualified to exercise the franchise. Then if household suffrage be democracy, what is this all about?[2]

In that speech at Edinburgh, already mentioned,[3] he said:

. . . We have not established household suffrage in England.
There are, I think I may say, probably four million houses in
England. Under our ancient laws, and under the Act of
Lord Grey, about a million of those householders possess the
franchise. Under the new Act of 1867, something more than
500,000 will be added to that million. Well, then, I want to
know if there are four million householders, and a million and
a half in round numbers have the suffrage, how can household
suffrage be said to be established in England?[4] . . . Are we

[1] *Cf. Westminster Review*, July, 1867, p. 185.

[2] *Hansard*, vol. clxxxviii, p. 1113. This was as far along in the session
as July 5.

[3] *Cf. supra*, pp. 227-8.

[4] The obvious answer is that Disraeli was clouding the issue by trying
to prove that there was not household suffrage in England as a whole
when no one would suggest that the measure was democratic except as
it applied to the boroughs.

to be frightened at such a result as this? Are we really to believe that with a constituency of a million and a half—one million of whom we know of our own knowledge for a considerable space of time have exercised that suffrage according to the traditions of the country, and are now assisted in the fulfilment of that public duty by some half million more equally influenced by the traditions of the country—are we to believe that this is establishing a Democratic Government in England? If that can be maintained, even by an ex-Lord Advocate, I should look upon it as one of the most preposterous conclusions.[1]

Of course we may question whether Disraeli actually meant what he said or whether he was trying to smooth matters for some of the less radical people with whom he was dealing. No definite answer can be given. Disraeli will always remain to us, at least in certain respects, as he was to John Bright, the *mystery man*.

To those who believe that credit for the bill belongs neither to Disraeli nor to Bright, there is a fourth assumption open: that it was nobody's bill; that public opinion as stirred up partly by economic and social conditions, partly by the Reform League, partly by John Bright, partly by trade unions, dictated that a liberal bill should be passed; that one section of the House was merely trying to outbid, for popular favor, the other, and thus it happened that a radical Hodgkinson amendment proposed by the Liberals for political reasons was accepted by the Conservatives for like reasons. Considerable arguments can be adduced for this belief.

Before the year was very far advanced the *Times* had admitted that the House of Commons would probably shelve the subject of Reform at once if members could have the

[1] *The Chancellor of the Exchequer in Scotland*, pp. 14 and 15; *cf.* also the *Times*, October 30, 1867.

needful protection, and were not bound as gentlemen to tell
how they voted.[1]   After the measure had passed the third
reading, Lord Grey of the House of Lords said that it was
an admitted fact that a majority of the members of the
House of Commons really disapproved of the bill to which
they had formally assented.[2]   Earl Russell was rather
afraid of the measure, especially, he said, because of a probable increase of corruption among the classes who really
took no interest in politics.[3]   And Lord Derby, it will be
remembered, in spite of his " greatest confidence in the
sound sense " of his fellow countrymen, came out with the
phrase: " No doubt we are making a great experiment
and taking a leap in the dark." [4]

Lord Shaftesbury, great friend of the workingmen as
he was, spoke of the gross hypocrisy of the members of
Parliament; " with the exception of a few advanced Democrats, they all detest and fear the measure." [5]   Carlyle in
his " Shooting Niagara: And After?",[6] apropos of the Reform measure, declared—" Traitorous Politicians, grasping
at votes, even votes from the rabble, have brought it on."
The *Quarterly Review* before a bill was brought in, feared
lest politicians, working upon the pledges which the lower
ranks of the present constituencies had extorted from candidates, would create a fictitious political necessity to which
the present organization of the House of Commons might
induce the majority to submit, in spite of its convictions.[7]

[1] The *Times,* February 5, 1867 (mentioned *supra*, p. 122).

[2] *Cf. Annual Register*, 1867, p. 94.

[3] *Annual Register*, 1867, p. 108.

[4] *Hansard*, vol. clxxxix, p. 952.

[5] Edwin Hodder, *The Life and Work of the Seventh Earl of Shaftesbury*, 3 vols. (London, 1888), vol. iii, p. 218.

[6] To be found in *Macmillan's*, October, 1867.

[7] *Quarterly Review*, January, 1866, p. 256.

Blackwood's, in June of 1867, spoke of the meetings which had gone on all over the country, and at which the language held was always the same—that nothing would content the people except registered manhood suffrage protected by the ballot—and declared that a House of Commons of which the majority should refuse to concede all that was now conceded, would find itself at daggers-drawn with the bulk of the people.[1]   Disraeli himself, it is said,[2] heard the voice of the people and felt the force of the argument that " the pot was on the point of boiling over, and that those who kept it seething would get scalded for their pains."   In fact the *Edinburgh Review* states that in the great case of Mr. Hodgkinson's amendment Disraeli had made a concession to the popular stir threatening to grow into a tempest from without.[3]

It is probably true that this stir from without had its effect upon Disraeli and that he as the official who guided the bill through Parliament deserves approbation.

Disraeli deserves approbation provided, it may be suggested, he put through the bill not as a shrewd political act but on good faith that he was doing the country and the working class a benefit.   Thus it brought up the much mooted question as to the reason for Disraeli's action. Did he play successfully the part of a Vivian Grey in shrewdly outmanœuvering his opponents on the political field or was he putting into effect some of his social theories as displayed in *Sybil* in the belief that social betterment for the working classes would come with the franchise?   Or perhaps the real motive was a combination of these?

In the speech delivered at Edinburgh, Disraeli has given

[1] *Blackwood's,* June, 1867, p. 776.

[2] *Vide Frazer's,* November, 1867, p. 658.

[3] *Edinburgh Review,* October, 1867, p. 572; at least he could say this to his followers.

in general terms his view as to why the Conservatives dealt
with the question: everybody must have felt it to be absolutely necessary for Lord Derby in 1866, to deal with this
question. For fifteen years every prime minister and every
party had dealt with Reform and had proved itself inadequate to the occasion. "And what is that but a premium to
revolution?" Hence it was the duty of the Tories to try
to deal with it. The failure of another Reform bill would
have been a disadvantage to Lord Derby, he acknowledged,
but more than that it would have been a source of great
danger to the country.[1]

So because of patriotic sentiments, because of the impel-
ling force of popular opinion, Disraeli had been careful by
various manipulations to pass the bill. But not every one
living in 1867 and not every one of a later period has accepted
this statement of affairs as given by Disraeli. And granting
that the popular outcry did give Disraeli a leverage with
which to move his party from the old position on such a
question, and actually made the settlement of the question a
necessity, one may yet declare that the motive of Disraeli
was strictly political: that he desired to "dish" the Whigs.
The *Spectator* for August 10, 1867, for instance, declared
that Disraeli had admitted a party motive for the Reform
bill by his statement that he had disturbed the Whigs'
monopoly of Reform. The *Edinburgh Review* thought[2] the
Conservative party willing to bear anything and to do anything in order to make itself politically powerful by passing the bill: " That (the Conservative) party, sore at its
long exclusion, and determined to clutch the prize it had
obtained, was in a humor to bear much. Unlimited aban-
donment of principles and policy on Reform, deceit in any
quantity, vacillation without end—for these it was well pre-

[1] *The Chancellor of the Exchequer in Scotland*, pp. 6 and 7.

[2] *Edinburgh Review*, October, 1867, p. 543.

pared." Shaftesbury speaks of Disraeli and Gladstone as two tigers over a carcass—each for power and salary; and quotes Derby as telling his friends that if they passed his bill they would be in office for many years.[1]

But granting that political power was one of Disraeli's motives in passing the bill, that motive in him was no more unworthy than it was in Gladstone—the attacks of the Liberal papers and speakers notwithstanding. For the Liberals, says [2] *Blackwood's,* had palpably used the question of a further Reform of Parliament for the last six or eight years as a measure of keeping themselves in office and for no other earthly purpose. "Parliamentary Reform must always be a popular cry; and nothing could be more easy than for the Whigs, driven from office or threatened with expulsion, to raise that cry, and convert it, if need were, into a stern reality." [3]   Lowering the franchise to £7 would help the Liberals, said the pamphleteer,[4] as £10 did in 1832. "And then, when, under this new *régime,* the Conservative party had again succeeded in living down the obloquy which must necessarily attach to them with new electors admitted to the suffrage in spite of their opposition, the same game might be played once more, and a £5 suffrage be brought forward," *etc.* If this system could be followed and the Conservatives were inconsiderate enough to allow it, the Liberals might stay in power for the rest of their lives. If Disraeli thought such statements as these given above were facts, he can hardly be blamed for breaking the monopoly. If by granting the franchise to the ordinary

[1] Edwin Hodder, *The Life and Work of the Seventh Earl of Shaftesbury,* vol. iii, pp. 217 and 218.

[2] *Blackwood's,* July, 1867, " The Progress of the Question," p. 113.

[3] *Ibid.,* December, 1866, p. 781.

[4] H. W. Cole, *The Middle Classes and the Borough Franchise* (London, 1866), p. 26.

workingmen he could have their support to balance the support given the Liberals by the middle class and the *élite* of the working class, then might the Conservatives look for their share of the power of office.   At least that was the opinion of many of the leading writers of the day.   In the *North British Review* may be found a convenient summary of this view:

Mr. Disraeli believes that the lowest and most ignorant portion of the householders, both in town and country, are the most amenable to influence, the most likely to be managed and *exploité* by the Conservative party, most under the control of those above them, most dependent, both in circumstances and in mind, upon their employers, their landlords, their superiors.   He thinks, too,—and to a great extent he is right,—that their native sympathies, and mental habits, and old prejudices, will dispose them to side with the Conservatives, with the old families, with " the land," with the proprietors of great estates, and the inheritors of venerable names. . . . He knew that the *élite* of the artisan class, those intelligent and politically-interested workingmen, who lay immediately below the present electors, . . . were almost invariably Liberals and Radicals.[1]

And Disraeli and the Conservatives must have been pleased in case this assumption is a correct one, by the reports of the growth of Conservative feeling as mentioned in the newspapers during the summer of 1867.   The *Times* reported on the thirtieth of April the formation of a Conservative League to be called the Conservative Union and noted that in the last six months feeling for Disraeli's party had grown especially in the North where many Conservative organizations had sprung up.[2]   On the first of May it reported two deputations to Disraeli, one of workingmen from

---

[1] *North British Review*, September, 1867, " The Achievements and the Moral of 1867," pp. 211-212; also *vide infra*, p. 242.

[2] *Cf. supra*, p. 130, and also *News of the World*, May 5, 1867.

Norwich, the other of members of associations, who assured the Government that Conservative feeling was spreading throughout the country, that the workingmen of the North were prepared to support the Government, that the workingmen of Yorkshire had joined Conservative associations because they felt that the party was the true and only friend of the working classes. These and like reports at other times would lead the reader to think that Disraeli had a chance for success if he were really playing for the votes of the working class.

But was he not interested in the welfare of the lower classes? In the address to the workingmen of Edinburgh in October, 1867, he definitely made a statement of his interest. The country in general might well be congratulated, he said, that the bill the Government had introduced for the representation of the people in England had passed into law, and he was glad that the working classes of Edinburgh so entirely approved of it. Throwing his eye over a Parliamentary career that continuously had prevailed for upwards of thirty years, he could not find that he had ever taken any part hostile, or intentionally hostile, to the interests of the working classes, or that he had ever been connected with those who ought to be or who intended to be in antagonism with them. He continued:

Now, gentlemen, during those thirty years there has been a great mass of legislation which has been carried in Parliament affecting the interests of the working classes—measures in which they were deeply interested themselves, which they promoted by their presence, and which they showed by their conduct were dear in every sense to the innermost sentiments of their hearts and hearths. I have remarked, in looking over that period, that during that time, I think, if I recollect correctly — of course, upon an occasion like the present I must speak with that indulgence which I am sure you will afford to

one who has no blue-books to refer to, but I think there have
been thirty-two acts passed relative to the condition of the
people, and especially of the working classes in this country,
in which they took the deepest interest — laws affecting their
wages, their education, their hours of toil, their means of self-
improvement—laws the object of which was to elevate their
condition and soften the asperities which are the inevitable
consequence of probably any state of society that may exist.
Now, Gentlemen, I can say this, it is some gratification to me,
and I think it will be fairly admitted, it is some trial of the
disposition and career of a public man, that of those thirty-two
acts passed during those thirty years, I have invariably supported every one.   Gentlemen, allow me to tell you that
though that legislation is now considered as the result of a
philosophy the propriety and justice of which cannot be questioned, there was not one of those acts that was not bitterly
and ably opposed.   I will not say now by whom they were opposed, or by what party they were opposed, because it is
neither my wish, nor is it in any way necessary to a meeting
like the present, that we dwell upon those circumstances.   But
this I will say, they were not opposed by the political party
with which I am intimately connected. . . . Well, Gentlemen,
on this subject I may be perhaps permitted to remind you
that the present session of Parliament has given, I think, some
evidence that the feelings of her Majesty's Ministers are unchanged upon this subject, and that we have not forgotten
that which is one of the first and principal duties of any Minister, which is to consider whether, by legislation, the condition of the great body of the people can be improved.[1]

Again, if reference is made to the early writings of
Disraeli, there may be found at least quasi-democratic leanings.   The welfare of the People is to him an important
topic.   That political advantages, however, may be had from
care for the social welfare of the People is even more than
suggested.   He writes:

[1] *The Chancellor of the Exchequer in Scotland*, p. 34.

Even now it [Toryism] is not dead, but sleepeth; and, in an age of political materialism, of confused purposes and perplexed intelligence, that aspires only to wealth because it has faith in no other accomplishment, as men rifle cargoes on the verge of shipwreck, toryism will yet rise from the tomb over which Bolingbroke shed his last tear, to bring back strength to the Crown, liberty to the subject, and to announce that power has only one duty: to secure the social welfare of the PEOPLE.[1]

In another place he has Egremont's great speech in Parliament so interpreted:

"He spoke throughout in an exoteric vein," said the gray-headed gentleman, "and I apprehend was not very sure of his audience; but I took him to mean, indeed it was the gist of his speech, that if you wished for a time to retain your political power, you could only effect your purpose by securing for the people greater social felicity."[2]

Egremont's opinions are perhaps best stated in his discussion with Sybil:

"If there be a change," said Sybil, "it is because in some degree the People have learnt their strength."

"Ah! dismiss from your mind those fallacious fancies," said Egremont.

"The People are not strong; the People never can be strong. Their attempts at self-vindication will end only in their suffering and confusion. It is civilization that has effected, that is effecting, this change. It is that increased knowledge of themselves that teaches the educated their social duties. There is a dayspring in the history of this nation, which perhaps those only who are on the mountain tops can as yet recognize. You deem you are in darkness, and I see a dawn. The new generation of the aristocracy of England are not tyrants, not op-

[1] Disraeli, Benjamin, *Sybil or the Two Nations* (London, 1845), p. 82.

[2] *Ibid.*, p. 84.

pressors, Sybil, as you persist in believing. Their intelligence
—better than that, their hearts—are open to the responsibility
of their position. But the work that is before them is no holi-
day-work. It is not the fever of superficial impulse that can
remove the deep-fixed barriers of centuries of ignorance and
crime. Enough that their sympathies are awakened; time and
thought will bring the rest. They are the natural leaders of
the People, Sybil; believe me, they are the only ones." [1]

It can be said that the People, as portrayed in *Sybil,* are
not able, apparently, to carry on affairs successfully — the
time for political democracy has not yet come—but by 1867
Disraeli definitely stated [2] that those called upon to exercise the franchise were sufficiently educated to fulfill that
trust. It can be contended that Disraeli, the author of
1845, is not Disraeli, the statesman of 1867, but according
to Shaftesbury Disraeli's interest in the welfare of the
People had continued. The philanthropist wrote on August
9, 1866—" Have spoken to Disraeli, whom I found, as I
always found him in the House of Commons, decided and
true to the cause (of the working class)." [3] At least it can
be said for Disraeli that he knew of the condition of the
working classes and had been interested in their welfare
for a long period.

But, as the above-quoted passage from *Sybil* suggests,
it seems that neither interest in the well-being of the working class, nor the political motive, taken alone, actuated
Disraeli, but rather a combination of the two. Circumstances such as the revolt of Cranborne and the consequent
dependence on Radical support [4] and especially the already

[1] Disraeli, *op. cit.*, p. 83.

[2] *The Chancellor of the Exchequer in Scotland,* " Speech in Answer to
an Address Presented by the Working Men of Edinburgh," p. 40.

[3] *Vide* Hodder's *Life of Shaftesbury,* vol. iii, p. 214.

[4] *Cf.* view of Trevelyan, *Life of John Bright,* p. 373, on this point.

emphasized discontent with economic conditions, undoubtedly did much to effect the passage of a democratic measure, yet Disraeli's writings clearly show that he was alive to the fact that it would be possible to make the working classes see the Conservatives as the champions who would gain for them social justice; by causing his party to give them social and political justice, he could bid, cleverly, for their political support.[1] At Edinburgh he declared to the workingmen:

You are indebted . . . to the party with which I am connected, who upon that occasion evinced a devotion and an energy rarely to be equalled in the history of the Constitution of our country. They gave no churlish support; they gave no limited devotion to their leaders; but impelled by the conviction that the settlement of this question was one of vital necessity, they determined that it should be settled in a manner which should produce concord among all classes of her Majesty's subjects.[2]

Elsewhere in his speeches he said: " I have from my very earliest public life been of opinion that this assumed and affected antagonism between the interests of what are called the Conservative classes and the laboring classes is utterly unfounded ";[3] and " When the people are led by their natural leaders, and when, by their united influence, the national institutions fulfil their original intention, the Tory party is triumphant."[4] In fact, Disraeli's acts and his expression of opinions appeared to more than one writer as an attempt to get the support of the lower strata of workingmen. The Whigs had allied themselves with the middle classes for the benefit not only of the country but of themselves; the Conservatives might now ally themselves with

[1] *Vide supra*, p. 237, the *North British Review*.
[2] *The Chancellor of the Exchequer in Scotland*, p. 33.
[3] *Ibid.*, p. 35.
[4] *Ibid.*, p. 29.

part of the working class for the benefit not only of the country, and of the working class, but of themselves, said *Blackwoods*.[1] The *Spectator* was of the opinion that Disraeli believed as he believed when he wrote *Tancred* [2] that the uneducated people would always have a leaning in favor of Tory ideas.[3] It liked to quote [4] a part of his speech at Merchant Taylors' in June, 1867, where he said that he went to household suffrage because he believed that while the enfranchisement of the *élite* of the working classes alone would destroy his party, the enfranchisement of the residuum with the *élite* would renew its sources of strength.[5] *Frazer's* poked fun at him for "his discovery that the lower you descend in the social scale, the better materials do you find for a sound, safe, and Conservative system of representation." [6] Lord Shaftesbury denied the theory that though the middle classes were not Conservative, if you went deeper you could get into a vein of gold, and encounter the presence of a highly Conservative feeling.[7] Other writers, however, assured their readers that the experience of English boroughs, as they were, demonstrated that when-

[1] *Blackwood's*, December, 1866, p. 781.

[2] *Tancred*, possessed of a religious theme, when taken with *Coningsby* and *Sybil*, will give some idea of Disraeli's religious, political and social opinions: an excellent chapter on *Tancred* is to be found in Monypenny and Buckle, vol. iii, chapter ii.

[3] The *Spectator*, April 6, 1867.

[4] *Vide* the *Spectator*, September 21, 1867, and September 28, 1867, p. 1076.

[5] The *Spectator* does not give the exact words used by Disraeli; for his speech, *vide* the *Times*, June 12, 1867.

[6] *Frazer's*, November, 1867, p. 661 *et seq*. One of its writers quoted the sentence: "the right honorable Gentleman is not the first great Hebrew legislator who has led his people into the wilderness, and what is more, he resembles Moses in this—he will never live to lead them out of it." *Ibid.*, p. 668.

[7] *Vide Frazer's*, November, 1867, p. 663.

ever the majority in the constituency consisted of working-men, Tories were returned to Parliament; where the work-ingmen balanced other classes, and no more, Whigs were re-turned; wherever the working class happened to be in a minority, the boroughs returned Radicals. *Blackwood's* deduced from this even in January that a more liberal measure would probably be obtained from Lord Derby than any Lord Russell and Mr. Gladstone would venture to pro-pose.

This idea of having a new kind of support for their party must have appealed to the Conservatives as a body. In 1865 their attitude toward Reform was thus put by the *Quarterly Review*: "During the last five years . . . . they (Conservatives) have expressed themselves in opposition to all bare degradation of the suffrage, to all alterations in it that can in any degree increase the democratic element in the Constitution, with a frankness which leaves no room for misconstruction." [1]   Later it said in reference to the Conservative attitude toward Reform before 1867: "Any one who cares to refer to ' Hansard ' will find that the danger of lowering the franchise even to £6 or £7, because it would give to the working classes a preponderating power, was one on which the Conservative speakers constantly dwelt." [2] But by 1867 a change had come. Mr. Henley, who had long since [3] declared in favor of household suffrage, was not now alone. "By little and little," says *Blackwood's*, " the truth has made its way into their (Tories') convictions that there is far more of sympathy between the working-men and the aristocracy of England, than between either the aristocracy and what are called the middle classes, or

[1] *Quarterly Review*, July, 1865, p. 293.

[2] *Ibid.*, October, 1867, " The Conservative Surrender," p. 538.

[3] The *Spectator*, June 29, 1867.

the middle classes and the workingmen." [1]— It denied out
and out that the Tories were " mortified " by the action taken
by Disraeli.   The party had indeed wisely followed its great
leader: " In 1867 the party has not rebelled, indeed it has
scarcely murmured; it has answered in divisions to the
calls of its summoners with a discipline worthy of a more
honorable campaign; and the malcontents, who may be
counted on the fingers, have been voices crying in the wilderness." [2]   The malcontents had attacked Disraeli in the
Quarterly Review,[3] it is true, for passing a bill opposed to
party principles but they were not representative of the
party feeling.

Disraeli had seen a great Reform bill through Parliament.
The suggestive chapter title of Monypenny and Buckle—
" Disraeli's Parliamentary Triumph "—does not seem to be
unfitting, provided it is remembered that the Parliamentary
Triumph to Disraeli probably meant more than mere Parliamentary triumph—it signified also an anticipated success for
his attempt to lead the *People* to cherish the Conservative
party and those great institutions which that party held to
be most truly British.

[1] *Blackwood's*, July, 1867, p. 115.

[2] The *Edinburgh Review*, October, 1867, p. 542. The Tory dissenters
in 1867, unlike the forty Adullamites of 1866, were unable to destroy
party effectiveness.

[3] *Vide* October, 1867, p. 547. Cranborne wrote for this magazine.

CHAPTER VI

CONCLUSION

WHAT would be the effect of Disraeli's " triumph " upon
the political fortunes of the Conservative party? Would
the People, as he hoped, affirm that the monopoly of
Liberalism in Reform had been broken and would they now
have confidence in the ability of Toryism to gain for them
rights and privileges?

Disraeli had told a deputation in April, 1867, of his efforts for the People and of his expectations of their assistance:

The bill was the restoration of the old Constitution of this
country, it gave back to the working classes those rights and
privileges of which they were deprived by the bill of 1832
(loud cries of " Hear, hear "), and it sought to break down
the barriers which separated the people from their natural
leaders. . . . When you go back to your homes, tell your
friends and neighbors that the hour may arrive, and that perhaps shortly, when we must count upon the energy and public
spirit of the people (loud cheers). If the appeal is made, let
it not be made in vain (it shall not be) ; and if it is successful
you will do much more than support a ministry, you will save
a country (enthusiastic cheering).[1]

To the ministers, in a speech at the Mansion House banquet
just before the close of the 1867 session, he declared that the
Conservative party had " resumed its natural functions in
the government of the country:"

[1] *News of the World*, April 14, 1867.

I have seen in my time several monopolies terminated, and recently I have seen the termination of the monopoly of Liberalism. Nor are we to be surprised when we see that certain persons who believed that they had an hereditary right, whenever it was necessary, to renovate the institutions of their country, should be somewhat displeased that any other persons should presume to interfere with those changes which, I hope in the spirit of true patriotism, they believed the requirements of the State rendered necessary. But I am sure that when the hubbub has subsided, when the shrieks and screams which were heard some time ago, and which have already subsided into sobs and sighs, shall be thoroughly appeased, nothing more terrible will be discovered to have occurred than that the Tory party has resumed its natural functions in the government of the country. For what is the Tory party unless it represents national feeling? If it does not represent national feeling Toryism is nothing. . . . The Tory party is nothing unless it represents and upholds the institutions of the country. . . . I cannot help believing that, because my Lord Derby and his colleagues have taken a happy opportunity to enlarge the privileges of the people of England, we have not done anything but strengthen the institutions of the country, the essence of whose force is that they represent the interests and guard the rights of the people.[1]

Was Disraeli to have his hopes fulfilled? Had he really made the Conservative leaders the leaders of the people to such an extent that great political advantage would come to the Conservative party from the Act of 1867?

The answer to the questions was not to be clearly shown from the results of the next election—that of the autumn of 1868. The question at issue at that election was to be Irish disestablishment. Disraeli might well complain in his address to the electors of the county of Buckingham,[2]

[1] *Cf.* Monypenny and Buckle, vol. iv, pp. 553 *et seq.*, and the *Spectator*, August 10, 1867.

[2] In October, 1868.

that although his party had settled the question of Parliamentary Reform, had carried on foreign affairs successfully, especially in the handling of Abyssinia,[1] and had strengthened the army and navy, *etc.*, public verdict would not be given on such accomplishments but rather on a " proposal for the dissolution of the union between Church and State," brought forward by the Opposition.[2] Not the achievements of the past but the problems of the present and future were to receive the attention of the voters.

The state of Ireland, was, indeed, the great question of the day. For " while Parliament did many things in 1868, it thought only of one thing: Ireland, always Ireland." [3] Fenian activity in 1866 and 1867 causing a continuous suspension of the *habeas corpus* act in Ireland, Fenian attacks in England in 1867,[4] had forced[5] Irish affairs into prominence, and made them the paramount issue in domestic politics. In March, 1868, an Irish member moved that the House of Commons should resolve itself into a committee for considering the state of Ireland. He argued that England should either govern Ireland justly, or let her govern herself. On the question involved the Liberals once more became united. Gladstone, strongly supported by Lowe of

[1] British forces were sent into Abyssinia in the winter of 1867-68 to release British subjects held captive by the native ruler. The success of the expedition led Disraeli to declare that the standard of St. George had been hoisted on the mountains of Rasselas. For details on the Abyssinian War *vide* Walpole, *History of Twenty-five Years*, vol. ii, pp. 267-286.

[2] The *Times*, October 3, 1868.

[3] Herbert Paul, *A History of Modern England*, vol. iii, p. 130.

[4] For the attempt on Chester, *vide* Sidney Low and L. C. Sanders, *The Political History of England* (edited by William Hunt and R. L. Poole), vol. xii, p. 228; for the Manchester affair and the attempt on Clerkenwell jail, *vide* pp. 229-230.

[5] *Ibid.*, p. 219.

the Adullamites and Bright of the Radicals, declared that
the Irish Church as an establishment must cease, and brought
forward resolutions to that effect.   The case had to be considered in committee, but when the motion to go into committee was put, Lord Stanley [1] of the Government proposed an amendment which would have left the question for
the next House of Commons to consider.   Many of the
Conservatives, however, did not like Stanley's policy of delay; they stood for a policy of no surrender.   Disraeli himself was not able to defend the Government in the manner
expected of him by his followers [2] so that Lord Stanley's
amendment was defeated by a majority of sixty, and the
main question, that the House should resolve itself into a
committee, was carried by a majority of fifty-six.   And after
the Easter recess, Gladstone's resolution—" That it is necessary that the Established Church of Ireland should cease to
exist as an establishment, due regard being had to all personal interests and to all individual rights of property "—
was passed.   Yet Disraeli who since the retirement of Derby
in February, 1868, had been the head of the Conservative
party, did not resign or dissolve at once in spite of these de-
feats.   His work with regard to Reform had not been completed.   Bills dealing with Scotland and Ireland [3] had not
yet been passed and reports of boundary commissioners [4]
had not been considered.   Had Parliament been dissolved,
appeal must have been made to an obsolete constituency.
Hence the appeal to the people had to be postponed for some
time.   Before an election was held, Gladstone continued to
press his advantage by having the House pass other resolu-

[1] Secretary of State for Foreign Affairs.

[2] Walpole, *History of Twenty-five Years*, vol. ii, p. 327.

[3] *Cf. infra*, pp. 258-60.

[4] For the recommendations of the commissioners and the boundary bill
(the 31 and 32 Vict., c. 46), *vide Annual Register*, 1868, pp. 30-37.

tions not favored by the Conservatives. The Lords, however, refused to follow his dictations. Thus stood affairs when Parliament was dissolved by proclamation on the eleventh of November, 1868. The country was asked to give its opinion upon the disestablishment and the disendowment of the Irish church.

Naturally, however, both sides tried to gain popular support, not only by the appeal to the Irish question but also by claims to the authorship of the Reform bill of 1867. Disraeli told his constituents at Buckinghamshire how the Conservatives had passed the bill.[1] Gladstone, on the other hand, in his address to the electors of South-West Lancashire, spoke of the bill " introduced by the Government, but amended and almost transformed by the Opposition." [2] At Liverpool he spent much time describing the part successfully played by the Liberals in Reform.[3] And not only by the leaders but by speakers [4] less noted, by magazines, by newspapers, the question was debated. *Blackwood's* had great hopes and anticipations that the newly-created voters would prove worthy of a boon which a Conservative Government had bestowed upon them. These newly-created voters owed all to the Conservatives:

And now, in order that the workingmen may be able to look after their own interests, the Tories have received them within the pale of the Constitution, to an extent which their rivals never dreamed of; and to which, when the Reform Bill of 1867 was brought forward, Mr. Gladstone and his friends offered all the opposition in their power.[5]

[1] Speech is to be found in the *Times*, November 20, 1868.

[2] *Vide* the *Times*, October 10, 1868.

[3] *Vide* the *Times*, October 15, 1868.

[4] Some speeches are given in *Blackwood's*, November, 1868, pp. 637 *et seq.; vide* also the *Times*.

[5] *Blackwood's*, November, 1868, pp. 622 *et seq.*

To the *Spectator,* on the other hand, Mr. Gladstone might well claim confidence by what he had done to secure for the nation at large a wide and substantial representation in the new Parliament:

It was in that cause (*i. e.,* Reform) that he sacrificed office, and the country now knows that it was really that sacrifice of office which secured reform. . . . It was Mr. Gladstone who, amidst a storm of disapproval from Conservative Liberals and Liberal Conservatives, no less than the Tories, threw over the " wise " Palmerstonian policy of " Rest and be thankful," and insisted on redeeming the repeatedly broken promises of Reform. It was Mr. Gladstone who roused the enthusiasm of the working classes by asserting, in reply to the scornful taunts of the superfine Conservatives, that the working classes are " our own flesh and blood," and have a right to expect trust rather than dread. It was Mr. Gladstone, who, after parrying the unwearied thrusts of the Opposition for months, at last saw that he would do more for Reform by resignation than by perseverance in a measure so ruthlessly contested in every detail. It was Mr. Gladstone who obliged the Tory Ministry to abandon every one of their reactionary proposals, and to widen their mock reform into a real (one) by conceding nine out of the ten conditions which he dictated. . . . Mr. Gladstone said in April, 1866, " We stand or fall by this Bill, as has been declared by my noble friend; we stand with it now; we may fall with it a short time hence; and if we do, we shall rise with it hereafter." To the spirit, if not to the letter, that prophecy is about to be fulfilled. The new Constituencies are about to mark whom they regard as the true author of the great reform by using their new privileges for the very first time to realize that " hereafter ". What Mr. Disraeli resisted vehemently and even manfully in 1866, what he conceded contrary to his declared principles under compulsion and with mischievous qualifications in 1867, the people cannot profess to thank him for, with full hearts or true confidence in 1868.[1]

[1] The *Spectator*, October 17, 1868, p. 1209.

The election was favorable to the Liberals. Gladstone's party won in Scotland, Ireland and in the boroughs of South Britain.[1] In the English counties the Conservatives were successful. They also could point out that Lancashire went for them [2] even to the extent of rejecting Gladstone himself,[3] and comfort themselves with the phrase—" What Lancashire thinks to-day, all England thinks tomorrow." [4] Another statement which solaced them was the announcement that only one hundred and forty Tory members had been returned after 1832 as compared with about two hundred and seventy-five after 1867. Many of their members, too, represented the most powerful constituencies of the kingdom and not the small boroughs.[5] The wisdom of Derby and Disraeli had been established, it was said, for had the Liberals passed a £7 bill, the Conservative party would have been routed as it was routed after 1832. *Blackwood's* appeared to be quite cheerful over the situation:

There can be no doubt that the extension of the franchise has invigorated Conservatism. The Tory party has voluntarily widened its borders, and the experience of the elections demonstrates, as its leaders had believed, that it flourishes most vigorously when " broad-based upon the people's will." . . . Two hundred and seventy-six Tory Gentlemen have been returned to Parliament by the English democracy. . . . All men can see

---

[1] The *Spectator*, December 5, 1868, p. 1421, gives data.

[2] *Blackwood's*, January, 1869, p. 119; the *Spectator*, November 21, 1868, p. 1361—quotes as causes that either the majority of the new voters were generally Conservative, or they were specially anti-Catholic and anti-Irish, or they were not free voters at all, but under the influence of their employers.

[3] The *Spectator*, November 28, p. 1392, gives reasons for this.

[4] *Cf. Blackwood's*, January, 1869, p. 130.

[5] Conservatives said that the Liberals had won through small boroughs. *Vide* refutation of the *Times*, December 1, 1868 (quoting *Liverpool Albion*).

that the Tory party is still intact; but we are convinced that an examination of the electoral returns will show that it is at the present moment substantially more powerful than it has been at any time since 1846.[1]

The Liberals on their part could point out that they had a majority of over a hundred.[2] Some of their organs were unable to resist the temptation to twit opponents:

This at least, it should seem, is clear, that as far as electioneering results go, the course which Mr. Disraeli has taken is as damaging to the Conservatives as any course could possibly have been. The majority is enormous in mere numbers, exceeding anything in recent history except that of the Parliament which met after the first Reform Act. This is hard enough, considering the kind of promises by which the poor squires were induced to follow their leaders. Lord Derby laid it down that the great object of his Reform policy was " to take such measures as should turn his minority into a majority." Mr. Disraeli told them that he had resisted the line of £7, and accepted household suffrage, " because that measure would not injure the Conservative party." By promises such as these, scattered still more lavishly in private, the Conservative members, up to their ears in anti-democratic pledges, voted enthusiastically for the platform of the most extreme Reformers in the House. The " dodge " has ridiculously failed. . . . To a sacrifice of reputation, or a forgetfulness of scruple, a portion at least of the Conservative party might possibly have been reconciled, if it would have enabled them to " dish the Whigs." But to have gone through all this dirt in order to make their political condition exactly twice as bad

[1] *Blackwood's*, January, 1869, pp. 112 and 113.

[2] In the *Journal of the Statistical Society of London*, vol. xxxii, pp. 102-113, is to be found collected from the newspapers of the two leading political parties (*Daily News* and *Standard*) facts relating to the general election of 1868. The editor considered it desirable to preserve these statements, as exhibiting the manner in which the same class of facts was regarded by contemporaries of opposite politics.

as it was before must be irritating. . . . To have changed a majority of sixty into a majority of a hundred; to have changed their opponents from a rabble into a disciplined host; and to have made the Liberals into Radicals, is about the net result to the Conservatives of the Conservative strategy of 1867.[1]

As a matter of fact, Disraeli thought it best to resign at once. He had believed that the country would not sanction the disestablishment of the Church, and had advised an appeal to the new constituencies.[2] The appeal had not been successful. Gladstone, with the prospect of a general election, says Kebbel,[3] had played the trump card (*i. e.*, Irish Church Resolution). He knew well enough, the writer continues,[4] that a ministerial majority would have been returned, had the appeal to the people been on the merits of the Reform bill of 1867. It must be confessed, however, that Gladstone's attack on the Irish Church does not appear to a writer like Mr. Trevelyan as the attempt of a politician to catch votes.[5] To him it seems that the Liberal leader could not even be sure that the question would not finally and definitely break up a party already split into many sections.

Yet if the result of the election of 1868 was not the result hoped for by Disraeli, his idea of establishing the Conservative party on a national and popular basis, was destined to be successful, to a degree at least, in the long run. One authority has pointed out how events have largely justified Disraeli's policy:

[1] *Saturday Review*, November 28, 1868, pp. 702-703.
[2] *Vide* the *Spectator*, December 5, 1868.
[3] Kebbel, *Lord Beaconsfield and Other Tory Memories*, p. 41.
[4] *Ibid.*
[5] Trevelyan, *Life of John Bright*, p. 388.

The constituency which the Reform Act of 1867 created, and which was logically completed by the extension of household franchise to the counties in 1884, gave the Conservative party, either alone or in alliance with the Unionist Liberals, majorities at four General Elections—1874, 1886, 1895, and 1900; insuring a fair spell of power to Disraeli himself, and a much longer tenure, by one of the caprices of fortune, to the statesman who worked his hardest against Disraeli to prevent that constituency from coming into being—Lord Salisbury. The existence, in considerable numbers, of the Conservative working man, whom it was the fashion of the Liberals of the 'sixties to treat as a myth, has been shown over and over again by the immense polls cast for the party in the largest urban constituencies.[1]

Also Mr. Charles Seymour points out [2] that if the elections from 1867 to 1884 are taken as a whole, the effect of the bill of 1867 in so far as it altered the strength of parties was beneficial to the Conservatives. Their gain was most marked in the counties where the new voters became their enthusiastic supporters. In the agricultural divisions they took seventy-seven per cent of the county seats after 1867 in contrast to sixty-seven per cent carried before the passage of the Reform bill. It had been supposed, however, that those newly enfranchised would vote much as the £50 tenants had voted in this type of division. Much more striking was their gain in the industrial counties where the Liberals, owing to the numerical superiority of the urban elements over the tenant farmers, had been accustomed to a slight majority of seats. But the £12 electors, perhaps feeling that the Liberals were no longer bent on middle-class legislation, gave to the Conservatives sixty-six per cent of the seats in such divisions.

[1] Monypenny and Buckle, vol. iv, p. 564.

[2] Charles Seymour, *Electoral Reform in England and Wales* (New Haven, 1915), pp. 300-310.

In the boroughs the relative strength of the parties was not changed by the Act of 1867: the Liberals still carried as before, about sixty per cent of the seats. An analysis of the effect of the Act upon different types of boroughs, Mr. Seymour remarks, is a difficult task inasmuch as classification into types is quite artificial and, at times, almost impossible owing to the effect of corruption, the influence of the "tradition or sentiment of the community" and the activity of the controlling landlord who unlike the county landlord might belong to either party. But in the metropolis and in that type of borough which may be designated as the smaller centers of industry the Conservatives made important gains. In the metropolis they carried thirty-four per cent of the seats following 1867 in contrast to five per cent after 1832, and in important industrial towns they took over thirty-four per cent of the seats after 1867 in contrast to twenty-five per cent after 1832. It appeared that Disraeli had not appealed in vain to the working class. However, the Conservatives made no gain and even suffered losses in other types of boroughs. In the very great industrial towns the Liberals held their own. In fifty or more of the smallest boroughs they proved themselves to be as strong as formerly. They gained slightly in the boroughs of moderate size—the cathedral cities and county towns—and to a greater degree in the boroughs having a population from ten to twenty thousand [1] and in the boroughs of such territorial extent that they represented interests of a rural and agricultural character. [2]

The redistribution bill which was quite limited in charac-

[1] Mr. Seymour thinks that the Liberals may have been influenced to retain boroughs of this type in the redistribution of 1885 because of their value to the Liberal cause. *Vide Electoral Reform in England and Wales*, p. 308.

[2] The results of the elections in this type of borough would lead the Liberals to be willing to try the household franchise in the counties.

ter, favored the Conservatives very slightly, if, indeed, it may be said to have changed the relative strength of the parties at all.[1]   Hence the Act of 1867 in its total effect considerably strengthened the Conservative cause chiefly by the gain of county seats.   Moreover, it became clear as election succeeded election " that the Conservatives might without discouragement look to the workmen in the industrial towns, and that the Liberals had nothing to hope from the yeomen farmers." [2]

Thus far the result of the passing of the 1867 Act upon the fortunes of the Conservative party has been the chief matter of consideration.   What, on the other hand,—it may be asked—was the result of the passage of that Act upon the position of workingmen in the state?   So numerous, indeed, were the new householders that the working class was in a clear majority.   A return of 1869 shows that especially in the large industrial towns the electors entitled to vote as householders far outnumbered the electors entitled to vote as £10 occupiers.[3]   Birmingham with 42,880 as the total number of electors on the register had 35,172 electors entitled to vote as householders and 7,708 electors entitled to vote as £10 occupiers; Blackburn with a total of 9,712 electors on the register had 7,764 householders and 1,948 £10 occupiers; Bolton with a total of 12,745 had 9,880 householders and 2,861 £10 occupiers; Manchester with a total of 48,256 had 22,897 householders and 25,331 £10 occupiers; Leeds had 37,470 householders and 9,443 £10 occupiers; Preston, 11,021 and 2,442, and Sheffield, 19,928 and 10,027.   On the other hand, the new electors in the metropolis where the lodger franchise was not as effective as

[1] *Vide* Seymour, pp. 344 and 345.

[2] *Ibid.*, p. 310.

[3] *Accounts and Papers*, 1868-1869, 1 (419), 109.

its supporters had supposed it would be, were represented by a gain of only sixty-six per cent, in Liverpool by a gain of less than ninety per cent and in some of the smaller boroughs by a very slight increase.[1] Moreover, the proportion of electors to population in the boroughs became equalized so that no longer did the manufacturing towns have the low ratio of voters which prevailed before 1867.[2]

But the second Reform Act in spite of those democratic tendencies displayed by the strengthening of the position of the workingmen in the boroughs of England and Wales left problems to democratic advance in the future. Very pressing was the question of Parliamentary Reform for Scotland and Ireland. Effective changes in electoral registration, the curbing of bribery at elections, a radical redistribution of seats, the introduction of a democratic suffrage in the counties, were tasks to be completed before England could be said to be truly democratic.

Reform measures for Scotland and Ireland were soon taken up. A Reform bill for Scotland was introduced in 1867, but, for want of time, was postponed until the following year when a measure was introduced by the Lord Advocate for Scotland. This measure as it concerned the franchise was based on the English act.[3] In the boroughs the franchise was to be extended to all householders rated and paying rates; in the counties there was to be an ownership franchise of £5 clear annual value, and an occupation franchise of £12.[4] According to the distribution clauses seven new members were to be given to Scotland, which would be an addition to the aggregate numbers of the House. It

[1] Seymour, pp. 281-283.
[2] For data, *vide* Seymour, pp. 289 *et seq.*
[3] A clear account is to be found in the *Annual Register*, 1868, pp. 18-24.
[4] Later fixed at £14.

was in this last point that the Government again found
itself defeated.   Many were the protests against adding to
the number of members of the House.   When the measure
was taken up in committee a motion was made " That it be an
instruction to the committee that, instead of adding to the
numbers of the house, they have power to disfranchise
boroughs in England having by the census returns of 1861
less than 5000 inhabitants."   Disraeli, retaining his opinions
that the best way to give the entitled additional representation was by increasing the number of members of the House,
finally spoke in favor of an alternate motion, that instead of
disfranchising boroughs, the committee have instructions to
take one member from each of those boroughs in England
which in 1861 had less than 12,000 inhabitants.   But in spite
of Disraeli the first motion was carried and the Government
had to accept the situation.   On one other important amendment the Government was defeated : this was a motion proposing to get rid altogether of the rate-paying qualification
in Scotland by omitting the words making the payment
of rates a necessary condition of the franchise.[1]   When the
defeat came, Disraeli asked for time to consider the future
course of the Government, but finally accepted this amendment also.   With some minor changes the bill became law.[2]

Less difficulty was met in the Irish Reform bill.[3]   It was
proposed with regard to Ireland to make no change in the
occupation franchise in counties which had been fixed at
£12 but to reduce the borough franchise from £8 to £4 and

[1] But subsequently the committee agreed that no man should be entitled to be registered as a voter, " Who shall have been exempted from
assessment or payment of poor rates on the ground of inability to pay
. . . or who shall have failed to pay . . . all poor rates (if any) that
have become payable by him."   Cf. Hansard, vol. cxcii, p. 842.

[2] As the 31 and 32 Vict., c. 48.

[3] For an account of this, vide Annual Register, 1868, pp. 24-30.

to extend the lodger franchise to Ireland on the same conditions as to England.   Inasmuch as the landlord was to
pay the poor rates of all houses below £4, only those rated
for the poor as in England, would obtain the franchise.   A
redistribution scheme proposed met with so little favor on
either side of the House, that Disraeli withdrew that part
of the measure.   And, although the bill was passed [1] without causing the ministry the embarrassment met with during the passing of the Reform bill for Scotland, much dissatisfaction was expressed.   It was declared that the Irish
people would refuse to accept this as anything like an adequate measure of Reform for Ireland; that the borough
franchise was fixed at an unfair figure; that the county
franchise was not reduced below the figure at which it was
placed eighteen years ago and was in effect the equivalent
of a £30 county rating in England; and that by the bill only
9000 would be added to the total number of voters in Ireland, whereas if the English system were acted on in respect
to Ireland some 20,000 ought to be added to the Irish constituencies.

Another question connected with Parliamentary representation and needing change was the registration system.
The Act of 1867 made an already complex system of registration still more complex: the new franchises added to
those previously in effect, caused more labor for the overseers who made up the lists of voters, and the abolition of
composition and the requirement of " personal payment "
of rates led to confusion and dissatisfaction.   Under the
old system many landlords had included the rate in the rent.
Now the occupiers had to pay the rates themselves in addition to the rent which the landlord did not lower.   A " fine "
had been imposed after all by the franchise as had been predicted by certain members of Parliament during the de-

[1] The 31 and 32 Vict., c. 49.

bates on Reform. The situation became such that Lord
Henley declared to Parliament that " the feeling among the
small occupiers in the towns where the change from compounding to non-compounding was made was one of the
most serious dissatisfaction." [1]   The Conservatives who
had debated for " personal payment " of rates did nothing
notwithstanding the unpopularity of the requirement, but
the Liberals in 1869 passed legislation for composition.[2]
The compound occupiers, however, were to have their names
on the electoral lists.

Other forces causing disfranchisement had operated before 1867 and still persisted, as Mr. Seymour points out.[3]
The overseers because of ignorance, carelessness, inefficiency
or political bias drew up unsatisfactory lists.   Double en-
tries sometimes created fagot votes in the counties.   More
often complaint was made that the registration system disqualified.   For instance, red tape made the lodger franchise almost entirely ineffective.[4] Objections by the wholesale, moreover, were made by election managers to the qualifications of those electors of opposing party creed.   The protested voters were often unwilling or unable to sustain their
votes by appearing in the revision courts with the result
that the active and unscrupulous manager might get rid of a
hostile plurality.   The lawyer of the party association was
often in a position to uphold an elector's claim but would be
fairly sure to reap the benefit of the vote for his party.[5]

[1] *Hansard*, vol. cxc, p. 438.

[2] 32 and 33 Vict., c. 41.

[3] Seymour, chapter xii, gives a clear account of the various restrictions
which the system of registration put upon the franchise.

[4] Special claims had to be made in the revising courts which were open
only in the daytime.

[5] If the objection proved to be frivolous or vexatious the claimant
might get costs according to an existing law.   The law was not very
effective, however.

To do away with these and similar abuses a committee was
appointed in 1868 to investigate registration conditions.
Their suggestions, embodied in a bill introduced in 1871,
met with opposition to change, which was too strong to
permit any but slight reform until 1878. The Act of 1878 [1]
concerned with boroughs and the Act of 1885 [2] dealing with
the counties attempted to make the preliminary lists free
from errors. The relieving officials of the poor, the regis-
trars of births and deaths were to give necessary data to the
overseers. The latter officials were to enter the names of
compound householders in the rate book and thence place
them on the electoral register; the red tape involved in the
lodger's franchise was modified and a curb was put on the
system of wholesale objections. Although not radical the
legislation helped to make the system work fairly smoothly
after 1885.[3]

Corrupt practices did more to hinder democratic advance
than did the abuses of the registration system just mentioned. An attempt made to deal with the situation in
1854, had not been really effective. It was felt that even
with the greater number of electors after 1867 bribery
would continue as a problem. To overcome existing abuses
a tribunal more free from party spirit than the committee
chosen by lot in the House of Commons would be needed to
test the validity of elections, some method of combating intimidation in elections must be found, and direct bribery
must be strictly dealt with by law. Acts of 1868, 1872, and
1883 accomplished such results that political democracy was
greatly advanced. By the act of 1868 [4] judges selected

[1] 41 and 42 Vict., c. 26.
[2] 48 and 49 Vict., c. 15.
[3] For defects of the system, *vide* Seymour, pp. 381 and 382.
[4] 31 and 32 Vict., c. 125.

from the judges of superior courts were to try the petitions
alleging that elections were void because of the misconduct
of the successful candidates.   They were to decide on the
facts and on the law and had the power to report on the pre-
valence of bribery in the inculpated constituencies.   In contrast to the committees of the House of Commons the judges
performed their duties so impartially that charges of party
bias have been made infrequently and the reform has been
spoken of as a noteworthy landmark in political history.[1]
By passing the Ballot Act of 1872 [2] Parliament granted one
of the requirements made by the speakers of the Reform
League in 1866 and 1867.   It was pointed out that intimidation of the working class in their exercise of the franchise
could best be coped with through the adoption of secret voting.   The Liberal Government showed itself in favor of
the change in the method of conducting elections in 1870,
had a bill passed through the Commons in 1871,[3] and finally
was able to enact the measure in 1872.   The Act did protect the elector from intimidation.[4]   But bribery was still
practiced even when it could not be known whether the
bribed voter had fulfilled his bargain.   Moreover, general
entertainments and picnics, general treating at public houses,
payment of traveling expenses, as practiced by the parties in
the 'seventies and early 'eighties, may be called indirect
bribery.   Such forms of bribery because of their effectiveness were sure to continue so long as election expenses were
not more carefully checked up.   The measure passed to
curb the abuses—the Corrupt and Illegal Practices Preven-

[1] Spencer Walpole, *The History of Twenty-five Years*, vol. ii, p. 204.

[2] 35 and 36 Vict., c. 33.

[3] The bill was sent to the Lords so late in the session that they refused
to consider it.

[4] Sir Thomas Erskine May and Francis Holland, *The Constitutional
History of England*, 3 vols. (London, 1912), vol. iii, pp. 26 and 27.

tion Act [1]—limited, therefore, the expenses of elections and the use to which money might be put.[2] The candidate was not to have personal expenses amounting to more than £100. The returning officers were allowed maximums fixed according to the size of constituencies. Voters might no longer be brought to the polls in hired vehicles. One authorized agent and no paid canvassers were permitted to the candidate. Treating, defined as the giving, or paying the expense of giving, any meat, drink, entertainment, or provision with the object of corruptly influencing voters, was forbidden to all. Undue influence, defined as the making use or threatening to make use, of any force, violence, or restraint, or inflicting, or threatening to inflict any temporal or spiritual injury to any person in order to influence his vote, was likewise an offence. Corrupt practices were punishable by imprisonment with hard labor or by a fine of £200. A candidate found to have been knowingly guilty of breaking any of the regulations was to be excluded from representing the constituency forever and from sitting in Parliament for seven years. That the Act was successful in controlling expenses is seen from the fact that the election by 3,000,000 electors in 1880 cost £3,000,000 whereas the election by 5,670,000 electors in 1885 cost but £780,000.[3] But seats were still so costly as to limit the choice of candidates. Although the various acts against corrupt practices did not entirely stop bribery, complaints after the year 1883 were comparatively rare.

The question of further extension of the suffrage in counties and of radical redistribution was brought forward soon after 1867. The Act of that year was not regarded

[1] 46 and 47 Vict., c. 51.
[2] May and Holland, vol. iii, pp. 32 and 33.
[3] May and Holland, vol. iii, p. 33.

as having the mark of finality. In one sense the measure
was undemocratic: it actually increased the difference between the proportion of electors in counties and boroughs.
When it is considered that after 1867 only one man in fourteen was an elector in the counties in contrast to one man
in seven in the boroughs,[1] that the voting increase as a result of the second Reform Act was only forty per cent in
the counties in contrast to one hundred and forty-five per
cent in the boroughs and that the boroughs had one and a
half as many electors as the counties in spite of a population
smaller by two millions,[2] that the property qualification
dating to 1430 was the most important franchise in the counties, claim might well be made that the miners and the artisans and small tradesmen of the towns not to mention the
agricultural laborers were being unjustly discriminated
against simply because they lived on the wrong side of an
imaginary line. Hence Mr. Trevelyan[3] in 1872, 1873
and 1874 brought before the House of Commons either by
resolution or bill his opinion that the " householders outside
the boundary of Parliamentary boroughs" should be in possession of the franchise. But the Liberals thought that the
time had hardly come for a new extension of the suffrage,
and Disraeli as Prime Minister in 1874 was opposed to extension without a large measure of redistribution. In 1875
Lord Hartington of the Opposition also pointed out that
serious anomalies would be created by any new bill unless
redistribution were included in the measure.

In fact, redistribution measures in 1867 and 1868 had
been slight in character. Agricultural counties still upheld

---

[1] Before 1867 the proportion had been one man in twenty-one an
elector in the counties and one in sixteen in the boroughs. *Vide*
Seymour, p. 287.

[2] *Ibid.*, p. 295.

[3] George Otto Trevelyan was a Liberal.

the power of the landowners as formerly. Slight gains had been made by the manufacturing groups of the Midlands and Northwest, it is true, but even with this gain the manufacturing county divisions as against the agricultural divisions were represented, in proportion to their population, by far too few members. The proportion of seats to population in the South-Midlands was two and a half that of the Northwest.[1] And with the growth of the industrial divisions after 1868 the anomalies became more striking. Should 1,000,000 new voters be created, Disraeli declared, there would be necessity for a large measure of redistribution and a system of equal electoral districts.

Mr. Trevelyan in 1876 and 1877 tried, therefore, to meet objections by introducing resolutions in favor of redistribution. But the Prime Minister contended that the increase in the number of voters in the counties would call for such redistribution as to cause the dissolution of the existing borough constituency and the destruction of the variety of character derived by the House from the municipal communities.[2] Hence the resolutions were defeated in 1876 and 1877.

In the meantime, the public was showing interest in the question of Reform. The Reform League which had gone out of existence in 1869 was revived in 1876. John Bright spoke at great public meetings and Gladstone wrote in favor of a further extension of the suffrage. Yet nothing was accomplished before the Liberal victory in the general election of 1880. By 1884 Gladstone was ready to deal with the franchise. The bill which he championed gave to the rural classes such privileges of voting as were

[1] Seymour, pp. 345 and 346.
[2] May and Holland, vol. iii, p. 30.

enjoyed by the workingmen in the boroughs.[1] Extension to the counties of household and lodger franchises which had prevailed in the boroughs since 1867 and a service franchise for those who occupied houses or separate rooms by virtue of their employment, caused an increase of two million to the number of electors of the United Kingdom. The Liberals acknowledged the necessity of a redistribution scheme but did not plan to present it until the following year. It was to this arrangement[2] that the Conservatives gave opposition, as they had done in 1866. After some difficulty the bill passed the House of Commons only to be rejected by the House of Lords. Conservatives, feeling that in case of a dissolution before redistribution, Radical influence would become paramount and would dictate such a redistribution bill that the Conservative party would long be out of control and landed interests would suffer, demanded a complete bill. The ministers did not give way, agricultural laborers paraded for their rights, and threats of ending or mending the House of Lords began to be heard. That body, it was supposed, was using its demands as a means to escape from passing the bill. Compromises, however, soon were mentioned, and the passage of the bill became assured when the leaders, brought together in private conferences partly through the influence of the Queen, made an agreement as to the coming redistribution. The redistribution bill soon followed. Boroughs having a population less than 15,000 were merged in the counties and boroughs under 50,000 which had been returning two members now were allowed one.

[1] *Vide* Paul, *op. cit.*, vol. iv, pp. 326-336.

[2] Also to the inclusion of Ireland in the scheme, where the electorate was increased from 200,000 to 700,000 voters. It was said that forty per cent of the new electors were illiterate and would be a power for Parnell.

Of the seats liberated for distribution in England and Wales almost an equal number was given to the counties and the boroughs. Boroughs and county members now represented approximately the same population and in counties, at least, the ratio of seats to population was for the most part, constant.[1] Industrial county divisions and manufacturing towns of the North had been granted their full proportion of representatives and the Southwest had lost, therefore, a considerable number of seats. It was determined that single-member districts should be made in the new constituencies and in the larger towns so that minorities which were majorities in certain sections might obtain representation. For the purpose of giving additional representation to Scotland twelve more members were added to the House. Thus by 1885 England was approaching[2] manhood suffrage, although not until 1918 was there further lowering of qualifications and the granting of woman suffrage.

But did the fact that the workingman had obtained the franchise really make better his position in the state? Did all those reforms which the Reform speakers were wont to talk about, come as expected, with the vote? As a matter of fact, the welfare of the workingman did not immediately occupy the attention of the parties after 1867, to the extent predicted; nor did the workingmen themselves have much success in obtaining representation in the House. Indeed, they did not put forth much effort, at least, in the beginning, to return members of their class; they voted, some of the papers proudly proclaimed, like good Englishmen. The *Spectator* was one paper, however, which preached against

[1] For anomalies in the representation of boroughs *vide* Seymour, pp. 515 *et seq.*

[2] Bachelors living with parents, domestic servants, and those who did not meet residence qualifications were excluded.

this lack of representation of the working classes, for no-
where in 1868 were workmen returned and in scarcely a
borough could they be said to have selected separately the
representative.   Not until 1874 did trade union leaders try
a general campaign for direct representation in Parliament.[1]
And although even then no success resulted when Labor
candidates ran without support from the other parties, aid
from the official Liberals enabled Mr. Alexander Macdonald
and Mr. Thomas Burt, the two chief officials of the
National Union of Miners, to enter Parliament as the first
Labor members.

Of course something was done for the workingman, the
historian can point out.   Even in 1867 [2] Lord Elcho had
succeeded in carrying through the Master and Servant Act.[3]
The condition existing previously, namely, that a workingman in case of breach of contract, could be arrested on
warrant and imprisoned, subjected to hard labor by the
justice, while the employer could be attacked only by civil
action, had been much complained of and was now remedied by the law which put both employer and employee
on the same level by making it possible to summon either
for breach of contract before the magistrates who might
fine or order the contracts to be fulfilled.   Leaders of the
trade unions had agitated for an amended law since 1863
and with the passage of the measure of 1867 not only " won
the first positive success of the trade unions in the legislative
field" but "did much to increase their confidence in
Parliamentary agitation." [4]

In the same year was passed the Factory Acts Extension

[1] Slater, *The Making of Modern England*, p. 210.

[2] The bill received the royal assent on August 20, 1867; a select committee had been appointed for inquiry in 1866.

[3] The 30 and 31 Vict., c. 141.

[4] Sidney and Beatrice Webb, *The History of Trade Unionism*, p. 236.

Act [1] whereby the restrictions on the employment of women
and children in dangerous trades were extended and the
powers of inspectors increased, and also the Workshop Re-
gulation Act [2] applicable to an establishment in which fewer
than fifty persons were employed in any manufacturing
process, except those already included under factory acts.
This Act defined " employed " as work in any handicraft,
whether for wages or not, under a master or under a parent
and hence was supposed to control home-workers. [3] A law
which limited hours of work but gave no fixed times was
easily evaded and often proved, of course, a dead letter.

There was the Factory Act [4] of 1874 whereby the hours
of labor for women and children were still further reduced,
i. e., to a maximum of fifty-six and one half a week. The
men who would find their day's work completed when the
machinery was shut down with the departure of the women
and children, had hoped for a fifty-four hour week from the
Conservatives whom they had helped to elect in 1874. [5] The
new Government, reputed, at the time, to be more favorably
inclined than the Liberals toward labor, nevertheless disappointed trade union demands by effecting but slight improvement on existing conditions. [6] There was the Employers' Liability Bill [7] of 1880 which met in part a griev-
ance often protested against by the trade union world.
Since 1837 the courts had decided that although an employer

---

[1] The 30 and 31 Vict., c. 103. Disraeli spoke of this in one of the
Edinburgh speeches, as an instance of interest on the part of the Government in the welfare of the working class.

[2] 30 and 31 Vict., c. 146.

[3] Hutchins and Harrison, *A History of Factory Legislation*, p. 171.

[4] 37 and 38 Vict., c. 44.

[5] *Cf.* Hutchins and Harrison, p. 175.

[6] For the Consolidation and Amendment Bill of 1878 *vide* Hutchins and
Harrison, pp. 176 *et seq.*

[7] 43 and 44 Vict., c. 42.

was liable to a member of the public for the result of his workmen's negligence he was liable to those in his employ only for the result of negligence on his own part, and not for the result of negligence on the part of one employee to a worker in common employment. Injured persons living near a mine might get damages from the mine owner in case of an explosion due to the carelessness of a miner; fellow miners could not bring suit for damages on account of the doctrine of common employment.[1] The influence of great employers in both the Conservative and the Liberal parties prevented an abolition of this doctrine of common employment but it could not prevent the Act of 1880 which made the employer liable to his workingmen for negligence on the part of superintendents or foremen " to whose orders the workmen were bound to conform." There was the Artisans' Dwellings Act [2] of 1875 which, intended to be the cause of better dwellings for the working classes, was never of great effect.

The passage of the Education Bill [3] of 1870, too, met the oft-voiced demands of the workingmen. Mr. Forster was chiefly responsible for this Act by the terms of which the supply of efficient elementary schools was to become adequate for needs in all sections of the country. It was felt that the Act of 1867 by entrusting to the urban workingmen the responsibilities of citizenship had made it necessary that illiteracy as a peril to a democratic state should be removed. Mr. Lowe had correctly forecast the future legislation in 1867 when he declared to the House of Commons: " I believe it will be absolutely necessary that you should prevail on our future masters to learn their letters." [4]

[1] Paul, *op. cit.*, vol. iv, p. 153.
[2] 38 and 39 Vict., c. 36.
[3] 33 and 34 Vict., c. 75.
[4] *Hansard*, vol. clxxxviii, p. 1549.

In 1871, moreover, the Government found itself forced to legislate on the subject of trade unions.[1] The influence of trade unions had assisted, it has been seen, in accomplishing the passage of the Representation of the People bill in 1867. Nevertheless, the leaders of the societies had little feeling of security in 1867. Because of outrages, especially at Sheffield, the public viewed the movement with the eyes of a Charles Reade; and in a case involving the funds of the Boiler-makers' society, the Court of Queen's Bench declared that trade unions were illegal associations. Hence they could not seek legal protection for their accumulated funds. In the early part of 1867 the leaders convened a " Conference of Amalgamated Trades." It was little more than a meeting of the " Junta," the informal cabinet of five trade union leaders living in London,[2] and a few friends. Assisted by Mr. Tom Hughes in Parliament and by the writers, Professor Beesly and Mr. Frederic Harrison, out of doors, it tried to obtain a legal status for the societies. The majority report of a royal commission appointed to inquire into the whole subject of trade unionism, was not hostile, while a minority report advocated the removal of all special legislation relating to labor contracts and contended that no act by a combination of men should be regarded as criminal if it would not have been criminal in a single person. Mr. Harrison was anxious to bring the trade unions under existing acts for the protection of their funds against fraud or theft but to have them retain a legal privilege of being incapable of being sued or otherwise proceeded against as a corporate

[1] *Vide* Webb, *History of Trade Unionism*, chap. v.

[2] The men in this group were William Allan and Robert Applegarth, the general secretaries of the two amalgamated societies of Engineers and Carpenters, Daniel Guile, general secretary of the national society of Ironfounders, Edwin Coulson, general secretary of the " London Order " of Bricklayers, and George Odger—the Reform speaker—a member of the union of makers of ladies' shoes.

entity. A bill embodying such proposals was introduced in the first Parliament elected after the passage of the Reform Act of 1867. The Liberal Government was against it but demonstrations by the workingmen led to the promise that the cabinet would soon bring in a bill of its own. Accordingly in 1871 legislation [1] was passed, providing that no trade union was to be illegal merely because it was in restraint of trade, but an important additional bill [2] provided that any violence, threat or molestation for the purpose of coercing either employer or employed should be severely punished. The terms used in this latter bill were not defined, and the trade unionists knew that no effective policy could be carried out under such a law. Their protests, however, were without result—until the elections of 1874 when the Liberals found themselves out of power. Conservatives alive to the political influence of the unions repealed the Criminal Law Amendment Act in 1875 and passed a new bill expressly permitting peaceful picketing.[3] Moreover, by replacing the Master and Servant Act of 1867 by an Employers and Workmen Act,[4] master and servant became, as employer and employee, two equal parties to a civil contract and imprisonment for breach of engagement was abolished. Trade union demands were completely satisfied.

But for some time after the passage of the Reform bill of 1867 the workingmen followed the two great parties too closely to obtain great and important results for themselves. Trade unionism after its triumph in 1875 passed through financial trials during the trade depression of following years until by 1879 its total membership had decreased to that of the year 1871. And, as a result of the *laisser faire*

[1] The 34 and 35 Vict., c. 31.
[2] The 34 and 35 Vict., c. 32.
[3] The 38 and 39 Vict., c. 86.
[4] The 38 and 39 Vict., c. 90

political and social creed of the leaders, the trade union world failed to exercise any effective influence upon Parliament between 1876 and 1885.[1]   Hence the bill of 1867 did not bear its chief fruits until many years later.   Distrust of the promises of the Liberals and the Conservatives, however, was to be seen at times, and among the workingmen and their leaders there cropped up occasionally the idea that real emancipation of labor would come only through their banding together, through strikes, and perhaps through a complete international social revolution, rather than through the promised, though too often deferred, activity of any of the political parties.   That politics did count, however, was to be shown in a quarter of a century by the formation and activity of the Labor party.   That party formed from the union of a Social Democratic party founded in the early 'eighties on the Marxian gospel, a Fabian Society founded shortly afterward with the idea of educating the public in Socialism, and an Independent Labor party founded in the early 'nineties on Socialistic principles but acknowledging the need of occasional compromise, was brought into being in 1901 as a result of the Taff Vale decision by the House of Lords.   By that decision trade unions were held responsible for damages done by individual members.   Labor interests, therefore, called for defense; hence the Labor party.   The Labor party was fortunate, too, in finding the Liberals willing to work with it.   The Liberals, influenced by the writings of Henry George, by the Fabians, and perhaps even more by the actual facts concerning the physical condition of the English workingman as brought out by the examination of Boer War recruits, decided that something must be done for the lower classes.   The opening years of the twentieth century, therefore, witnessed a great amount

[1] Webb. *History of Trade Unionism*, p. 356.

of social legislation in Great Britain. The people were using their democratic representative mastery over government as a means through which to undertake general social control.[1] The Reform Bill of 1867 had borne its fruit. Demands of the Reform speakers of 1867 were being realized; socialization of politics had come. And, to the student of to-day it seems unlikely that the Workmen's Compensation Act[2] of 1906, the provisions for Child Welfare[3] in 1908, for the Old Age Pensions[4] in 1908, the work for the unemployed and the Labor Exchange[5] Act of 1909, the Measure[6] of 1909 dealing with sweated labor, as well as Great Britain's imperialistic policy, would have been viewed[7] with displeasure by the author of *Sybil*. Further reforms of the franchise have advanced democracy; and although political leaders had but little opportunity to attempt a remedy for social sores during the course of the Great War, it is safe to predict that, with the coming of peace and the triumph of democracy's cause, England's statesmen and England's Government will give more time and more attention than ever before to the demands and needs of the workingman.

[1] *Cf.* Carlton Hayes, *British Social Politics* (Boston, 1913), pp. 2 and 3.
[2] The 6 Edw. VII, c. 58.
[3] The 8 Edw. VII, c. 67.
[4] The 8 Edw. VII, c. 40.
[5] The 9 Edw. VII, c. 7.
[6] The 9 Edw. VII, c. 22.
[7] It is easy to imagine, on the other hand, what would have been Disraeli's attitude on the curbing of the Lords.

BIBLIOGRAPHY

Adams, Charles Francis, *Charles Francis Adams*. Boston and New York, 1900.

Annuaire des Deux Mondes.

Annual Register.

Anstey, Thomas Chisholm, *Notes upon the Representation of the People Act, 1867*. London, 1867.

Argyll, Duke of (George Douglas Campbell), *Autobiography and Memoirs*, edited by the Dowager Duchess of Argyll. 2 vols. New York, 1906.

Arnold, R. Arthur, *The History of the Cotton Famine from the Fall of Sumter to the Passing of the Public Works Act*. New edition. London, 1865.

Ashwell, Arthur Rawson, *Life of the Right Reverend Samuel Wilberforce*. 3 vols. London, 1880-82.

Bagehot, Walter. *Essays on Parliamentary Reform*. London, 1883.

Bassett, Arthur Tinley, *Gladstone's Speeches*. Descriptive Index and Bibliography. London, 1916.

Baxter, Robert, *The Panic of 1866 with its Lessons on the Currency Act*. London, 1866.

Baxter, R. Dudley, *National Income*. London, 1868.

——, *The New Reform Bill*. London, 1866.

——, *The Taxation of the United Kingdom*. London, 1869.

Blackie, John Stuart, *On Government*. Edinburgh, 1867.

Blanc, Louis, *Letters on England*. Translated from the French by James Hutton and revised by the author. 2 vols. London, 1866.

——, *Lettres sur l'Angleterre*. Deuxième Série. Paris, 1866.

Bowley, A. L., *A Short Account of England's Foreign Trade in the Nineteenth Century*. Revised edition. London, 1905.

——, *Wages in the United Kingdom in the Nineteenth Century*. Cambridge, 1900.

Brassey, Thomas B., *On Work and Wages*. 3rd edition. London, 1872.

Bright, John, *The Public Letters of John Bright*. Collected and edited by H. J. Leech. London, 1885.

——, *Speeches on the American Question*. Boston, 1865.

——, *Speeches on Parliamentary Reform*. London, 1866.

——, *Speeches on Questions of Public Policy*. Edited by James E. Thorold Rogers. London, 1868.

Brodrick, G. C., *The Utilitarian Argument against Reform as Stated by Mr. Lowe.* London, 1867.

Bryce, James, *The Historical Aspect of Democracy.* London, 1867.

——, *Studies in Contemporary Biography.* London, 1903.

Buxton, Sydney, *Finance and Politics; an Historical Study 1783-1885.* 2 vols. London, 1888.

Carlyle, Thomas, *Shooting Niagara: And After?* London, 1867.

Chesterton, G. K., *The Victorian Age in Literature.* London, 1913.

Cole, H. W., *The Middle Classes and the Borough Franchise.* London, 1866.

Cooper, Thomas. *Life, Written by Himself.* 2nd edition. London, 1872.

Cox, Homersham, *A History of the Reform Bills of 1866 and 1867.* London, 1868.

——, *Whig and Tory Administrations.* London, 1868.

Cracroft, Bernard, *The Analysis of the House of Commons, or Indirect Representation.* London, 1867.

Dickinson, G. Lowes, *The Development of Parliament during the Nineteenth Century.* London, 1895.

Dictionary of National Biography.

Disraeli, Benjamin, *The Chancellor of the Exchequer in Scotland, being Two Speeches delivered by Him in the City of Edinburgh.* Edinburgh and London, 1867.

——, *Sybil or the Two Nations.* London, 1845.

——, *Vivian Grey.* London, 1881. Original edition 1826-1827.

——, *Whigs and Whiggism. Political Writings.* London, 1913.

Dover, Richard. *Progress versus Collapse.* Westminster, 1869.

Dunning, William Archibald, *The British Empire and the United States.* New York, 1914.

Fawcett, Henry, *The Economic Position of the British Labourer.* Cambridge and London, 1865.

Fox, Wilson, *Report on the Wages and Earnings of Agricultural Labourers with Statistical Tables and Charts.* London, 1900.

Fraser, Sir William, *Disraeli and his Day.* 2nd edition. London, 1891.

Frost, Thomas, *Forty Years' Recollections.* London, 1880.

Giffin, Sir Robert, *Essays in Finance.* 2nd series. New York, 1886.

Gladstone, W. E., *Gleanings of Past Years.* 7 vols. London, 1879.

Green, Willoughby, *Workingmen and Their Wages.* Leeds, 1869.

Hansard.

Hardy, Gathorne, *A Memoir.* 2 vols. London, 1910.

Hare, Thomas, *Memorandum on the History, Working, and Results of Cumulative Voting.* London, 1871.

——, *A Treatise on the Election of Representatives, Parliamentary and Municipal.* 3rd edition. London, 1865.

Harris, William, *History of the Radical Party in Parliament.* London, 1885.

Harrison, Frederic, *Foreign Policy.* London, 1867.

Hayes, Carlton J. H., *British Social Politics.* Boston, 1913.

——, *A Political and Social History of Modern Europe.* 2 vols. New York, 1917.

Heaton, William, *The Three Reforms of Parliament.* London, 1885.

Hickson, W. E., *Tracts for Inquirers.* London, 1867.

Hill, Frederic, *Parliamentary Reform.* London, 1865.

Hodder, Edwin, *The Life and Work of the Seventh Earl of Shaftesbury.* 3 vols. London, 1888.

Holland, Bernard, *The Life of Spencer Compton, Eighth Duke of Devonshire.* 2 vols. London, 1911.

Holt, Winifred, *A Beacon for the Blind Being a Life of Henry Fawcett the Blind Postmaster General.* Boston, 1914.

Holyoake, George Jacob, *Sixty Years of an Agitator's Life.* 4th edition. 2 vols. London, 1900.

Hunt, William, and Poole, Reginald L., *The Political History of England.* 12 vols. London, 1906.

Hutchins, B. L., and Harrison, A., *A History of Factory Legislation.* 2nd edition revised. London, 1911.

Hutton, R. H., *The Political Character of the Working Class.* London, 1867.

Hyndman, H. M., *Commercial Crises of the Nineteenth Century.* London, 1892.

Irving, Joseph, *The Annals of Our Time.* London, 1875.

Jones, Ernest, *Democracy Vindicated.* Edinburgh, 1867.

Kebbel, T. E., *Lord Beaconsfield and other Tory Memories.* New York, 1907.

Kent, C. B. R., *The English Radicals.* London, 1899.

Kinnear, John Boyd, *Redistribution of Seats.* London, 1867.

L., *Queries on the Franchise.* Norwich, 1866.

Lang, Andrew, *Life, Letters, and Diaries of Sir Stafford Northcote.* New edition. Edinburgh and London, 1891.

Lecky, William E. H., *Democracy and Liberty.* 2 vols. New York and London, 1896.

Levi, Leone, *The History of British Commerce and of the Economic Progress of the British Nation 1763-1878.* 2nd edition. London, 1880.

——, *Wages and Earnings of the Working Classes.* London, 1867.

Lowell, A. Lawrence, *The Government of England.* New edition. 2 vols. New York, 1917.

Ludlow, J. M., and Jones, Lloyd, *The Progress of the Working Classes.* London, 1867.

Lushington, Godfrey, *Workmen and Trade Unions.* London, 1867.

McCarthy, Justin, *A History of Our Own Times.* 2 vols. New York, 1880.

MacDonald, William, *The Government of Maine.* New York and London, 1902.

Mackey, Thomas, *History of the English Poor Law.* London, 1899.

Malmesbury, James Howard Harris, *Memoirs of an Ex-Minister; an Autobiography.* 2 vols. London, 1884.

May, Sir Thomas Erskine, and Holland, Francis, *Constitutional History of England.* 3 vols. London, 1912.

Mill, John Stuart, *Autobiography.* 3rd edition. New York, 1874.

Molesworth, W. N., *History of the Reform Question from 1832 to 1866.* Fortnightly Review, vol. vii.

Monypenny, William F., and Buckle, George E., *The Life of Benjamin Disraeli.* 4 vols. New York, 1910-16.

Morley, John, *The Life of William Ewart Gladstone.* 3 vols. London, 1903.

Mulhall, M. G., *The Dictionary of Statistics.* London, 1899.

Murchison, J. H., *The Conservatives and " Liberals," Their Principles and Policy.* 2nd edition. London, 1866.

Murdock, James, *A History of Constitutional Reform in Great Britain and Ireland.* Glasgow, 1885.

Nadaud, M., *Histoire des Classes Ouvrières en Angleterre.* Paris, 1872.

Noble, John, *Free Trade, Reciprocity and the Revivers.* London, 1867.'

O'Brien, R. Barry, *John Bright; a Monograph.* London, 1910.

Ostrogorski, M., *Democracy and the Organization of Political Parties.* Translated from the French by Frederick Clarke. 2 vols. New York, 1902.

Palmer, Roundell, *Memorials.* 4 vols. London, 1896-1898.

Parliamentary *Reports, Accounts and Papers.*

Parker, Charles Stuart, *Popular Education.* London, 1867.

Paul, Herbert, *A History of Modern England.* 5 vols. New York, 1904.

Periodicals:
Athenaeum.
Beehive.
Blackwood's.
British Workman.
Contemporary Review.
Dublin Review.
Economic Review.
Economist.
Edinburgh Review.
Era.
Fortnightly Review.
Frazer's.
Home and Foreign Review.
Illustrated London News.

Journal of the Statistical Society of London.
London Review.
Macmillan's.
National Review.
News of the World.
Nineteenth Century.
North British Review.
Public Opinion.
Punch.
Quarterly Review.
Revue des Deux Mondes.
Saturday Review.
Spectator.
Times.
Westminster Review.

Political Euclid, *The Reform Problem.* London, 1866.

Porter, G. R., *The Progress of the Nation.* Revised by F. W. Hirst. London, 1912.

The Public General Statutes.

Rathbone, William, *The Rock Ahead. A few Thoughts on Parliamentary Reform.* Edinburgh and London, 1867.

——, *Soundings in Political Waters; an Inquiry into the Principles of Parliamentary Representation.* Edinburgh, 1867.

Reade, Charles, *Put Yourself in His Place.* New York, 1870. Originally published in the Cornhill Magazine, 1869-70.

Reid, Stuart J., *Memoirs of Sir Wemyss Reid.* London, 1905.

Reid, T. Wemyss, *Life of the Right Honorable W. E. Forster.* 2nd edition. 2 vols. London, 1888.

Representative Reform. Report of the Committee appointed by the Conference of Members of the Reform League, and Others, on Mr. Hare's Scheme of Representation. London, 1868.

Rhodes, J. F., *History of the United States.* 8 vols. New York, 1900-1919.

Rogers, James E. Thorold, *Bribery.* London, 1867.

Rose, J. H., *The Rise of Democracy.* London, 1897.

Russell (1st Earl), John, *Essay on the History of the English Government and Constitution.* New edition. London, 1866.

——, *Recollections and Suggestions.* London, 1875.

Rutson, A. O., *Opportunities and Shortcomings of Government in England.* London, 1867.

Saintsbury, George, *The Earl of Derby.* New York, 1892.

Scrope, G. Poullett, *No Vote, No Rate.* London, 1867.

Seymour, Charles, *Electoral Reform in England and Wales.* New Haven, 1915.

Seymour, Charles, and Frary, Donald Paige, *How the World Votes.* 2 vols. Springfield, Mass., 1918.

Slater, Gilbert, *The Making of Modern England.* New revised edition. Boston, 1915.

Slosson, Preston W., *The Decline of the Chartist Movement.* New York, 1916.

Smith, George Barnett, *The Life and Speeches of the Right Honorable John Bright.* 2 vols. London, 1885.

Smith, Goldwin, *The Experience of the American Commonwealth.* London, 1867.

Stanley, W. F., *Proposition for a New Reform Bill.* London, 1867.

Stephen, Sir Leslie, *Life of Henry Fawcett.* 2nd edition. London, 1885.

——, *The " Times" on the American War.* In Magazine of History, vol. x.

Sybel, Heinrich von, *Die Begründung des Deutschen Reiches durch Wilhelm I.* 7 vols. Munich, 1890-94. There exists a translation into English by M. L. Perris and G. Bradford.

Taylor, F. Isabel, *A Bibliography of Unemployment and the Unemployed.* London, 1909.

Townsend, Meredith, *The Poor.* London, 1867.

Toynbee, A., *Lectures on the Industrial Revolution.* 3rd impression. London, 1913.

Traill, H. D., *Social England.* 6 vols. London, 1897.

Trevelyan, George Macaulay, *The Life of John Bright.* London, 1913.

Walpole, Sir Spencer, *History of Twenty-five Years.* 4 vols. London, 1904-08.

——, *Life of Lord John Russell.* 2nd edition. 2 vols. London, 1889.

Ward, Robert, *Thoughts on the Reform Question, and Proposals for its Solution.* Newcastle-upon-Tyne, 1867.

Wason, Rigby, *The Currency Question.* London, 1869.

Webb, Sidney, and Beatrice, *Industrial Democracy.* London, 1902.

——, *The History of Trade Unionism.* New edition. London, 1911.

White, William Hale, *An Argument for an Extension of the Franchise.* London, 1866.

Wood, George H., *The History of Wages in the Cotton Trade during the Past Hundred Years.* London, 1910.

Wright, Thomas, *Some Habits and Customs of the Working Classes.* London, 1867.

INDEX

TEXAS A&M UNIVERSITY-TEXARKANA